The Emerging Democratic Majority

LESSONS AND LEGACIES FROM THE NEW POLITICS

Lanny J. Davis

With a Foreword by Senator Harold E. Hughes

STEIN AND DAY/*Publishers*/**New York**

First published in 1974
Copyright © 1974 by Lanny J. Davis
Library of Congress Catalog Card No. 73–82142
All rights reserved
Designed by Bernard Schleifer
Printed in the United States of America
Stein and Day/*Publishers*/Scarborough House, Briarcliff Manor, N.Y. 10510
ISBN 0-8128-1643-9

*To Leonard
and Judith,
who understood
the decency instinct
more than most*

CONTENTS

Part IV: The Emerging Democratic Majority

FOREWORD
By Senator Harold E. Hughes

OF THE NUMEROUS BOOKS on political trends that have blossomed out in the McCarthy to McGovern era, this, in my judgment, is one of the better ones. Lanny Davis has related and interpreted the developments in the Democratic Party during these years with unaffected directness and a minimum of personal bias. A seasoned veteran of the campaigns of the New Politics at twenty-eight, he has spiced his narrative with personal experience in several campaigns, and, in analyzing the roots of the 1972 Democratic defeat, he directs a good deal of his critical scrutiny—refreshingly—to himself and other young political activists with whom he held common cause. He then proceeds to predict future trends in American politics—problems, potentials, and probabilities—in a way that makes good sense to me.

His basic thesis is that the wave of the future is the emergence of a new coalition under the umbrella of the Democratic Party, combining segments of the electorate successfully aligned in the New Deal era with the constituency of the New Politics. He rejects—and, I must say, I believe rightly rejects—the frequently heard assumption that the American electorate is in the throes of a massive right-wing swing away from human-value issues and government with compassion for the rank and file and disadvantaged citizens.

9

One of the significant contributions of this book is to put the landslide McGovern defeat in the 1972 election in more objective perspective than most commentators have done thus far. He explains the downfall of the Democratic presidential slate not merely in terms of mistakes, ideological and personal, but more basically as the result of attitudes and political forces that had been developing within the Democratic Party long before George McGovern's candidacy.

I support this interpretation over the personal scapegoat explanations. The positions that the McGovern forces were compelled to take to win the primaries, Mr. Davis argues persuasively, went a long way toward foreclosing their chances in the general election.

Mr. Davis proceeds to point out that the alienation of many middle-class voters, including blue-collar workers, from Democratic ranks in 1972 was an aberration limited, for the most part, to the presidential contest. He cites the 1972 Democratic victories in many congressional and state elections to prove his point. Readers who actively participated in the political events Lanny Davis describes will no doubt differ with him here and there on details and interpretations, but basically, I think, most will agree that he is on target. Coalition-building is the imperative of the American political process. America is a nation of widely diverse people from different backgrounds and perspectives. The political coalition is the best—perhaps the only—instrument available in a democracy to unite people who disagree on some issues but are willing to work together nonetheless on others.

Combinations of circumstances sometimes make it incredibly difficult, if not impossible, to field a winning coalition. Mr. Davis's insight into the difficulties Ed Muskie faced in his attempt to bring together the new and old politics under one tent in 1972 is a particularly valuable contribution because, as far as I know, this key problem of the Muskie effort has not been given adequate attention in other chronicles of the campaign. Beyond the mistakes and now-known political sabotage to which Muskie's campaign was subjected, his campaign effort was more suited to the general election than to the primaries, and, of course, it foundered in the primaries. As one who was involved in the Muskie campaign, I am pleased that this accurate and sensitive account of the Maine senator's presidential bid is now on the record.

Some may, at the outset, find Mr. Davis overly optimistic in his prediction that a new coalition, combining the old Roosevelt coalition with the forces of the New Politics, is emerging and that this coalition can be based on progressive principles of economic and social justice. However, I believe he has made a convincing case. Indeed, he has compiled an impressive array of evidence that the coalition was in existence in the 1970 and 1972 state and congressional elections and should reach new levels of strength in the elections ahead.

Obviously some of the mistakes of the recent past, which the author has pointed out so vividly, must be avoided and some progressive new actions taken if this new coalition is to become the dominant political party of the future.

In his epilogue on Watergate, he cautions us "to come to understand that there's a little bit of Herbert Porter in all of us, that we are all subject to the pressures of superloyalty leading to acceptance of unseemly means to justify desired ends."

This is wise counsel and is, I believe, placed in proper perspective. But Watergate doesn't cause Lanny Davis to change his basic thesis about the future direction of American politics. Nor does it submerge his implicit belief that idealism is required if a political party is to live and prosper and forge effective coalitions.

Underlying all of what Lanny Davis has written is a wholesome faith in the decency of the electorate and in the capacity of the American people to change and grow and work together despite their differences.

I have been through some political wars myself and some of the stars of yesteryear have faded from my eyes, but I share this view wholeheartedly.

PART I

Roots of the
New Politics

one

THE CIVIL RIGHTS MOVEMENT: DISCOVERING DEMONS

> "You had this feeling that you were up against absolute evil, and that you were part of a movement of absolute righteousness."
> —Gregory Craig, 1966 Harvard
> student body president, remembering
> his trips to Mississippi

IN A HOT, STUFFY OFFICE in the late spring of 1964, fifty Yale students listened, mesmerized, to a New York lawyer named Allard K. Lowenstein talk about the oppression of blacks in the state of Mississippi and why white college students were needed to help.

"Bullshit, Al, bullshit." The speaker was the head of a newly formed, politically radical organization at Yale called Students for a Democratic Society. He believed that the political system was beyond repair, that change in the society could come about only through militant confrontation and, perhaps, violent revolution.

"All of us good liberal white kids will go down to Mississippi," the SDS student said. "And when we get there, we'll make sure we do some good charitable work, and we'll feel real good about ourselves. Then we'll leave, and behind us will be the same conditions, the same oppression. Maybe it will be worse for the Negroes. They'll have to take the crap we've stirred up."

Lowenstein was livid. *"That's* bullshit. You're not coming down to Mississippi to change Mississippi. You're coming down to change your parents in order to get *them* to change the press, the Congress, the President."

The civil rights-integrationist movement was not new to the indefatigable Allard Lowenstein. As an undergraduate at the University of North Carolina in 1950, Lowenstein had organized a successful effort to force a local student-frequented hotel to accept black lodgers by getting a few hundred students to telephone the hotel twenty-four hours a day and make room reservations, thereby tying up the telephone lines and impeding the business operations of the hotel.

Now, more than ten years later, he was still urging college students to share his sense of outrage and to do something about it.

Lowenstein's eloquence and ardor moved most of us in that room. But the timing was also right. John Kennedy—young, Harvard, urbane, witty—was President. One of us, so to speak, had finally made it to the White House. Suddenly a career in public service and politics was worth thinking about, worth planning for. Lowenstein himself seemed the perfect combination—idealistic, committed, and, well, practical too.

And so we went South—white, comfortable, sons of privilege and liberal enlightenment—to do battle against the racist demon rednecks of Mississippi. Some, who were arrested, wore a generational badge of honor when they returned to their campuses. Some, like Andrew Goodman, James Chaney, and Michael Schwerner, did not come back at all. Whatever the actual effects of our pilgrimages to the South in 1964 and 1965, it was clear that we had enriched our own lives at least as much as the lives of those we had sought to help, if not far more.

"I remember attending a rally in an old, rickety church outside Clarksdale, Mississippi," recalled Gregory Craig, who, as a sophomore at Harvard University, was one of those who made the pilgrimage to Mississippi in 1965. "There I was, the only white face in the place. It was a revival meeting, except I was the one everyone was praying to. One old man came up to me and kissed my hand. Different people would stand up and talk about brotherhood and love. We sang, and prayed, and preached all night long. It was the most moving experience of my life."

The trip back North sometimes took us through the neighborhoods around our college campuses. Had we looked, we might have seen the poverty and despair of the blacks who lived a few blocks from our dormitories. Had we known, we might have felt outrage that black children would be bitten by rats not far from the place where we gathered for a beer to reminisce about the unforgettable spiritual uplift in Mississippi. But Mississippi was distant. New Haven was, well, too close, too unglamorous. Anyway, there were no demons, no Bull Connors, in New Haven. Only us.

In early 1967, antiwar political activists around the country, myself included, began to nurture the then visionary scenario that an incumbent president could be denied renomination by his own party. We could hardly have anticipated, even in our most optimistic moments, that our efforts would result in the rapid evolution of a national political movement whose ultimate impact on the American political process, for good or bad, would have few parallels in American history.

Within five years, this movement, which came to be called the New Politics, succeeded in forcing Lyndon Johnson to renounce a bid for reelection just four years after his unprecedented landslide victory over Barry Goldwater; revolutionized a presidential nominating system which had governed the Democratic Party, with minor variations, through nearly two centuries of American history; invented and refined techniques of grass-roots political organization which will influence the conduct of election campaigns in this country for years to come; expanded the political base of the Democratic Party into suburban, upper-middle-class constituencies; and gave birth to a new generation of young political professionals within the Democratic Party whose impact on the national political process, and on the country as a whole, is yet to be felt.

It took the Populists almost twenty years to capture control of the national Democratic Party and to secure the presidential nomination of one of its own. It took the New Politics constituency less than five years. And less than five months after that constituency's greatest moment of success—the nomination of George McGovern in 1972—it was faced with the stark reality of bearing an important share of responsibility for one of the worst political defeats of a presidential candidate in American history and for the alienation of millions of traditional working-class and middle-income Democrats.

How did a political movement which seemed to be so efficient in intraparty political battles produce such a disaster in the national political arena?

Tracing the development of the New Politics movement from the early days of the civil rights movement, through the anti-Vietnam War effort and the McCarthy and Kennedy campaigns of 1968, and finally, through the Muskie-McGovern clash of 1971–72, we find that at each stage, a central divisive question recurred: What is the best strategy for bringing about major changes in governmental policy in a free society?

Superficially, the division within the New Politics movement seems to be merely one over tactics. But beneath the surface of the tactical disagreements on how best to achieve social change came to be fundamentally different conceptions of the nature of the political process and a clash of personal values.

One group—whom I shall call the "purists"—begins with the premise that the American political system is corrupt, rigged by the holders of wealth and power to maintain the status quo (give or take a few insignificant reforms every so often). It follows that in order to bring about desired social changes one must confront the economic and political system and force individuals to face up to the need for a major overhaul rather than piecemeal reform.

Translating these premises into political organization means motivating like-minded people who are then willing to resist any form of compromise on goals, since compromise is seen as the system's method of blurring the lines of real grievance. Sometimes violence or disruption may be justifiable: such tactics might in the short run alienate some possible supporters, but in the long run, the purist will argue, the raising of the society's consciousness brings us closer to the desired changes.

The second group within the New Politics—the "coalitionists" —begins with the premise that, while there are grave economic and social injustices in American society, people who want to correct those injustices can act effectively within the political process. According to this view, the essence of the political process is persuasion, and change cannot come about in a free society unless ordinary people can be convinced that change is in their interest. The key to the process of persuasion is the political coali-

tion—bringing together different kinds of people, with different
interests and loyalties, and convincing them that there are overriding common interests which warrant a joint political effort. Of
necessity, those who seek to build political coalitions must be sensitive to the needs and experiences of others, which may mean accepting less than 100 per cent of their own goals, some of which will
inevitably be in conflict with those of other interest groups in the
coalition.

These two strategies for social change are not necessarily mu-
tually exclusive. In fact, a good argument can be made that each one
needs the other. The antielectoral-politics purists are frequently out
in front on controversial issues and often help dramatize such issues
to the point where they begin to become part of the American consciousness. The electoral-process coalitionists are then able to
translate the goals of the purists into the political framework and
elect people who are ideologically sympathetic.

A difficulty arises, however, when the purist elements turn to the
political process and try to impose values and tactics which are
essentially incompatible with the coalitionist necessities of
American politics. As we shall see, to a considerable extent, that was
what happened in the Democratic Party in 1972. It also happened
many years earlier during the middle years of the civil rights
movement.

The fight over the seating of an integrated Mississippi delegation
at the 1964 Democratic convention highlighted an inherent inconsistency in the application of an electoral-process coalitionist strategy to the civil rights movement. How could a cause of moral and
political absolutes be adapted to the political process, where
progress depended on compromise, concession, flexibility? How was
compromise possible when the issue was whether a racist Mississippi
delegation should be recognized by a national Democratic Party
which supported the civil rights movement?

But politics was a game: two steps forward, one backward. A
little here, a little there. We can't embarrass President Johnson too
much; just a little. And so, at a hot, crowded, tense meeting across
the street from the famous Atlantic City boardwalk, a "compromise"
was proposed: the integrated Mississippi Freedom Democratic Party

(MFDP) could have two seats on the delegation. And, four years hence, the entire Mississippi delegation would have to be integrated.

Allard Lowenstein, Joseph Rauh, a widely respected Washington civil rights lawyer, and black moderate civil rights leaders Roy Wilkins and Bayard Rustin urged acceptance of the compromise as an important political victory that could lay the groundwork for future victories.

The young, increasingly radical leaders of the Student Non-Violent Coordinating Committee (SNCC), largely responsible for the organization of the MFDP delegation, would not accept a compromise with racists. Period. After bitter debate, the Mississippi delegation of poor black sharecroppers, maids, and cotton-choppers unanimously voted to reject the compromise.

Although many liberal civil rights activists didn't realize it then, the failure of the MFDP compromise in 1964 signaled the beginning of a new phase in the civil rights movement. "SNCC and MFDP discovered their liberal friends cared more about the threat of Goldwater and the ambitions of Humphrey than about the absolute morality of a cause," Jack Newfield would later write in his thoughtful book, *A Prophetic Minority*, a study of the New Left. "They discovered that even the best liberals, those who sometimes supported civil disobedience, would at some point divide politics and morality and bend their knees to reality."

By late 1965 and 1966, the inner councils of SNCC became less and less amenable to the involvement of white liberals. In the North, the elite college campuses turned their attention to the war in Vietnam and the draft. Finally, in May 1966, Stokely Carmichael was named head of SNCC on a platform of "black power." Antipolitics purism had begun to take over the movement to achieve civil rights for blacks, and the coalition of white liberals and black moderates which had dominated the civil rights movement in the early sixties was dead.

two

THE ANTIWAR MOVEMENT: THE POLITICS OF PEACE

"The question comes down to this: Do you stop the war by bashing people over the head and ordering them to stop the war, or do you stop it by making our case in the political process and reclaiming the Democratic Party and the America we all believe in? Is there really any choice?"

—Allard K. Lowenstein, leader of
the "Dump Johnson" movement,
National Student Association Congress,
August 1967

JUST AT THE TIME—1965–66—when the civil rights movement appeared to be overtaken by the more purist, antipolitical-process elements, Lyndon Johnson escalated America's involvement in the war in Vietnam. White radical students from SNCC and the Students for a Democratic Society now transferred their absolute moralism and their perception of the opposition as demons from the cause of civil rights to the issue of the Vietnam war.

These student radicals who opposed Johnson's policies saw the war in Vietnam as an outgrowth of the imperialism and colonialism of a capitalistic, industrialized nation. They viewed Johnson's policies as fundamentally immoral; the policies, these students believed, were wrong from the start, even if they had a chance of succeeding (which, from their knowledge of Vietnamese history, they believed to be impossible).

Through the early period of escalation in 1965, these students bore the brunt of the effort to educate the American people about the war. They understood that in order to get attention from the press they would have to resort to symbolic acts of illegality and confrontations with governmental authorities.

During this period, most students were either indifferent to or mildly supported Johnson's policies on the war. A poll taken in March 1966 of 1000 Yale students, for example, showed that 44 per cent believed in the "domino theory." Pluralities also favored increasing U.S. ground commitments and the institution of a naval blockade of Haiphong. Only 10 per cent favored unilateral withdrawal by U.S. forces and 12 per cent, a coalition government modeled after Laos.

Six months later, an editorial appeared in the *Yale Daily News* endorsing a petition which urged President Johnson to cease the bombing, halt further troop increases, and announce a willingness to negotiate directly with the National Liberation Front and to allow the NLF to participate in a coalition government. In a campuswide mock election, a peace candidate running for Congress from New Haven defeated the hawkish incumbent by more than two to one, and Mark Hatfield, well known for his dovish views, defeated an outspoken hawk, Robert Duncan, by a margin of 81 to 18 per cent.

What had happened to cause the antiwar movement to move so rapidly from the radical left into the mainstream of campus opinion?

Two factors were at work here, each of which fed on the other. One was the cumulative effect of the tactics used by the radicals to "raise consciousness," as they would say, about the war, the most important of which was the use of classroom techniques—the "teach-in"—to impart basic information. As more students learned more about Vietnam, its past history, the character of its people, and the details of French and American involvement since World War II, substantial numbers began to turn against Johnson's policies not for moral or ideological reasons, but for purely pragmatic ones, i.e. the U. S. was bound to lose if we got involved in a civil war in Southeast Asia.

A second important factor was the draft. If it was true that a number of students came to oppose the war the more they learned about Vietnam, it was also true that most of them would never have been interested in learning anything at all had it not been for the growing worry that someday the United States government might be asking them to fight and perhaps die in Vietnam.

As the draft calls went up and the war continued to escalate, it became increasingly apparent that the fighting in Vietnam was becoming the most important reality in our lives. It wasn't just the fear of fighting in a war and maybe getting hurt, although that obviously lurked not too far back in the minds of those of us who were students at the elite colleges and universities. More important, we resented the danger of being drafted because of the inconvenience of it all. We were the high achievers who were accustomed to a secure future, all laid out neatly in front of us. Now, suddenly, all was uncertain. Would we be able to go to graduate school? Could we plan a few years traveling? There were no answers, only the growing apprehension that somehow the future had gotten outside our control.

The draft also brought us face to face with what we thought were deeply felt values. Student activists in the privileged colleges had gone South to bring justice to the oppressed, professing social selflessness and public responsibility. The draft now made that sort of commitment a bit expensive. We enjoyed the benefits of our privilege through the protection of our student deferments.[1] Meanwhile, those young people without our economic resources, including the sons of black parents whom we had traveled thousands of miles to help a few years before, were being drafted and bearing the ugly realities of the war, not just the inconvenience of an uncertain future. In the crunch, in the contest between our liberal compassion and our personal security, for too many of us, there was no contest.

By the fall of 1966, the mainstream of student opinion on the campuses of the major colleges and universities in the country had turned against the war. Few people in the Johnson administration or the press understood that such a change had taken place. But there was one person who saw it happening and immediately understood the political consequences.

Allard Lowenstein had kept his ties with the moderate student leadership he had recruited for the 1964 Mississippi Summer Project

1. At the United States Student Press Association conference in the spring of 1966, Robert Kennedy asked an audience of student editors how many students supported the war in Vietnam. A majority of the audience raised their hands. Then Kennedy asked, "How many of you are willing to give up your student deferments and volunteer to fight over there?" Not surprisingly, no one raised his hand. "In other words," Kennedy said quietly, "you like the fighting as long as someone else is doing it for you."

and other civil rights movement activities. He watched with growing dismay as the purist militance which he believed had set back the civil rights effort was now being used on the campuses to force a change in Johnson's war policies.

While Lowenstein's early opposition to the war arose from a moral revulsion similar to that of the early radical war dissenters, he believed that violent and disruptive tactics would only strengthen Johnson's political position. The only way Johnson would change his war policies, Lowenstein believed, would be to convince him that a political disaster awaited him if he failed to do so. Johnson would never be convinced of that until the antiwar movement was taken out of the counterculture of the purist left and taken over by the moderate student leaders who represented the mainstream of campus opinion and, more important, whose parents had political muscle within the Democratic Party and would be much influenced by the activities of their kids.

Gregory Craig was a good example of the kind of student moderate Lowenstein turned to. The son of a university administrator, Craig was raised in Palo Alto, California, while his father was dean of Stanford. He went to prep school at the prestigious Phillips Exeter Academy and on to Harvard in 1963. Prior to John Kennedy's election in 1960, he recalls, he had been only casually interested in politics. But "when Kennedy said 'the torch has been passed to a new generation of Americans,' I really believed him."

Craig won the presidency of the Harvard Undergraduate Council in 1966. "I loved my political position . . . it was just perfect," he remembers. "To my left was the SDS—loud, obscene, vulgar—screaming antiwar epithets, turning everyone off. To my right was 95 per cent of the student body. In contrast to SDS, everyone loved me."

Craig had come to oppose the war sometime in 1966, but never, he recalls, with the ideological or moral commitment of the more radical left. When Lowenstein, whom he had known through his father during Lowenstein's years at Stanford, approached Craig to help organize a letter from college student leaders to Lyndon Johnson, Craig immediately joined up.

At the 1966 National Student Association Conference, Lowenstein, a former president of NSA, had organized a working commit-

tee of student body presidents to solicit signatures for the letter.
There was, however, substantial opposition to the letter idea and to
the overall strategy of pressuring Johnson to change his strategy
through traditional political channels. The president of Stanford's
student body, David Harris, bitterly denounced Lowenstein for the
move. "The political system is corrupt and we'll never end the war
by joining in the corruption ourselves. The only way to end the war
is to confront the President, disrupt the institutions of government,
and deny the military the manpower they need to fight this rotten
war." Lowenstein was quickly on his feet. "You may be right . . . the
system may be corrupt. But how do we know? We haven't tried it
yet. That's all I'm asking."

On December 28, 1966, the front page of *The New York Times* led
with the story about the student moderates' letter to Johnson, which
urged in carefully respectful language that Johnson should seek a
"negotiated settlement." The front-page play signaled a new phase
in the antiwar movement. Suddenly, dissent on the war had become
respectable.

The student leaders met with Secretary of State Dean Rusk a few
weeks later. "Why are you here? Why don't you write Ho Chi
Minh?" Rusk asked repeatedly. "It was like two ships passing in the
night," Greg Craig recalls. "There we were, the most moderate and
establishment elements of the antiwar movement, wanting to open
the lines of communication with the administration, and he was
treating us like a bunch of crazy radicals." The attitude of the
administration accelerated student opposition to the war—and,
eventually, opposition by the parents of those students.

Lowenstein, in early 1967, began to take steps to establish a
national political organization to "dump Johnson." He rested his
hopes on winning the commitment of the 1967 NSA Congress at
College Park, Maryland. But when Congress convened, it was clear
the old basic split remained. As it turned out, the purist-coalitionist
division within the student organization crystallized around an essentially peripheral but highly symbolic issue. The so-called Black
Caucus had introduced a resolution supporting "national liberation,
at home or abroad, by any means necessary." "By any means necessary" was interpreted by all as a euphemism for violence.

Lowenstein and the student moderates, including Greg Craig, a

Harvard Divinity student named Sam Brown, and Steven Cohen, president of the Amherst College student body, immediately recognized that any suggestion that violence was an acceptable political tactic was inimical to a strategy of taking the antiwar movement into the mainstream of American politics.

For much of the debate, the antiviolence position seemed to be losing ground, as the blacks made good use of what they knew was a hypersensitivity of the student left to any suggestion that they were as racist as the rest of the country. Then a black student body president named Clinton Deveaux from the State University of New York at Buffalo took the platform. He denounced his fellow blacks for their "bullying reverse racist tactics, whipping up the white liberal consciences so that they are helpless to resist endorsing the irrational." The "irrational," as far as Deveaux was concerned, was to suggest that violence was any kind of answer to the problems faced by blacks or to ending the war in Vietnam. "There's only one way we're going to get the changes we want in this country," he said. "And that's by winning over the minds, the consciences, of the people who govern us and the voters who give them the power to govern us."

Deveaux's speech was roundly booed by the Black Caucus. Shouts of "Uncle Tom" interrupted him throughout. The "change-by-any-means-necessary" resolution ultimately passed by a small margin, and the writing was on the wall. The next day, Sam Brown, representing the student moderates, lost his race for the presidency of NSA to a candidate who, the day before, had endorsed the "by any means necessary" language. When Steven Cohen of Amherst also lost his bid for vice president, he took the platform and proclaimed: "I want to thank all of you for not electing me vice president. Now, while NSA spends its time passing resolutions about the political utility of throwing rocks and taking over classrooms, I'm going to be able to devote every ounce of my time and strength to dumping Lyndon Baines Johnson."

That night, Lowenstein, Craig, Brown, Deveaux, Cohen, and about a hundred other student body presidents made plans to launch a national political effort to prepare for an electoral challenge to Lyndon Johnson. Now all they needed was money and support from the liberal establishment in the Democratic Party and a candidate to work for.

The "adult" liberal establishment, meanwhile, had tried its best to maintain its loyalty to the president who had beaten Barry Goldwater and who, since then, had compiled an unprecedented record of domestic legislative achievement. As late as the fall of 1967, the national board of the Americans for Democratic Action, the most important national liberal organization, refused to endorse Lowenstein's Dump Johnson movement.

But the Democratic Party liberals were subjected with increasing frequency to the same forces which their children had experienced some months before. These were the lawyers, businessmen, engineers, and educators who had coalesced around Eleanor Roosevelt and Adlai Stevenson during the fifties and who supported Stevenson in 1960, suspicious of Kennedy's former "softness" on Joe McCarthy and his close relations with the uncouth Irish political bosses of the big-city machines. They had grown increasingly uncomfortable by the end of 1966 and 1967 with Johnson's policies in Vietnam as they learned more about the background of the war. And, not surprisingly, their learning incentive was heightened by the realization that their children's future was threatened by the draft.

And so, two growing political constituencies opposing Lyndon Johnson's war policies had evolved by the middle of 1967. Each needed the other in order to make possible a frontal political challenge to Lyndon Johnson. The student activists needed the linkage to the adult political establishment, the resources and national organization which the liberal reformers within the Democratic Party could provide. And the liberals needed the kids to give them what they rarely had had in their former battles against party regulars: political muscle, the ability to match the regulars in campaign workers and precinct organization.

No one in the country had closer ties and more extensive experiences with both groups than Allard Lowenstein. For more than ten years he had scurried around the country, a pile of newspapers typically under his arm, shirttail hanging out, rarely sleeping, always running, always meeting people, collecting names and telephone numbers. Now, in the fall of 1967, his moment had arrived. He had convinced a substantial portion of the leadership of the college student community from the nation's elite campuses that the future lay within the political process, not in throwing rocks at the Pentagon. He had convinced a substantial portion of the Democratic Party's liberal establishment that it could be respectable to challenge an incumbent president of their own party. And, under a superstructure called the National Conference of Concerned Democrats, he had brought these two groups together as a political movement which perceived itself as the beginning of a "new kind of politics in America."

When Eugene McCarthy finally accepted Lowenstein's invitation to run against Johnson (after Robert Kennedy, Lowenstein's first choice, had turned him down for pragmatic reasons), there was already a national constituency and the beginnings of a national political organization awaiting him, with local leadership identified and a fund-raising apparatus already established.

What is important here, however, is not who made up this constituency, but who did not. Lowenstein never had the time or the resources to go to the trade schools and junior colleges, or to the street corners, to convince the sons of working-class families that they had an even greater stake in opposing the war than the Harvards, Yales, and Stanfords. Nor did Lowenstein or his associates have the time or resources to visit many shop gates and union halls during these early days of the antiwar movement, making the case to blue-collar workers and their wives about the economic costs of the war.

The result was that when Eugene McCarthy launched his campaign to begin a "New Politics movement" in America, his constituency was white, culturally homogeneous, well educated, and totally insulated from (and indifferent to) the bread-and-butter grievances basic to the winning of political power in America. As the 1968 presidential campaign unfolded, that particular reality—that there was no chance of actually winning—not only didn't discourage the more purist elements of the New Politics but, in fact, confirmed the fact that they must be doing something right.

three

McCARTHY v. KENNEDY: THE LINES DRAWN

> "Somewhere along the line they had stopped listening. Our rallies had become rituals of the good and the pure. [But] you don't prove America is yours just by filling ball parks with college kids."
>
> —Jeremy Larner, speechwriter for Senator Eugene McCarthy during 1968 presidential campaign

THE CLASH BETWEEN Eugene McCarthy and Robert Kennedy for the backing of the New Politics constituency in 1968 was a classic confrontation between the purist and coalitionist philosophies.

McCarthy—the Antipolitician

At first glance it seemed that Senator McCarthy and his followers had opted for the political-process strategy. After all, McCarthy had responded to Lowenstein's offer to challenge Lyndon Johnson. He frequently told his young audiences that he was "testing" the political system to see if it would respond. His campaign organization, despite its youth and lack of experience, had chosen very traditional political techniques to win political support—press releases, canvassing, vote pulling on election day.

Nevertheless, from the very beginning of his campaign, McCarthy made it clear that he intended to launch a "New Politics" in the country. As he articulated the values and attitudes he believed that the "New Politics" should represent, it became clear that his brand of "new politics" bore a closer resemblance to the antipolitics purism of the latter-day civil rights movement and early antiwar movement than to the coalitionist philosophies of people like Al Lowenstein and Greg Craig.

The first time I heard McCarthy speak was in early January 1968 in a high school auditorium in Nashua, New Hampshire. My first impression of him, as he talked quietly about the necessity of making a "reasoned judgment" about the Vietnam War, was that he was *different* from other politicians I had seen. He used words, spoke in a style, new to my political experience. It was supposed to be a political rally, but we didn't interrupt him with applause; we listened, as if he were delivering a college lecture.

During the question and answer session a student asked him: "First, do you want to be president and, second, do you think you will ever be president?" McCarthy smiled, as if it were a question he had especially looked forward to answering. "My answer is, first, no; second, no."

There was a stunned silence. I remember thinking to myself, What the hell am I doing here? How the hell is this guy ever going to end the war? Suddenly, a Yale student whom I recognized as one of the most anti-Lowenstein, antipolitical-process people on campus stood up and started clapping. Within seconds, the entire audience was on its feet clapping and cheering. I found myself on my feet as well, and as I clapped, I kept thinking, he sure is different . . . he sure is different.

McCarthy liked to remind us that we were part of a brand-new political movement, with a higher level of political morality than others in the political system. He always liked to say that he had the A students, while Kennedy had the B students.

It was heady stuff. We got so accustomed to hearing it, and reading about ourselves as carriers of a new morality and a new kind of politics, that we began to believe it.

How much of it was really new? Certainly never before in American political history had so many citizen-amateurs—especially young people—invaded the precincts and volunteered their time on behalf of a cause or a set of principles. The degree of commitment and sacrifice these volunteers exhibited was extraordinary. It indicated the significant political potential of a highly motivated group of volunteers to outproduce the pros, who had been accustomed to regarding the political process as a closed club.

As it turned out, much of our perception of our newness was nothing more than delusion. The canvassing and vote-pulling techniques we used in New Hampshire may have been new and shiny to us, but Dick Daley had been using them long before the New Hampshire primary. As to personal self-interest, of course we were motivated by great issues of American foreign policy and the allocation of domestic resources; but many of us had a little self-interest involved in our motives as well—like not wanting to have our heads blown off in Vietnam, or liking the idea of the political power we would possess if McCarthy were ever elected president.

And despite all our press notices, we discovered that we weren't above doing whatever was necessary to win a vote. One night in the spring of 1968, I was canvassing with a friend in New Haven, Connecticut, in preparation for the coming primary. My friend knocked on a door and an elderly woman appeared. "Good evening, ma'am," he said. "We're here to ask you to consider supporting Senator McCarthy in next Tuesday's primary." The lady smiled brightly. "Oh, Senator McCarthy. Ain't he the one who's out to get rid of all them Commies in the government? Sure, I'll vote for him next Tuesday." I started to protest, but something stopped me. My friend gave me a wink, and quickly said: "That's right, ma'am, that's the same McCarthy. We'll be back in touch with you on election day and get you a ride to the polls."

There *was* an important difference between us and the old pols. They winked at each other and laughed about it. We did the same thing, got embarrassed about it, then justified it in the name of the high principles that motivated us.

Kennedy—the Ultimate Coalitionist

Robert Kennedy had never liked liberals who held purist values, which, he believed, did not belong in the political process. Many of the people behind Eugene McCarthy reminded him of the group who had supported Adlai Stevenson (who was nominated by none other than Eugene McCarthy over John Kennedy at the 1960 convention). The Kennedys were always suspicious of the Stevensonians, David Halberstam has written, because, while it was "all right . . . to present an image as the citizen-leader rather than the politician who made deals, . . . it was dangerous to believe it yourself." [1]

On the night of the Indiana primary, Kennedy was incredulous at the glorious ovation which rang from McCarthy headquarters and over the national TV networks, even though McCarthy had come in a poor third. It reminded Robert Kennedy of the "exhilaration" of Stevenson's followers after every defeat. "That very exhilaration had left the Kennedys, especially Robert Kennedy, with a vague suspicion that liberals would rather lose gallantly than win pragmatically," Halberstam observed, "that they viewed the irony and charm of Stevenson's election-night concessions more than they valued the power and patronage of victory." [2]

There were two sides to this Kennedy pragmatism. On the one hand, it often led him to measure the political currents first before taking a particular position. One of the most dramatic manifestations of this side of Kennedy's pragmatism was his refusal of Lowenstein's invitation to run in 1968. He chose to listen to people who based their political advice on past election returns and current polls, not on moral imperatives or on a firsthand sense of what the country wanted. As a consequence he was forced to watch with growing frustration as Gene McCarthy, for whom he had little respect, reaped the rewards of acting first and measuring the political realities later.

On the other hand, Kennedy's political pragmatism proved itself in his understanding that the essence of the political process is the ability to understand and to speak to the needs of ordinary people—people who had real, immediate economic and social fears and who, in 1968, would vote on the basis of those fears unless someone showed them a better alternative.

By January and February 1968, Kennedy's instincts (encouraged by his young Senate staff, including Adam Walinsky and Peter Edelman) prevailed over his pragmatism and the older advisers from

1. David Halberstam, *The Best and the Brightest* (New York, Random House, 1969), p. 27.
2. Halberstam, *op.cit.*, p. 72

President Kennedy's entourage, who had counseled caution. The war continued, the country grew increasingly troubled, and Kennedy could no longer remain on the sidelines—all the more so in deference to Eugene McCarthy, whom he neither liked nor respected. Shortly after the New Hampshire primary (too shortly, most people thought), Robert Kennedy declared for the presidency.

Kennedy did not shrink from addressing himself to issues other liberals avoided for fear of being accused of "selling out" to the conservatives or of being too opportunistic. In Indiana, for example, Kennedy began all his speeches in the white, ethnic, blue-collar neighborhoods of Gary, Indiana, with the line: "As the former Attorney General of the United States, I know the importance of tough law enforcement in this country."

Few of Kennedy's tactics drew as much contempt from McCarthy and his followers as that law-and-order pitch in Indiana. We regarded it as a thinly disguised appeal to white racism, just as we would think the same thing when it came out of the mouths of Richard Nixon and Spiro Agnew in 1970 and 1972. But we never asked ourselves at the time whether the blue-collar workers in Gary had a right to be concerned about their families being mugged on the street or their kids being shot up with dope in the schoolyards, and more importantly, whether some liberal Democrat ought to address himself to their fears and grievances.

As the 1968 primary campaign progressed, a number of McCarthy workers, myself included, became increasingly troubled by the venomous personal attacks on Kennedy by McCarthy, attacks gleefully emulated by the antipolitics purists who by now had thronged to the antipolitician's campaign. Suddenly everyone seemed to have lost perspective: the war, Hubert Humphrey's possible nomination—everything that had led us to turn to the political process in 1967—seemed to have become unimportant. Now the McCarthy campaign seemed motivated principally by hatred for Robert Kennedy.

A key incident in our growing disappointment with McCarthy came during the latter days of the Wisconsin primary, when McCarthy indicated a reluctance to campaign in the Milwaukee ghetto. Two of his best staff people, press aides Mary Lou Oates and Seymour Hersh, resigned in disgust. His explanation—"I don't have to prove myself to anyone, they know my record"—struck us not only as arrogant toward black voters but as utterly contemptuous of those of us who believed a politician was obligated to go to the people and prove himself.

The degree of our isolation from those "ordinary people" to whom Kennedy was trying to speak was brought home to me at a McCarthy-for-President meeting held at Yale late in the spring of 1968. I looked around the room and saw mirror images of myself. I had been to hundreds of such meetings all around the country and all of them, in effect, had been attended by the same people. We all thought the same, agreed with each other, applauded each other. We even looked like each other. We all felt immensely special, immensely important, and heady with the history we knew, and were constantly being told by the press, we were making.

Southern Connecticut State College, a commuter working-class school, is down the road from Yale. I had just read an article in the New Haven *Register* reporting that a Southern Connecticut undergraduate, drafted the year before, had been killed in Vietnam. I suddenly realized that we had not only neglected to publicize this particular meeting at Southern Connecticut; we had *never* invited Southern Connecticut students to join us. It wasn't just cultural snobbery, though there was surely some of that. The truth was, we simply hadn't thought of it. For us, those working-class kids simply didn't exist. They were, to the generation of college students who had marched for civil rights in Mississippi and Alabama, as invisible as Ralph Ellison's Invisible Man.

Those of us who had been fighting the battle over the years for a political-process strategy and for broad-based coalitions to achieve social change came to realize during the last days of the McCarthy campaign that we were part of an elitist, arrogant, exclusive movement that had adopted those very attitudes and tactics we had always argued were incompatible with the political process.

Not surprisingly, we began to look to Robert Kennedy with increasing hope, not because we thought he had a better chance to win—we all assumed Hubert Humphrey had already wrapped it up—but because he *wanted* to win. To us that meant he was committed to building a coalition of the black and white underclass, those who had previously spent much of their time fighting each other over crumbs while those who owned the cake urged them on. We were excited by the thought that, in the 1968 Indiana primary, Kennedy had won 90 per cent of the black vote at the same time that he was sweeping those counties in which George Wallace had done best during the 1964 primary.

We still felt a loyalty to McCarthy; after all, we kept telling ourselves, he had been there first, when Kennedy was hiding on the sidelines. But slowly, one by one, many members of McCarthy's national staff and local leadership became convinced that if Kennedy won in California, it was time to back Kennedy.

A bullet in a Los Angeles kitchen destroyed our chance to see whether an entirely new Democratic coalition was possible between McCarthy's New Politics constituency of comfortable suburbanites, intellectual elite, and the activist A students, and Kennedy's coalition of blacks, white ethnics, browns, reds, and the B students and working-class young people.

For the purists among us, the 1968 convention and Mayor Daley's police were final proof that such a coalition was both impossible and undesirable. The future lay in a realigned party system, the purists would agree, with liberal intellectuals, liberated women, activist kids, and minorities all under one roof. That roof *could* be the Democratic Party, which, many resolved, could be captured with the right kind of strategy by the next national convention. If that didn't happen, a new fourth party could be formed under the leadership of people like McCarthy, who hinted at such an idea, or even John Lindsay.

But the opportunity lost through Robert Kennedy's death haunted many of us in the months and years ahead. Many of us vowed that, the next time around, we would do something more than travel around the country from meeting to meeting, talking to ourselves.

PART II

The Quest
for Power

WHATEVER DISAGREEMENTS there were on future strategies within
the New Politics movement in the aftermath of the 1968 campaign,
large numbers of New Politics activists had come to a similar
conclusion about future goals. They were no longer interested
merely in symbolic protest or in "raising issues" in an otherwise
hopeless cause; that had its place, but not now. Now it was time to
win real political power and to get real change. The name of the
game was power, and they believed they now had the resources and
expertise to play the game successfully, although it might be
necessary to change some of the rules to give their side maximum
advantage.

This quest for power would proceed on two fronts. One involved
1972 and the national Democratic Party. Its major focus was
procedural: to alter the rules governing the selection of national
convention delegates to enable the New Politics constituency to
control the 1972 convention and nominate one of its own for
president.

The second line of attack was based on the determination to
expand the base of the movement, to take the issues of the New
Politics back into the political process and persuade a broad coalition of people beyond the college campuses and liberal intellectuals
of the need for their support. Some former McCarthy leaders such

as Joseph Duffey, the McCarthy campaign coordinator in Connecticut, in 1968, tried to build such a coalition through his own candidacy for public office. Others, like McCarthy's student coordinator, Sam Brown, sought to expand the antiwar movement into working class and Middle American communities. And, of course, in everyone's mind was building a strong base for the next go-round at the big prize—the Democratic presidential nomination in 1972.

The success of the procedural effort and the failure of the political one were to have profound effects on the political events of 1972.

four

POWER AND PROCESS: PARTY REFORM

> "We are concerned with the opportunity to participate rather than [with] the actual level of participation, less concerned with the product of the meetings than [with] the process."
> —Commission on Party Structure and Delegate Selection ("McGovern Commission"), April 1970

AUGUST 27, 1968, the second day of the Democratic National Convention, had been a long day. The credentials challenges on the seating of state delegations lay ahead; the roll call was proceeding on something called the Minority Report of the Rules Committee. Most of the delegates had no idea of what the Majority Report contained, much less the Minority Report.

The roll call got to the Missouri delegation. According to one account, Governor Warren Hearnes stood up at this point and shouted:

"Does anyone know what the hell this is all about?"

"Carl Albert [convention chairman] called it a unit rule vote," a voice shouted back.

"What's Humphrey say?"

"He's against it."

"Against what? The Minority Report resolution or the unit rule?"

"He's against the unit rule, which means he's for the resolution. Or maybe the other way around."

Hearnes apparently shook his head in disgust. "The hell with it.

All in favor say 'aye.' " There was silence. "All opposed say 'nay.' "
More silence. Hearnes took the delegation microphone. He announced to the convention and the nation that Missouri cast all 78
votes in favor of the minority resolution.

Those 78 votes from Missouri were decisive. The resolution
carried by a small margin of 1350 to 1206.

More than four years later, Eli Segal, a thirty-year-old attorney
who was one of those principally responsible for converting that
minority resolution into a revolutionary change in the Democratic
Party's nominating system, remembered that historic vote with some
poignancy. "The Democratic Party reform movement was born out
of confusion and thanks to the support of a governor who had
presided over one of the most undemocratic systems of delegate
selection in the country. What poetic justice."

What Warren Hearnes and other Humphrey supporters at the
convention hadn't understood was that, while they had concentrated
their attention on defeating Eugene McCarthy, many New Politics
activists had already abandoned that ship. More important business
was at hand. It wasn't just that they were tired of the futility of the
McCarthy candidacy. But they were ready to begin looking
ahead—to the next presidential campaign—and to begin the work
necessary to turn the tables in 1972.

By the summer of 1968 most of the New Politics forces were no
longer primarily concerned about the prospects of the McCarthy
candidacy; most assumed by then that it was utterly hopeless. Instead, the major point of attention was what was perceived as two
inherently undemocratic characteristics of the delegate-selection
process: first, the barriers to public participation in the process; and
second, the failure of the end product of that process to be
representative of the political preferences of all Democrats.

The liberal reformers in the New Politics constituency had had
prior experience over the years with what they had long regarded as
undemocratic practices by party regulars. Among the student activists in the campaign, however, the first contact with rules and
practices blocking public participation was traumatic, especially
since the tradition of democratic participation was so strong on the
elite college campuses during the early and mid-sixties. The "Port

Huron Statement" founding the Students for a Democratic Society in 1962 was based on the concept of "participatory democracy." The Berkeley demonstrations and the Free Speech Movement of 1964, the Yale protests against the failure of a popular teacher to receive academic tenure in 1965, and other protests in the mid-sixties were all essentially an effort by students to participate more directly in decision making on their university campuses.

Over and over again in the spring and early summer of 1968, these students were confronted by what appeared to be a deliberate, concerted effort to exclude "ordinary people"—among whom they saw themselves—from the nominating process, and hence, maintain control in as few hands as possible.

The examples were numerous. In 1968 there were no written party rules at all for the selection of convention delegates in at least ten states, and in ten others they were in existence but unavailable to individuals who wanted to read them. Party leaders had discouraged insurgents from mounting successful challenges by various means: using phony proxy ballots (in one instance, for example, the voting of 492 unwritten proxies by a local ward leader at a township caucus, a number constituting three times the number of party members physically present at the meeting); holding local caucuses in private homes without public knowledge or invitation; selecting delegates to the national convention long before issues and candidates had emerged (in 1968, two out of five convention delegates had already been selected prior to Eugene McCarthy's announcement to challenge Lyndon Johnson). In Connecticut, challengers to the party-endorsed slates of delegates to the state convention had to pay $14,000 in filing fees to mount a statewide challenge, but the party slates were entitled to free access to the ballot and a special designation on the ballot as the "Party Endorsed Slate."

There was particular outrage over the discovery that even the results of a statewide primary, in which all Democrats were free to participate, could be utterly ignored by party leaders. The most frequently cited example was the April 1968 Pennsylvania primary, in which Senator McCarthy received 430,000 votes, compared to 65,500 for Robert Kennedy and 72,000 for Humphrey. The primary was "preferential": elected delegates, and party leaders who controlled them, were free to ignore the results of the primary, and they did. Mayor Joseph Barr of Pittsburgh, Mayor James Tate of Philadelphia, and I. W. Abel, the Steelworkers' president, were the triumvirate who controlled the Pennsylvania delegation. The final delegation voted 103 for Humphrey and only 26 for McCarthy.

Attacking these undemocratic—and not so subtle—techniques of exclusion, we would often add together the votes of McCarthy and Kennedy in each primary state—70 per cent in Indiana, 80 per cent in Oregon, 85 per cent in California—to prove that Hubert Humphrey was in fact supported by only a small minority of Democrats. We perceived the so-called New Politics as the politics of the "people." "This is the year when the people are right and the politicians are wrong," John Kenneth Galbraith would say again and again.

We agreed. But we failed to see other things: despite our rhetoric about "public participation," fewer than one out of five Democrats participated in the Pennsylvania primary, which we kept citing as evidence of McCarthy's great popularity. And, despite our rhetorical flourishes about the combined McCarthy-Kennedy peace vote, we ignored the fact that 75 per cent of the Kennedy vote would have supported Humphrey over McCarthy, including—we were shocked to learn later—Robert Kennedy himself; or the fact that the national polls indicated that Hubert Humphrey was far more representative of rank-and-file Democrats than Eugene McCarthy.

We were already paying the penalty for having spent too much of our time talking to each other.

Our shock at the undemocratic delegate selection procedures was mild compared to the trauma of the Chicago convention of 1968.

The police-state atmosphere within the convention hall, the microphone cutting, the heavy-handed thugs who roamed the floor as Mayor Daley's security force, and, most of all, the police riots outside the convention hall unified the New Politics movement, McCarthy and Kennedy people, radicals and liberals and moderates, purists and coalitionists, as nothing had before.

Hubert Humphrey had several opportunities to express sympathy for those young people whose heads had been senselessly bloodied by Mayor Daley's police. After the police had raided the McCarthy staff floor in the Hilton Hotel and dragged young people out of their beds early in the morning of August 29, beating every head in sight, a number of McCarthy staffers raced up to Humphrey's suite a few floors above and asked him, through one of his aides, to come down and at least help to quiet down the hysteria which then prevailed. The Vice President, they were told, flatly refused. More than that, the next day, at a press conference, Humphrey avoided any mention of the incident and instead praised Mayor Daley and his police.

Humphrey's association with Mayor Daley was far more responsible for the refusal of many McCarthy workers to support him in the weeks following the convention than his association with Johnson's war policies. Had Humphrey appeared among the McCarthy young people that night in the Hilton and at least made it known that he was concerned about this type of mindless violence, that single gesture would certainly have done more than anything else to reconcile the New Politics forces and heal divisions within the party.

On the other hand, few of us stopped to consider whether our actions—or inactions—would result in the election of Richard Nixon and what that might mean for the Supreme Court, the poor, blacks, and other minority groups. We were so involved in our own sense of being wronged, in our own self-righteousness, that some of us even admitted we preferred a Nixon victory (whose consequences for us, since we were neither poor nor black, were more theoretical than real) to a Humphrey victory. With Humphrey defeated, we reasoned, it would be easier for us to pick up the pieces and take over the Democratic Party. So we set out to take full advantage of the sleeper resolution a few McCarthy staffers had slipped by an unsuspecting convention. We vowed that the next time around, the "people"—meaning us, of course—would be in control of the Democratic Party.

At first glance, Eli Segal seems an unlikely candidate to have played such a critical role in revolutionizing a nominating system which had prevailed in the Democratic Party for more than a century.

Like many of the best of the New Politics young professionals who graduated from the McCarthy and Kennedy campaigns of 1968,

Eli Segal's political roots were from the more moderate, less politically activist elements of the elite college campuses during the early
and mid-sixties. Born and raised in Brooklyn, Segal graduated in 1964
from Brandeis University. While at Brandeis, his political activity
was confined to some casual involvement in student government.

As late as the summer of 1967, his last year at the University of
Michigan Law School, Segal was still relatively indifferent to the war
issue. Upon graduation from law school, he served as legislative
assistant to the late New York congressman Joseph Resnick, a
pronounced hawk and an outspoken Johnson supporter. Segal had
little problem explaining this apparent contradiction. "Joe was a
unique guy . . . a domestic liberal, a maverick who had a penchant
for socking it to the 'big boys' on issues. I did his domestic work and
argued with him on Vietnam."

When he finally did join the McCarthy campaign in the middle of
1968 as an advance man, he was motivated primarily by his growing
opposition to Johnson's war policies and not by any unusual emotional commitment to McCarthy. During the Indiana primary campaign, however, Segal became increasingly bitter at the type of
campaign Kennedy was waging, especially what he perceived as
Kennedy's blatant attempts to take advantage of the law-and-order
issue. From that point on, he preferred McCarthy to Kennedy.

In June 1968, after the California primary, Segal was one of those
who began to discuss ways to shift the focus of the New Politics effort
from McCarthy's candidacy to the issue of the delegate-selection
process. A Yale Law School student, Geoffrey Cowan, suggested to
Segal one evening that an independent commission be organized
which could prepare a report, publicize the injustices of the current
system, and lay the groundwork for future change.

Governor (now Senator) Harold Hughes of Iowa agreed to serve
as chairman of that commission, which was quickly organized by
early July 1968, and included representatives from the McCarthy
and Kennedy campaigns, organized labor and minorities. Within six
weeks, the commission had published a report detailing the
undemocratic practices of the current delegate-selection process
and recommending, in the form of a resolution submitted to the
Convention Rules Committee, that the unit rule, which had permitted a majority to bind an entire delegation, be abolished for all

future conventions and that the delegate-selection process thenceforth ensure that "all Democratic voters have ... full and timely opportunity to participate."

The Hughes Commission resolution lost by a large margin within the Convention Rules Committee but was submitted as a minority report before the full convention and, with the aforementioned help from Governor Hearnes, narrowly won. The convention also adopted, without debate, a Credentials Committee resolution which established a "Special Committee" to "aid State Parties ... to assure broader citizen participation in the delegate selection process."

In February 1969, Senator Fred Harris of Oklahoma, the new chairman of the Democratic National Committee, on the basis of these two resolutions, appointed the National Commission on Party Structure and Delegate Selection. The obvious choice for chairman of this commission, Senator Harold Hughes, was vetoed by the Humphrey/labor forces because of his close association with the 1968 McCarthy campaign (Hughes had nominated McCarthy at the convention). Instead, Humphrey recommended Senator George McGovern of South Dakota. After all, McGovern had immediately supported Humphrey in 1968, even before the Chicago convention was over. McGovern seemed safer to those who were beginning to get a little worried about where all this reform talk was going to take the Democratic Party in the days ahead.

Eli Segal, who joined the commission shortly after its creation to serve as general counsel, saw immediately the serious inconsistency between two announced goals of the reformers: public participation in the delegate-selection process and the desire to establish standards for the type of people who would ultimately be selected as delegates.

"There was a difficult question which I saw on the horizon from the very beginning: What happens if a state party follows democratic procedures and then the delegation which is elected is composed of fifty-five-year-old white, Anglo-Saxon males? Which principle should prevail? Participation or representativeness?"

The commission's final report had opted in favor of participation and equal access. "We are less concerned with the product of the meetings than the process," the commission concluded. "The guidelines which we have adopted are designed to open the door to all Democrats who seek a voice in their Party's most important decision: the choice of its presidential nominee."

With little or no debate, the McGovern Commission decided to require state Democratic parties to permit full public participation in all phases of the delegate-selection process, including guaranteeing that all nominating meetings would remain open to the public.

Despite this commitment in favor of process over product, the commission went on to outline new rules aimed at guaranteeing that the selection of people who would ultimately be chosen as convention delegates would be representative. Unlike the open-democracy provisions, these suggested rules aroused considerable controversy. From the beginning, both the New Politics commissioners and the representatives of the Johnson-Humphrey wing of the party anticipated a number of serious implications in terms of the power structure within the party and control of the 1972 convention.

After a good deal of heated debate, the commission voted, ten to nine, to require that "State Parties overcome the effects of past discrimination by affirmative steps" to encourage the representation on the national convention delegation of minority groups, young people, and women "in reasonable relationship to their presence in the population of the state."

Four years later, Senator McGovern was severely criticized by party regulars for this provision, but he was not responsible for its passage. Senator Birch Bayh proposed the "reasonable relationship" language. Bayh recognized from the beginning the apparent political opportunities which such a provision might offer a presidential candidate who had strength among some of these groups. At Eli Segal's urging, Senator McGovern proposed the now-forgotten footnote to this section: "It is the understanding of the Commission that [representation of these groups] is not to be accomplished by the mandatory imposition of quotas."

One seldom-noted irony here is that the man who in 1972 was outspokenly critical of Senator McGovern for allegedly taking political advantage of this so-called quota provision was himself chiefly responsible for its passage. I. W. Abel, president of the Steelworkers and a member of the commission, had decided to boycott commission meetings. Had he been present and voted against Senator Bayh's motion, it would have failed.

Why were "minorities, young people, and women" singled out

for special treatment? The commission report cited past discriminatory practices against these three groups. In 1968, for example, only 5.5 per cent of the delegates were black; in 1964, the figure was 2 per cent, despite the fact that blacks are at least 11 per cent of the total population and an even higher percentage of Democratic voters. Approximately 4 per cent of the delegates in 1968 were under thirty and 13 per cent were women.

But why did the commission omit statistics concerning the underrepresentation of other ethnic groups?

"That's pretty simple," Eli Segal explained. "They had no one there pushing for them. Who spoke for the Italian construction worker or the Polish gas station attendant? They should have had someone pushing for them. It's the American way—get organized, or get overlooked."

A great distance remained between the written report and the actual selection process, so the New Politics-oriented commission staff members, especially Eli Segal, the research director, Kenneth Bode, and Anne Wexler, who had helped lead the McCarthy forces in Connecticut, engaged in a determined effort to protect the commission's report from subsequent modification and to ensure that the rules of the state parties would conform in time for the 1972 campaign.

There were three aspects of the effort. The first step was to ensure that the Democratic National Committee did not decide on the substance of the guidelines, since some staff members assumed that conservative party regulars would seek to change a number of the reforms, especially the representation requirement.

This was done by convincing the National Committee's general counsel, former LBJ aide Joseph Califano, that since the commission was created by the 1968 convention, its work was subject to the review only by the 1972 convention. The best that can be said for the staff's theory was that the mandate was ambiguous. The Reform Commission was actually created by the Majority Report of the Credentials Committee as a "Special Committee" to "recommend to the Democratic National Committee such improvements as can assure even broader citizen participation in the delegate selection process" and to "aid the state Democratic parties" to adopt rules which assured such participation.

It appears that the Democratic National Committee did have

authority to accept or reject the "recommendations." [1] On the other hand, the commission staff cited the precedent of the Special Equal Rights Committee, which was created by the 1964 convention after the Mississippi Freedom Democratic Party controversy. Governor Richard Hughes, chairman of the committee, made recommendations directly to the Credentials Committee of the 1968 convention. But, of course, the founding resolution for Governor Hughes' committee said nothing about the necessity of making recommendations to the Democratic National Committee, as did the resolution which created the McGovern Commission.

In any event, on February 19, 1971, Califano convinced a relatively confused Democratic National Committee that the words "recommend" and "report to" didn't give the National Committee the right to pass on the work of the McGovern Commission. On the other hand, Califano explained, the committee could—and should —include the new rules in the formal "call" to the 1972 convention (the "call" is the formal authority for the national convention and includes all the rules for the convening of the convention). In other words, the National Committee couldn't disapprove the new rules but they could approve them. Clear? Not very. And so, without any significant debate or discussion on these enormously important proposed reforms, the Democratic National Committee, not surprisingly, followed Califano's advice and voted unanimously to include the McGovern Commission's new rules on delegate selection in the formal "call" to the 1972 convention.

The second phase of the effort to protect the final commission report from modification was to ensure that the state parties complied with the new rules *prior to* the 1972 convention, even though, by Califano's own interpretation, such rules were supposed to be formally approved by that convention. Research director Kenneth Bode set up his own organization, funded by millionaire liberal Stewart Mott, to pressure state parties to adopt the commission guidelines in time for the 1972 campaigns. For its part, the

1. The McGovern staff seemed to recognize the problem raised by that language in a memo delivered to Senator McGovern shortly before the National Committee meeting: "The DNC is having a meeting in January 1970. Do we want to submit our guidelines to them as a report, as mandated by the convention . . . if submitted to the DNC and rejected, what are the consequences?"

commission staff exerted its own pressure on state party leaders. Since most state party chairmen were busy people who didn't have much time to sort through the complexities of who had authority to force them to do what, most decided to go along rather than risk embarrassment at the convention.

Thus, when the Credentials Committee of the 1972 convention met formally for the first time, its responsibility to pass on the McGovern Commission reforms had been rendered totally academic. Joseph Califano, who had previously told the National Committee that only the National Convention could alter the reforms, now told the Credentials Committee of the National Convention that the McGovern Commission reforms are "the rules that have been set up and adopted by your national party. They are no longer the McGovern Commission Rules, or the Fraser Commission Rules. They are the Democratic Party Rules." Once again, without debate about the substance of the new rules, the reforms were approved.

The third effort was aimed at ensuring that all delegations included numbers of minorities, young people, and women in "reasonable relationship" to their presence in the general population. Actually, the guidelines required only that the states take "affirmative action" to meet those numerical goals: the McGovern-inserted footnote had specifically foresworn the use of mandatory quotas. However, the commission staff understood from the beginning that whoever had the burden of proof to show "affirmative action" would, under the heated political circumstances of a national convention, be at a considerable disadvantage. After a lengthy series of meetings in midsummer and the fall of 1971, chairman Lawrence O'Brien made the crucial decision that the burden of proof should be on the *challenged* delegation, rather than on the challengers. Ironically, this so-called *prima facie* rule—that delegations lacking the numerical goals would be assumed to be in violation of the "affirmative action" requirement unless they proved otherwise—was formulated by Mrs. Patricia Harris, the Credentials Committee chairwoman, whom organized labor and the party regulars had supported for the post because she seemed to be "safer" on the party reform issue than her rival for the job, Senator Harold Hughes of Iowa.

Minnesota Congressman Donald Fraser, who had taken over the commission chairmanship after Senator McGovern began his race for the presidency, did make an effort to outline objective criteria for "affirmative action." He sent out a memorandum to all state party leaders on October 18, 1971, which suggested various techniques using publicity and educational efforts to help undo "past discriminatory patterns and restrictive practices" which he claimed had previously caused the underrepresentation of minorities, young people, and women at national conventions.

Most of those close to the commission in those days, however, understood fully the significance of the *"prima facie* rule" decision by O'Brien and Mrs. Harris. A short time after his nomination, Senator McGovern, with typical blunt candor, told the *National Journal:* "The way we got the quota thing through was by not using the word 'quota.'"

Of all the many ironies involved in this story, probably the greatest was that, as it turned out, both the New Politics forces and the organized labor/party professional axis that opposed the reforms had focused their attention on the wrong issue.

The "public participation" sections of the commission report, as already pointed out, sailed through with no opposition and no debate. The "representativeness" issue got most of the energy and produced most of the heat. Yet the rules requiring public participation in the delegate-selection process turned out to have a much greater political impact, advantaging the New Politics constituency far more than the provision regarding quotas.

Perhaps if the commission report had been debated within the Democratic National Committee and at the National Convention, some of its more questionable premises might have been subjected to greater scrutiny. Some might have urged, for example, that the emphasis be placed on enforcing objectively defined "affirmative action" steps, along the lines suggested by Congressman Fraser, by nonpolitical hearing examiners rather than by a Credentials Committee which had already divided itself into the political camps of the presidential campaign advisers. Some might have insisted more strongly on proportional representation of voter candidate preferences on all delegations so that minority candidates would not have a disproportionate advantage in multicandidate primaries; and some might have questioned the premise that only minorities, young people and women deserved special attention in the final report.

Perhaps all the details weren't adequately thought through and perhaps some of the tactics used by the reformers in the name of democratizing the party were less than democratic. Nevertheless, what had begun as a hopeless effort by a small group of Eugene McCarthy supporters to reform certain party rules had resulted in the adoption of the most truly democratic rules for the conduct of party affairs in the history of political parties in America.

That revolution—and that is not too strong a word—in the Democratic Party was fully understood, at least in terms of its political consequences for 1972, by very few people. As will be seen, one of those who understood better than most was George McGovern.

five

POWER AND PERSUASION: THE JOE DUFFEY SENATE CAMPAIGN

> possible for the new [politics] constituency to score election victories in 1970 without attention to the blue-collar voters ... but such victories will be at the expense of further division within the society. The answer ... rests with our capacity to take on the task of putting together, defining, and giving concrete political expression to all the discontent in America."
>
> —Joseph Duffey, July 26, 1969, in a speech entitled "Forging a Winning Coalition"

WHILE THE EFFORT was under way at the national level to alter the delegate-selection rules, some of the New Politics leadership from the 1968 campaign turned their attention to the political process at the state and local level in an attempt to build a political coalition which went beyond the New Politics constituency.

One of these was Joseph Duffey, an urban scholar and theologian from Hartford, Connecticut, who had led the Connecticut McCarthy organization in 1968 and won the Democratic Senate nomination in an upset victory in 1970.

Duffey's race for the Senate is important for a number of reasons. For one thing, it was the most successful effort by a New Politics leader to run for high office and win significant support in blue-collar communities. Furthermore, his experiences in seeking and winning the nomination—depending on solid support from the New Politics

53

political base in a contested Democratic primary—and the difficulties he faced in the general election, in large part because of the requirements of his primary campaign, bear striking similarities to those faced by Senator McGovern two years later. The Duffey campaign experience also dramatically affected the attitudes of Duffey, Anne Wexler, his campaign manager, and the many New Politics activists who came to Connecticut to work in the campaign as they thought about who would make the best presidential nominee for the Democratic Party in 1972.

Joe Duffey and Mrs. Anne Wexler, a Westport, Connecticut, veteran of numerous liberal causes in the past, put together probably the best organized grass-roots effort in the 1968 McCarthy campaign. Mrs. Wexler, in particular, became one of the most respected political professionals to come out of the New Politics ranks. One of her greatest admirers was her chief opponent in the Connecticut Democratic Party, state chairman John Bailey. "I sure wish she was on my side," Bailey was heard to say more than once during the 1968 campaign.

It wasn't long before Duffey and his McCarthy organization of suburban liberals, intellectuals, and student activists began to look beyond the increasingly hopeless McCarthy candidacy to the possibility of an ongoing effort to win control of the state Democratic Party. Duffey outlined such long-range plans in a May 1968 speech delivered to a caucus of more than two hundred McCarthy state convention delegates.

The speech accurately reflected the purist attitudes of his audience. Duffey spent much of his time putting down coalition politics, the "old politics" of political "consensus," conceived as the "art of merging the interest of ethnic groups and economic blocs in such a way as to hold power in a kind of balance of expediency." This type of coalitionist politics, Duffey contended then, "tends to avoid debate and . . . discourages participation of the electorate in policy making." In contrast, the "New Politics . . . consists in seeing political action as the shaping of a mandate rather than the accommodation to the widest spectrum of opinion."

Joe Duffey was addressing a typical New Politics audience of comfortable liberals and, as he later said regretfully in recalling this speech, "It's easy to get carried away into liberal self-righteousness among fellow liberals and to play the moralistic demagogue."

Nothing in Duffey's personal background suggested that he would be comfortable with an audience of upper-class liberals. He was born in 1932 in Huntington, West Virginia, a small town in the southern part of the state. Duffey's mother died when he was fourteen. His father, a one-time prizefighter, bulldog trainer, and—after he lost his leg to a mule car in a coal mine—barber, was a Roosevelt Democrat who became involved in local politics. He was elected as a councilman and state legislator, and Duffey recalls with warmth the hours he spent in his father's barbershop listening to the local political gossip.

While Duffey never experienced poverty, he always had a deep sense of his working-class origins. He lived in a white lower-income ethnic neighborhood. His father got him into a private school on the wealthier side of town and it was during those years that Duffey experienced what he recalls as a "deep contrast in classes" between the life and values of the rich and those who live in poverty or on the edge of it.

Beginning in 1965, after the first escalation of U.S. involvement, Duffey immersed himself in the political activities of the antiwar movement, ultimately helping Allard Lowenstein found the Dump Johnson movement.

Throughout the McCarthy campaign, however, Duffey had increasing doubts about the political attitudes of the "comfortable liberals" of the New Politics. He felt a great deal of personal affection for McCarthy, but by the late spring of 1968, he had developed serious doubts about McCarthy's ability to operate effectively within the political process. "McCarthy crossed over from skepticism to cynicism at some point," Duffey explained, "which is good for a philosopher but devastating for a public leader."

Not long after the McCarthy insurgency began in Connecticut, Duffey came under fire from the more purist elements of the New Politics constituency. To begin with, he seemed suspiciously "soft" on Robert Kennedy (in fact, he always deeply admired Kennedy and would undoubtedly have supported him prior to the National Convention, had Kennedy lived).

Suspicion increased as a result of Duffey's (and Anne Wexler's) negotiations with John Bailey over the number of McCarthy delegates who would go to the National Convention. The McCarthy Steering Committee had instructed Duffey to accept no less than 25 per cent of the delegation—eleven delegates—which they felt was reasonable since McCarthy appeared to have more than that percentage of the delegates at the state convention. Bailey at first offered two, then four, then seven, and finally eight delegates.

Duffey recalls with some pleasure those all-night negotiating sessions with Bailey, watching the "master at work." He realized that Bailey's power came not from any kind of absolute authority but from his "ability to broker competing interests." Duffey was also reminded, during these sessions, "what I had learned from my father in West Virginia but sometimes forgot in the McCarthy campaign—that politics is persuasion and advocacy, that you must always give the other person room to maneuver, and that you don't win a victory that's worth anything if, in the process, you alienate the other guy."

The negotiations with Bailey, not surprisingly, went down to the wire. Bailey's final offer of eight delegates was quite unprecedented and extraordinary for the previously unchallenged, tightly run Bailey machine. At this point, Senator Abraham Ribicoff, up for reelection and one of the few men in the state who had credibility with the New Politics activists and the party regulars, gave up his place on the National Convention delegation on the condition that it go to a McCarthy delegate. Bailey accepted Ribicoff's offer and the general assumption was that the McCarthy people would come down two delegates and accept nine.

Duffey and Anne Wexler took the final offer back to the state McCarthy Steering Committee and recommended that it be accepted.

I was an alternate McCarthy delegate from New Haven and attended the Steering Committee meeting firmly opposed to any compromise with the Bailey organization. I remember preferring the drama of a walkout from the convention as a way to embarrass Bailey and to give a morale boost to other McCarthy state organizations. (Now that I think about it, I wanted to walk out even if Bailey had offered us what we wanted—we could have then upped the demand one more delegate.)

For more than two hours, with the entire state convention impatiently waiting for a decision, the debate within the Steering Committee raged. It was a classic confrontation between the purist and the pragmatic wings of the New Politics movement, reminiscent of the debate four years before within the Mississippi Freedom Democratic Party at the 1964 Democratic Convention.

"I want to remind you," Duffey said at one point, "that a few months ago, if I had suggested to any of you that we would have a few delegates to the National Convention who would vote for Senator McCarthy, you would have all denounced me as an overoptimistic visionary. I urge all of you to think about what we are throwing away if we walk out of this convention because we wanted eleven delegates and got only nine. We not only lose nine votes at the convention, which may be important to pass a peace plank, but we may be giving up our credibility . . . our seriousness as people who intend to work within the Democratic Party for the long haul."

A McCarthy delegate from West Hartford stood up and shook his finger at Duffey. "I'm sick of this pragmatic kind of bullshit," he said. "Who cares about those ten goddamned delegates, and who cares about losing our credibility with the hacks of the Democratic Party? We didn't get into politics to play the same old games, the same crappy compromises that led to our getting into Vietnam in the first place. We're better than that. If we walk out of this convention, we're telling the world that we stand for a different kind of politics, better than anything the John Bailey types could possibly understand. We'll get page one in tomorrow's *New York Times* . . . and we'll give a big morale boost to peace people from Massachusetts to Wisconsin to California."

We finally decided to walk out. I remember a great sense of exaltation among the McCarthy delegates as Joe Duffey walked slowly onto the stage of the Bushnell auditorium before a packed crowd of over two thousand to announce the decision. I stood on my feet and cheered till my throat was hoarse, taking pride in the fact that our student-packed galleries were drowning out the boos from the bitter party regulars. It felt so good, so pure. There we were, the

enemy booing, and we were ready to spit in his face. We finally
quieted down, anticipating a ringing denunciation by Duffey of the
party bosses who wouldn't let the "people" of Connecticut come
into the Democratic Party—all that familiar New Politics rhetoric
we all knew by heart.

But Duffey didn't give us what we wanted. He was quiet. He
seemed sad. He spoke slowly and thoughtfully. He talked about the
need to reconcile the conflicting forces in the Democratic Party.
("Reconciliation," someone whispered in my ear, "that's utter
bullshit. What's Duffey trying to do, anyway?") Finally he paused
and said with a measured dignity: "We walk out of here today
because we believe we help the Democratic Party by doing so, not
because we are walking out of the Democratic Party. We disagree
today. But in the future we will need to work together . . . for the
larger things we have in common. And I believe we can—and we
will."

With that, Duffey walked down the steps of the stage, and up the
aisle, and all of us followed him. I remember feeling a little unhappy
that none of the regulars were booing us. What's wrong? I thought.
Then I looked ahead, and saw a party regular town chairman lean
out as Duffey walked by him. They shook hands. And I was even
more disappointed.

In the aftermath of the November 1968 elections (Duffey had
endorsed Humphrey, to the dismay of some of his purist backers, in
early October), Duffey began to think more and more seriously of
challenging the incumbent, Senator Thomas Dodd, for the
Democratic nomination. He was especially encouraged to do so by
Senator Ribicoff, who had won by a landslide in his own reelection
bid, helped considerably by his nationally televised denunciation of
Mayor Daley's police and their "gestapo tactics" on the streets of
Chicago.

From the very beginning of his campaign for the Senate
nomination, Duffey resisted running a reenactment of the 1968
McCarthy crusade. "Anne Wexler and I agreed before we began that
I would do it only if we had something more to offer than simply
replacing someone else, which is usually the only program liberal
reformers offered the voter," Duffey explained. "I was determined to

prove that an alliance was possible between the working class, with whom I felt such a strong, personal identity, and the newer forces who were part of the 1968 insurgency. If I wasn't committed to that kind of a coalition—and if I didn't think it was possible—I never would have run."

At about the same time Joe Duffey was concentrating his energies on efforts to build a coalition beyond the New Politics constituency, substantial segments of the antiwar movement, for the first time, were also attempting to reorient their strategy.

In the fall of 1969, Sam Brown, the McCarthy student leader, and three other staff people from the McCarthy campaign, organized the Vietnam War Moratorium. They planned a series of peaceful demonstrations—one day in October, two days in November, three in December, and so on—which, th3y hoped, would involve leaders of organized labor, business and professional communities, and, perhaps, antiwar Republicans.

Given such a strategy, Moratorium coordinators were bound to clash with the more radical, purist elements of the antiwar movement, who were urging violent, confrontational tactics. The issues divided and the sides lined up along familiar lines. Brown and the Moratorium committee insisted on tactics that might appeal to blue-collar and Middle American communities. The radical left—represented by Rennie Davis's New Mobilization to End the War (New Mobe) committee—insisted that the political process could not be used to end the war: the nomination of Humphrey and the election of Nixon proved that. Instead, they insisted, the atmosphere of normalcy must be disrupted and the ordinary functioning of the government halted as much as possible.

This was the time when Mark Rudd and his brave followers thought they were accomplishing something by taking over buildings and breaking windows. Al Lowenstein continued to urge the Moratorium coordinators to denounce publicly the use of violence for any purpose. While they agreed with Lowenstein's sentiments, however, the Moratorium leaders somehow couldn't stomach the concept of attacking the left and diverting attention from Nixon and Agnew.

The argument between Lowenstein and the coordinators became

so bitter on this question that Lowenstein, for the most part, refused to help the Moratorium effort in any way. "You're going to learn that unless you have the guts to stand up to the violent left," Lowenstein warned during one of many heated arguments with Moratorium representatives, "you'll never be able to win political power from the right."

The dispute between the more moderate Moratorium coordinators and the New Mobilization radicals remained essentially a private one. Meanwhile, the Moratorium proceeded with its plans to try to involve a broader base of people, beyond the college campuses, in the antiwar movement. In October 1969, the first Moratorium demonstrations occurred around the country. There were some breakthroughs. In New Haven, three brilliant Yale Law School student organizers—Steven Cohen, a veteran of the McCarthy campaign, Michael Medved, who would later become Joe Duffey's speechwriter, and Gregory Craig, previously mentioned as a key moderate student leader in the antiwar movement—succeeded in convincing several leaders of organized labor, a leading Republican businessman who had headed the Nixon campaign in Connecticut in 1968, the Republican president of Yale, Kingman Brewster, Jr., and the popular mayor of New Haven, Richard C. Lee—to take part in the Moratorium rally. It was the first time that any of these men had participated in a public anti-Vietnam War activity. But the New Haven crowd of more than thirty thousand was still overwhelmingly white middle-class students from the elite campuses. This was also the case in other Moratorium rallies around the country. Once again, the junior colleges and trade schools had been totally overlooked; so had the invisible young people who had full-time jobs.

Like the Moratorium organizers, Joe Duffey realized that in theory, creating such a broad coalition through "peaceful persuasion" was desirable, but in practice it would prove very difficult. Despite some significant breakthroughs in blue-collar areas during his senatorial campaign, Duffey was never really able to alter completely many voters' perception of him as a candidate of the New Politics constituency of student activists and affluent liberals. He learned painfully, as the primary campaign and then the general election ensued, that identification with that constituency tended to create a communication barrier between what he was trying to say and what many voters insisted on hearing.

In retrospect, it is apparent that such a barrier was inevitable once Duffey ran for the nomination from a New Politics political base. That is not to suggest that he had any choice. In spite of his efforts to win labor backing, it was clear to him and his campaign manager, Anne Wexler, that to win the Democratic primary, he would have to receive solid political and financial backing from the New Politics constituency. There was nowhere else to go.

John Bailey's party regulars had abandoned Senator Dodd in favor of Stamford millionaire Alphonsus Donahue, a close friend of Bailey's, a political centrist, and, most important, a candidate who promised to finance his own campaign. Once Senator Dodd announced he would not seek the Democratic nomination but would run as an independent, the right-wing majority leader of the State Senate, Edward Marcus of New Haven, announced his candidacy and made a determined effort to capture the far right of the Democratic Party. His campaign slogan was "Tough ... very tough." With such a political lineup—Duffey supported solidly by a leftist-New Politics constituency, Donahue straddling the middle and depending on the party-regular base, and Marcus running to the right of Spiro Agnew—Duffey's primary campaign reinforced his image as a New Politics candidate. In addition, Duffey had to contend with three other problems as a result of his dependence on New Politics purists' support.

First, a candidate is usually perceived through the people who are most active in his behalf at the local level. This is especially so in a primary campaign, in which media budgets are limited and few people get a chance to meet and hear the candidate directly. No matter what Joe Duffey was saying about the need to reconcile all the factions of the Democratic Party, especially labor, his earliest supporters, who came to lead and speak for his local organization, were almost always the most purist, politically doctrinaire of the New Politics constituency, and thus least interested in reconciliation with the old guard.

Campaign manager Anne Wexler, who had never gotten along with these purist elements, did her best to keep them under control. But she also realized that Duffey needed them, for they were the only ones who had the motivation and the commitment to work for what appeared to be a totally hopeless political cause. Despite all her efforts, these local supporters frequently defied her advice, insisting on confrontation with the regular organization. In the small rural town of Monroe, Connecticut, for example, the Duffey forces could have settled for two out of four delegates to the state convention. But, against Anne Wexler's instructions, they insisted on waging a full primary for all four. They not only lost the primary but so exacerbated the divisions within the party that in the November election the party regulars refused to help Duffey in any way.

Duffey also had to deal with the political reality that a party primary in which the party leadership is threatened is more divisive than in an ordinary primary, which is usually a personality squabble. Once in a while one party faction may be challenging another for a share of the party apparatus, but even then, most of the leadership and power bases will remain intact irrespective of the outcome. In the case of Duffey's campaign, however, the entire party leadership perceived itself to be threatened by a cultural and ideological perspective which it saw as completely alien to its own. Reconciliation after the primary would be even more difficult.

In the days before the June state nominating convention, when it appeared that the Bailey organization might be able to prevent Duffey from getting the 20 per cent of the convention delegates required to qualify for a primary, Duffey and Wexler began to threaten publicly that if they couldn't get a primary they would form an independent party and Duffey would run anyway. Bailey and the party regulars—especially the Democratic candidate for governor, Representative Emilio "Mim" Daddario, a popular liberal congressman from Hartford [1]—were furious. Many party regulars

---

1. Daddario had supported Robert Kennedy in 1968 and was one of the two members of the "regular" delegates to the 1968 convention who defied Bailey and voted for the so-called peace plank. Daddario also defied Bailey's intense pressure and refused to endorse the organization's choice, Al Donahue, for the Senate nomination, even after Donahue received the formal party endorsement by getting more than 50 per cent on the first ballot at the state convention. Daddario opted for neutrality, which he regarded as a step which would favor Duffey's chances. Ironically, Daddario's neutrality was most criticized not by Donahue's people but by some of Duffey's purist supporters who, before and after the primary, would never forgive Daddario's failure to endorse Duffey directly. Daddario, faced with resentment from both the Duffey supporters and the party regulars, as well as the legacy of a $220 million deficit left over from Democratic Governor John Dempsey's administration, lost to Representative Thomas Meskill by 80,000 votes.

remembered that threat—and reminded Duffey of it—when, after he won the primary, he came to them and asked for their support on grounds of party loyalty.

The third problem for Duffey was that the New Politics constit- uency, whose solid support he required, often demanded that he take public positions on issues which would hurt his candidacy in the general election. It wasn't a question of Duffey's saying things he didn't believe to please the left-liberal constituency. He could never have done that. Rather, he was forced to publicize his positions on controversial issues of importance to college student activists and doctrinaire liberals but to no one else.

In the middle of a debate shortly before the primary, for example, at a time when Duffey was under increasing criticism from purists because of his appeals to the blue-collar voter, he was asked about amnesty for political prisoners like draft resisters and the antiwar priest Daniel Berrigan. The question of amnesty for political prisoners was hardly near the top of his list of priorities. But he also knew that if he completely evaded the question, he would lose substantial support from the New Politics people he needed to win the primary. And so he answered, honestly: "Let me say that I respect Father Berrigan and I believe that such men of conscience have often been sent to prison essentially because of their political views. Amnesty is a tradition throughout American history. Once this war is over, I hope we can face this question of amnesty in a way best aimed at reconciling the bitterness which the war produced."

The right-wing candidate, Ed Marcus, immediately accused Duffey of supporting "instant amnesty" for "criminals" and demanded that Duffey apologize to the people of Connecticut. Duffey, of course, had not said he was in favor of immediate amnesty, but the more he explained his position in subsequent days, the more the public grew to identify him with the "instant amnesty" position of the radical left.

Duffey's past actions and statements also came back to haunt him. At the time of his arrest in Bedford-Stuyvesant, he had stated that he "chose" to violate the law; and, in an interview with the British authors of the 1968 campaign book, *An American Melodrama,* he had said he considered himself "something of a Marxist-revisionist." (He made the latter comment in order to separate himself from the more radical, violence-prone doctrinaire Marxists on the left.) During the primary campaign, Duffey was forced to explain, clarify, and reclarify both remarks. In the general-election campaign, neither Republican Lowell Weicker nor Senator Dodd let the voter forget that Duffey had "chosen" to violate the law and considered himself a "Marxist-revisionist."

In a multicandidate primary, Duffey's committed, solid constituency of New Politics activists and affluent suburban liberals constituted the best grass-roots organization in the history of Connecticut, and was able to deliver a winning plurality of the vote. Anne Wexler was so well organized, so on top of the statewide canvass and election-day vote-pulling operation, that she was able to predict the night before the election within 5000 votes of the actual totals Duffey received (she had predicted 75,000; Duffey got almost 80,000). The left voted solidly together. Al Donahue's campaign had never taken off, and he spent most of his time guarding the middle by saying very little on any controversial issues and beating back Marcus's raids on his right flank. The result should have been predictable, although it was greeted all over the country as a major political upset. Duffey won with 43 per cent of the vote; Donahue received 37 per cent, Marcus 20 per cent.

Duffey's victory was, however, not entirely sweet. After the primary, he had to convince 57 per cent of the Democratic vote which had supported Marcus and Donahue that he was more than a left-wing children's crusader. He and Wexler made a determined effort to minimize the influence of the purists in his campaign and to present him as a candidate concerned about the blue-collar voter and the average citizen.

By early October, Duffey's determined efforts to win support from working-class voters seemed to be bearing fruit. For one thing, the State Central Labor Council endorsed him, with only minor opposition from within the ranks. In speeches and public appearances, he continued to talk about the problems of the workingman, about the need to build broad coalitions of the discontented and the average citizen caught in the middle. He and his local supporters found that as election day approached, and local newspapers reported rising unemployment, more and more ethnic and blue-collar voters expressed support and admiration for Duffey.

Duffey's growing momentum among these voters was aided by Senators Edward Kennedy and Edmund Muskie, both of whom campaigned with Duffey in late October. Kennedy spun his magic wherever he went. He sang Irish melodies late in the evening before 30,000 people in the town square of Waterbury, where John Kennedy had been greeted by 75,000 people at two o'clock in the morning a day before the November 1960 election. Kennedy's message was simple and direct: The war was wrong; Nixon's economic policies were a disaster; Joe Duffey stood for the best the Democratic Party could represent. The crowd roared its approval.

Muskie flew in from Maine and accompanied Duffey into a conservative, working-class Polish neighborhood. It was a cold October evening, but some 10,000 people had crammed into a small parking lot in front of the New Britain Pulaski Club to see their fellow Pole from Maine, who had won national recognition for his 1968 vice-presidential campaign. Wallace stickers and Dodd buttons could be seen everywhere. Muskie was greeted with shouts of recognition and words of welcome in Polish from ladies hanging out of their windows. Muskie waved and exchanged his own Polish greetings. As he and Duffey climbed on the platform and raised their clasped hands in the air, there were some scattered boos from some of the crowd. Muskie stepped forward and the crowd quieted down.

In a somber voice, Muskie talked about the divisions he saw in the country, about how the president and the vice president had decided to go to the country and arouse their fears and their worst instincts. He talked about Joe Duffey, how Duffey had convinced young people that the political system would respond, that violence wasn't the answer. As he spoke, you could see the audience beginning to respond. Not in the usual way political audiences respond, for there was little cheering or applause to interrupt. Heads began to nod, and people murmured, "He's right." Muskie concluded: "Joe Duffey is the only man in this race who is committed to talking to people who won't talk to each other. The Democratic Party needs that kind of man. America needs that kind of a man. I introduce to you my good friend, Joseph Duffey."

The crowd cheered wildly. Duffey came forward to speak but for five minutes the crowd continued to applaud and cheer. Duffey seemed taken aback by the response. When he finally began, he spoke movingly about his father's hard work in the coal mines of West Virginia, about his father's lack of workman's compensation after he lost his leg. His voice rose in outrage when he spoke of a president who deliberately put men and women out of work as a means of stopping inflation, a president who refused to support job-safety legislation while workers were injured and died on their jobs every day. When he finished, the entire neighborhood rang with applause and cheers. Dodd banners disappeared.

Joe Duffey carried that neighborhood in New Britain in the general election; he also carried Waterbury. You couldn't have gotten very many people in the state to bet on his being able to do both. Duffey had clearly made considerable progress toward his goal of building a coalition which included blacks, workers, and liberals of the New Politics—a coalition which current conventional wisdom believed impossible.

But it was too little, too late. A week before the election, the polls had put Weicker slightly ahead, Duffey running second, and Dodd third; but the sizable undecided vote—still over 25 per cent—appeared to be moving to Weicker. The final totals on election night showed Weicker with 42 per cent, Duffey with 36 per cent, Dodd with 24 per cent.

Duffey's concession speech reflected his continuing conviction that the coalition of hardhats and kids for which he had worked would someday be a reality. "I am especially proud of the spirit of this campaign," he told a deliriously cheering, predominantly young crowd who gathered in the Hartford Hilton ballroom. "I am especially proud of the fathers and sons and daughters who have stood together." Pausing, he looked around and saw Vinnie Sirabella, the tough labor leader from New Haven who had nominated him and stuck by him throughout the campaign. He smiled at Sirabella and added, with obvious emotion: "I am proud of the workingmen and -women of this state who, in a crucial moment, made a very key decision in the labor movement—to go with the future and not with the past. I am proud of all of us.

"The battle is not finished. I'll be there again. Someday soon, if not this year then in 1972, we are going to come together as citizens and Americans and work for a future we can be proud of. I know the day is coming—not because of fate and not because of nature and not because of some irresistible tide of history—but because you and I are going to work together and bring it."

On the eve of the November 1970 elections, I was sitting in a hotel room with a group of staff people from the Muskie and Daddario (the Democratic gubernatorial candidate) campaign. We were talking about Nixon's demagoguery on the law-and-order issue and some speculated about how much Duffey had been hurt by Agnew's portrayal of him as a left-winger, soft on radicals and crime. We watched with incredulity as Richard Nixon appeared on the screen and, arms waving in the air, denounced a few rock-throwers who had participated in a questionable incident a few days before in California and urged the American people to hold the Democratic Party accountable.

Then Ed Muskie came on the screen. "There are those," he began, "who seek to turn our common distress to partisan advantage—not by offering better solutions—but with empty threat and malicious slander. They imply that Democratic candidates for high office in Texas and California, in Illinois and Tennessee, in Utah and Maryland, and among my New England neighbors from Vermont and Connecticut, men who have courageously pursued their convictions in the service of the republic in war and peace—that these men actually favor violence and champion the wrongdoer.

"That is a lie.

"And the American people know it is a lie."

The words—written by Richard Goodwin, we later learned— were eloquent. But it was the delivery of that speech, Muskie's soft-spoken style and demeanor, that made the moment powerful and unforgettable.

Muskie concluded: "There are only two kinds of politics. They are not radical and reactionary . . . or conservative and liberal. Or even Democratic and Republican. There are only the politics of fear and the politics of trust."

When he had finished, there was a stunned silence in the room. It lasted almost five minutes. Finally somebody said: "That's the greatest political speech I've ever heard in my life."

PART III

Muskie v. McGovern: The Fight for Leadership

THE 1970 ELECTIONS OVER, New Politics activists from the McCarthy and Kennedy campaigns of 1968 and from state and local "peace" campaigns in 1970 looked to the 1972 presidential race with considerable optimism. They knew they had three important advantages: an extensive network of political activists and financial supporters across the country; a new set of rules for delegate selection that could be used to their advantage, especially with the passage of the eighteen-year-old vote; and finally, despite their constant internal rivalries, a unifying goal: the nomination of a presidential candidate in 1972 who was sympathetic to their views on the issues, especially the war in Vietnam and party reform.

The three other political subdivisions within the Democratic Party—the party regulars, organized labor, and the Wallaceites—were, for the 1970–72 period, not as well positioned as the New Politics organization. The party regulars were confined to a narrowing political base in Northern urban areas, beyond which their control over large blocs of votes had deteriorated drastically. Organized labor had the money and the manpower to exert a respectable amount of political muscle, as had been demonstrated by

69

labor's prodigious efforts on behalf of Hubert Humphrey in 1968. But between 1970 and 1972, the more important union chiefs, especially AFL-CIO president George Meany and Steelworkers president I. W. Abel, were never able to focus organized labor's energies to work for one candidate, at least not until it was too late.

Wallace supporters had little cohesive direction; they needed no organization. They knew who they were for. They didn't need to be canvassed or pulled out to vote on election day. Because their man didn't decide to run in the Democratic primaries until January 1972, they never had the time to take advantage of the new rules, which offered them similar advantages to those enjoyed by the New Politics activists.

But New Politics forces knew that organizational advantages meant little unless they found a someone to lead them in 1972. Should they support someone who would re-create the McCarthy constituency of student activists and affluent liberals, except, this time, with a more serious commitment to actually winning the nomination? Or someone who was committed to building a broader type of coalition, one which included working people, Southern moderates, and Middle Americans as well as the newer forces of the New Politics?

Two men with serious plans to run for the Democratic nomination seemed best positioned to compete for the support of the New Politics constituency. The irony was that both Ed Muskie and George McGovern had been generally suspect to the New Politics activists during and immediately after the 1968 convention.

Muskie was bitterly remembered for his moderate and effective defense of the Humphrey plank on Vietnam during the debate over the 1968 party platform. McGovern had alienated McCarthy and his supporters around the country by refusing to endorse McCarthy over Lyndon Johnson in the 1968 New Hampshire primary; by refusing to endorse McCarthy after the assassination of Robert Kennedy, and instead, choosing to run himself; and, worst of all, by appearing on the platform with his arm around Hubert Humphrey the night he was nominated in Chicago—just at the time that Mayor Daley's police were at the height of their police riot on the streets of Chicago.

Yet by the end of 1971 the more purist elements of the 1968

McCarthy campaign—those who were most opposed to any form of compromise with the regular organization and more conservative elements in the Democratic Party—rallied to Senator McGovern. Meanwhile, many of Senator McCarthy's top staff and state political leadership had rallied to Senator Muskie as someone who was right on the issues and who, most importantly, could build a broad coalition within the Democratic Party and defeat President Nixon.

How did McGovern and Muskie achieve that kind of political turnaround? How did McGovern achieve the image of political purity and radicalism among New Politics activists who, a few years before, contemptuously viewed him as a political opportunist?

And how did Senator Muskie escape his image as an apologist for the Johnson-Humphrey war policies? How did he become (at least for a good while) the only man who seemed to be able to unite New Politics kids with Old Politics pols?

And finally, how did the candidate with the broadest political support in the Democratic Party—Ed Muskie—lose to a candidate with a narrow base of support in the party? Was it all attributable to Muskie's mistakes and McGovern's strategic brilliance? Or was it, in the end, an inevitae result of the political circumstances that prevailed in the Democratic Party in 1972? What role did the news media play in influencing the outcome? What role the Committee to Re-elect the President?

As the story of the Muskie-McGovern clash unfolds, it will become clear that the very reasons Muskie seemed to be in the best position to build such a broad coalition and defeat President Nixon were also the reasons why he was doomed as a candidate for the Democratic presidential nomination under the circumstances which prevailed in the Democratic Party in 1972. And, conversely, the same reasons which permitted Senator McGovern to convert his narrow purist New Politics base into a majority of the delegates at the 1972 Democratic National Convention were also responsible for his doomed candidacy against President Nixon in November.

six

MUSKIE IN THE CROSS FIRE

"Muskie's in danger of becoming identified suddenly and right away as the candidate of the LBJ-John Connally wing of the Democratic Party."
—Tom Wicker, *New York Review of Books*, February 11, 1971

"The Muskie campaign faces a continuing test to prevent his romantic attachment to the left being followed so far that it undermines the broad-based appeal that now makes Muskie President Nixon's most likely opponent."
—Evans and Novak, "The Left Fringe and Muskie," April 25, 1971

EDMUND MUSKIE'S STRATEGY of trying to speak to people in the Democratic Party who wouldn't speak to each other followed from his conception of himself as a political bridge-builder, which in turn was traceable to his experiences in Maine politics. Maine is a small, largely rural state. Politics in such a state is unusually personal. Campaign time is spent primarily in speeches before small groups of people. Personalized politics was especially necessary to a Pole, a liberal and a Democrat—a triple handicap which Muskie had to overcome in conservative, solidly Republican Maine. Elected governor in 1954 and U.S. Senator in 1958, he was accustomed to being able to convince voters to put aside their ideological differences and to vote on the basis of judgments of character more than on issues.

The 1968 vice-presidential campaign solidified Muskie's sense of himself as a healer and reconciler. In a time of turbulence and polarization, Ed Muskie—who thought before he spoke, who seemed to really listen when people spoke to him, the man who had invited a young radical who had disrupted his speech in September 1968 to take the platform and state his point of view—seemed far more responsive to what the country wanted than the frenetic Hubert Humphrey or the sealed-off, programmed Richard Nixon.

If the 1968 campaign solidified Muskie's conception of himself as a reconciler, then the November 1970 election-eve speech fixed it in steel. Once again, the need of the times and the nature of the man seemed to mesh perfectly. Some Muskie critics attempted to minimize Muskie's accomplishment in the speech, emphasizing that speechwriter Richard Goodwin deserved the credit. The criticism completely missed the real impact of Muskie's speech on the American public. What Muskie said wasn't as important as how he said it. Mary McGrory, nationally syndicated columnist, as is frequently her habit, came up with the best description of the Nixon-Muskie comparison. "We saw a president acting like a candidate," she wrote, "and a candidate acting like a president."

The avalanche of mail Muskie's office received in the weeks following the speech—more than fifteen thousand letters in the first three weeks—reflected a common theme: gratitude for the aura of calm and reconciliation in Muskie's tone and demeanor. "You made me proud to call myself a Democrat," wrote a California man. "Your calmness and serenity instills confidence." "Your broadcast was the voice of reason in the land—calm, reassuring, dignified and eloquent," wrote a Chicago woman. A Minneapolis man wrote: "I work with average Americans. I'm younger than many, twenty-eight, but earn an average wage, and put in long, hard hours for that money. And I can assure you that we average Americans are waiting, longing for a man to lead us with dignity, wisdom, and forbearance. Even here in Minnesota we have been subject to a campaign from both sides that has been disgusting. Even as once noble a man as Hubert Humphrey has succumbed to the politics of fear. Such politics may win an election, but they lose a country. You're the kind of man who can help save it. Run in '72. My wife and I will give you our full support. And above all, don't lose faith in us. . . . America is ripe for a return to decency."

The reaction to the speech was uniformly nonideological and

nonpartisan, the same kind of reaction to which Muskie had been accustomed in his kaffeeklatching days in Maine politics. As he began an active campaign for the presidency in 1971, there was no doubt in his mind what political strategy he should pursue—to be himself, to be what he'd always been. He would follow a coalitionist strategy for the nomination, building the broadest possible coalition prior to the nomination, leaving him with a unified Democratic Party and a strong position to defeat President Nixon in the general election.

Most political analysts tend to overestimate the ability of a candidate to choose a particular strategy among various options. This permits the analyst to describe the winning candidate as a genius, since he obviously selected the right strategy, or the losing candidate as a bum, since he obviously picked the wrong one.

In fact, this scenario of a deliberative, rational selection of one strategy is largely mythology. The less dramatic reality is that campaign strategies often follow from factors beyond the candidate's control, including the relative strengths and weaknesses of the opposition and, in some cases, his own personality traits. A candidate does not select a strategy as much as he reacts to political realities and, within those limits, does the best he can.

Muskie was able to pursue coalitionist strategy because he was the front runner, for it was easier to convince people to forget their differences if they all thought they were on the winning side. And, as Muskie liked to point out privately and sometimes publicly, he was the front runner only by a series of happenstances for which he could claim little personal credit—for example, the accident at Chappiquidick, not to mention the election-eve speech, initiated and made possible by others.

With Kennedy out of the race and Humphrey having been just reelected to the Senate and still bearing too many scars from 1968, Muskie found himself at the end of 1970 the only nationally known Democrat in a position to run for president—nationally known, it might be added, as a result of his selection as Humphrey's running mate in 1968. With the polls already indicating that he was the front runner, and his own vision of himself as a reconciler stronger than ever, Muskie's coalitionist strategy followed.

He understood from the start, however, that such a strategy

would inevitably place him in an ideological and factional cross fire between New Politics purists and liberals on the one hand, and the party regulars, organized labor, and conservative factions on the other. But, remembering what he had achieved in Maine, Muskie was confident he could survive the cross fire. In the end, the need to defeat Richard Nixon would convince the most hostile foes to put down their weapons and work together.

At least, that's what he thought.

While Muskie insisted throughout the campaign on pursuing a coalitionist strategy which could unite the party, he stubbornly resisted efforts by advisers on the right and left to mold his public positions to please (or to avoid the displeasure of) one side or the other.

One of the greatest myths of the Muskie campaign, which gained wide acceptance in the press by the end of 1971, was that Muskie deliberately refused to "take positions" because he was running a "centrist" campaign. A corollary to that myth was that George McGovern was more "liberal" than Muskie.

In fact, Muskie's record in the Senate was consistently as liberal as McGovern's. His rating by the liberal Americans for Democratic Action consistently gave Muskie ratings between 90 and 100. Moreover, Muskie did not avoid speaking out on controversial issues which were sure to anger Democratic Party conservatives. In April 1971, for example, when Muskie learned that the FBI had assigned agents to surveillance at one of the Earth Day meetings he had addressed, he was outraged.

He had always shown great sensitivity to issues involving civil liberties and First Amendment rights. In the heat of his 1970 reelection campaign in Maine, against the advice of political aides who were worried about the law-and-order issue, Muskie insisted on returning to Washington and casting a vote against Nixon's D.C. Crime Bill. Muskie called the bill's provisions on no-knock forcible entry and preventive detention "experiments in repression"—hardly the words of a man who refused to speak out on controversial issues. Muskie's denunciation of the FBI over the Earth Day rallies, and his call for the resignation of J. Edgar Hoover, were consistent with his past philosophy and record.

The FBI statement drew howls of protest from the conservative elements in the Democratic Party, who blitzed Muskie with phone calls warning him to stay away from such dangerously leftist tendencies. Especially upset was Governor Jimmy Carter of Georgia, who warned Muskie, as he would on many other occasions throughout 1971, against "coming on too liberal."

In the summer of 1971, Muskie received intense pressure from George Meany and the AFL-CIO to vote in favor of the $250 million loan to the Lockheed Corporation. Subtle threats were communicated that his failure to support the bill would make it difficult for him to get labor support in his presidential race. Hubert Humphrey, under similar pressure, caved. Muskie refused to support the bill. "I can't see bailing out that company, while lots of other programs are starving for funds, simply because you threaten me about my political future," he told one labor leader. "Running for president is not *that* important to me." It was a phrase he would use in a variety of contexts again and again through the campaign.

The most stubborn supporters of the Muskie wishy-washy myth would point to such incidents as explicable since the political fallout was too indirect and long range to present Muskie with any real political problems. That theory didn't take into account the danger, of which Muskie was always aware, that the more the center and the right were angered by his liberal positions on such issues, the more they would encourage Hubert Humphrey to try for the brass ring one more time. In any event, Muskie's position on the space shuttle should have put even the greatest doubters to rest. He knew that the space industry, and its related economic complexes, was central to the economy of Florida, which would hold the second major presidential primary of 1972. And he knew that, with his own probusing position, he could be serious trouble in the Florida primary, especially with the possibility of antibusing candidates like Henry Jackson or Hubert Humphrey—or even George Wallace—entering the primary. Yet, in the fall of 1971, in a question-and-answer session after a speech in Orlando, a short distance from Cape Kennedy, Muskie denounced the space shuttle as a waste of taxpayers' dollars at a time when resources were being cut from other domestic needs. The response in the Florida press was disastrous. "Muskie Turns His Back on Florida," one local Orlando paper headlined.

A few of the leading liberals in the party, as well as liberal newspaper columnists, were impressed by Muskie's stand on these issues. *New York Times* columnist Tom Wicker had previously criticized Muskie's "centrism" in an article in the *New York Review of Books* and flatly stated then that a Muskie presidency would not make "one damn bit of difference" from a Nixon presidency. In a September 1971, *New York Times* column entitled "Muskie Speaks Up," however, Wicker conceded that Muskie's recent speeches had tended "to unsettle the notion of a wishy-washy Muskie trying to win the nomination by saying nothing." Wicker was referring here to Muskie's statement, in response to a direct question on the subject, that he didn't believe a black man could be elected on the 1972 Democratic ticket. Muskie's answer, Wicker wrote, "represented more than candor. . . . It was an obvious effort to face hard facts, not to take refuge in comforting sophistry." Wicker also praised Muskie's speech on the massacre of the inmates at the Attica, New York, prison—a speech which he decided to deliver before the Governors' Conference in Puerto Rico. "What kind of country convinces men that it is better to die on the inside of prison walls than it is to want to live outside of them?" Muskie had asked.

Nonetheless, Muskie did not always enjoy speaking out on those controversial issues that most ruffled the feathers of the moderate and conservative wings of the Democratic Party. Obviously a man pursuing a strategy of trying to win trust and support from all factions of the ideological spectrum is not going to be happy when he appears to be alienating large numbers of Democrats from one particular faction. Throughout this period, Muskie often privately second-guessed himself on the political wisdom of making these statements, and often these afterthoughts reached the press. That habit certainly helped to create the wishy-washy image.

What made matters worse, encouraging Muskie to second-guess himself even more, was the fact that, despite his forthright statements and speeches, the attacks from the New Politics purists of the party were, if anything, more intense than the heat Muskie was getting from the right. His answer about the black vice president, for example, was denounced by a leader of the Black Caucus, Representative John Conyers, who accused Muskie of "moving to the right of George Wallace." George McGovern quickly joined in on the criticism, as did Richard Nixon.

Muskie was most vulnerable on the left on the Vietnam War issue. He had supported the majority plank at the 1968 convention and many New Politics people simply could never forgive him for that. By 1970, however, there was no doubt that Muskie was fully committed to the antiwar position. He had cosponsored the 1970 McGovern-Hatfield amendment cutting off funds for the war and, in February 1971, he made a widely publicized speech at the University of Pennsylvania, largely drafted by a former aide to Henry Kissinger, Tony Lake, who had resigned from the National Security Council staff after the Cambodian invasion.

Muskie stated, in part:

It should be clear to all of us by now that this war is essentially a war fought among the Vietnamese people for political ends. And therein lies a lesson of this tragedy. We cannot substitute our will and our political system for theirs. We cannot write the social contract for another people. We may, however, be able to reach agreements on those issues which concern us most, provided we make clear our intention to withdraw all our troops from Vietnam by a fixed and definite date. . . .

It should be clear to us by now that for too many years, we have pursued the wrong policy in the wrong place in the wrong way. . . . It is clear that the only light at the end of the tunnel will be the one we strike ourselves. We must withdraw our troops from Vietnam. We must do so by the end of this year. We must be willing—all of us—to say, "Enough."

The following week, Berl Bernhard, who had just taken over as Muskie's new campaign manager, asked me to send out the University of Pennsylvania speech to every delegate to the 1968 Democratic Convention, every Democratic senator, representative, and governor, and a large number of influential leaders in the business and professional communities. The possibility of sending the speech out to only antiwar liberals in the party was quickly eliminated. "This will convince people that Muskie is not hedging on his war position now," Bernhard said. "And if some hawks are upset by his position, they might as well know it now."

Neither the speech nor the subsequent publicity came close to satisfying the purists in the Democratic Party. Whatever Muskie said, he was still suspect. The night after Muskie's speech at the University of Pennsylvania, for example, I coordinated a Youth Coalition for Muskie organizational meeting at the university. About thirty students showed up, at least half of whom were wearing McGovern buttons. I asked one of the McGovern students what he thought of Muskie's speech.

"It was a lot of political bullshit," he said. "Where was he in 1968? Defending Johnson. He's changed his mind because the political winds have shifted." When I asked him whether he also held it against George McGovern for his vote in favor of the Tonkin Gulf resolution or for war appropriations between 1966 and 1969, he shrugged. "That's different," he said cryptically.

I was reminded of all those meetings, years before, during the McCarthy campaign. Things we condemned in others—well, for us, in our purity, it was always different.

By mid-1971 New Politics leaders were producing a continuing stream of anti-Muskie writings. All of them had two things in common: they seemed to apply one standard of judgment to Muskie and another to McGovern or Lindsay, and many distorted Muskie's record.

Joseph Rauh, the widely respected Washington civil rights lawyer and former chairman of the Americans for Democratic Action, in a widely circulated memo entitled "Liberals and 1972," criticized Muskie's "centrism," and urged liberals to support the "most liberal" Democrat—either George McGovern or John Lindsay.

"Isn't a man like George McGovern, who opposed the war when his own party was in office and when it was unpopular to do so, more likely to be an all-out liberal president than a man who supported the war when his party was in office and only changed after the other side had been in office a couple years?" Rauh asked.

Rauh neglected to point out McGovern's own change in position on the funding of the war in 1968–69. Rauh also neglected to mention that when Muskie was endorsing the majority Vietnam War plank at the 1968 Democratic Convention, John Lindsay was standing on the platform of the 1968 Republican Convention nominating Spiro Agnew.

The *New Democrat,* a monthly magazine aimed at the New

Politics constituency, published a series of anti-Muskie articles throughout 1971. While its circulation always remained small—less than five thousand—it was frequently quoted in the nationally syndicated columns of Rowland Evans and Robert Novak, multiplying its effect. In one *New Democrat* article, its editor, Steve Schlesinger, the son of historian Arthur Schlesinger, Jr., and an early McGovern supporter, accused Muskie of heading what he called the "Temperance Society" faction of the Democratic Party: "subversive to real change so long as it hangs its political hat on the concept of centrism." Another widely quoted article, entitled "The Muskie Puzzle," accused Muskie of being a prisoner of the Johnson wing of the Democratic Party because he was "surrounded" by the "King's Caucus" of old LBJ advisers, including Clark Clifford and Paul Warnke.

One of the more irresponsible attacks on Muskie was published under the auspices of the millionaire liberal McGovern backer Stewart Mott. Mott financed a project in the winter of 1971 called the Muskie Accountability Project, which produced a twenty-three-page, single-spaced document with handwritten headlines in red ink. Typical of the level of accuracy and constructive political dialogue in this document was one section with the roughly scrawled headline: "Muskie's ancestry: Draft dodgers!" followed by a short biography of Stephen Marciszewski, Muskie's father, who, according to Mr. Mott's researchers, "when he reached 17, . . . left for England and lived there three years, then moved on to the U.S., changed his name to Muskie and fifteen years later sired young Ed." How was the charge of Muskie's father being a "draft dodger" documented? "At the time, seventeen was the age of conscription into the czarist armies, and few Poles were anxious to serve in the army of their oppressor." The rest of this "Accountability Project" pamphlet was filled with material of a similar level of responsibility and taste. Included were distortions and blatant falsehoods about Muskie's record that made a John Birch society pamphlet look respectable.

The McGovern campaign line on the Mott material was, "We're not responsible . . . we can't do anything about it." Muskie campaign manager, Berl Bernhard says he made several calls to McGovern's top staff, urging—unsuccessfully—that somebody renounce the Mott material.

The conservatives attacked Muskie for being too liberal; the New Politics purists attacked him for being too centrist. The cross fire was even more intense over certain campaign appearances and actions which both sides viewed as especially symbolic.

Muskie was invited by Allard Lowenstein to address a "Dump Nixon" antiwar rally in Providence, Rhode Island. Muskie had campaigned for Lowenstein in 1970 (Lowenstein had been elected to Congress from a Long Island district in 1968, but lost his bid for reelection in 1970 after a Rockefeller-initiated gerrymander) and had a great deal of personal affection for him. He also greatly respected Lowenstein's political advice about what activist young people and the liberal left in the Democratic Party were thinking.

Lowenstein called me in Washington in early February 1971 to invite Muskie to his first Dump Nixon rally, which, he explained, ought to be an ideal opportunity for Muskie to show that he was anxious to win the trust, if not the political support, of the New Politics students and reformers. "Some of the antiwar people have objected to my insisting that Muskie be invited," Lowenstein told me, "but I've told them of my high regard for Muskie and stressed the importance of beating Nixon."

Concerned about alienating the organized labor/party regular faction by appearing to be too closely associated with Lowenstein at this kind of event, Muskie was at first opposed to accepting the invitation. He also worried that, no matter what he said about the war, he could not outperform George McGovern (who had also been invited) before an audience of student activists. And so I was informed that Lowenstein would have to be told there was a scheduling conflict.

When I called Lowenstein to tell him, Lowenstein exploded. "Doesn't he know that he can't get the nomination if he doesn't win those kids? Doesn't he know that if he gets the nomination without those kids behind him, it won't be worth anything?"

I had to concede that Lowenstein had a point. The best strategy for Muskie to secure the nomination, as far as I was concerned, was for him to preempt George McGovern on the left of the Democratic Party. Then he could worry about the center and the right. Lowenstein's sympathy to Muskie would be crucial: New Politics liberals all over the country looked to Lowenstein for guidance about the "acceptables" and "unacceptables" in 1972. The very fact that, in his speeches up to that point, Lowenstein had referred to Muskie as "not another Hubert Humphrey" had produced significant inroads for Muskie among some New Politics leaders.

I went to see Berl Bernhard, the Muskie campaign manager. Throughout the campaign, Bernhard more than Muskie had to live with the day-to-day realities of the political cross fire. Everyone turned to him to register complaints or to seek to pressure Muskie to do what he wanted him to do. Bernhard, who under John Kennedy had been a staff director of the Civil Rights Commission, was a committed liberal, an early opponent of Johnson's war policies, and a Robert Kennedy supporter in 1968. He had gotten to know Muskie intimately during the 1968 vice-presidential campaign and Muskie had turned to him in March of 1968 to take over the campaign.

Bernhard listened to my arguments about why Muskie should accept the Lowenstein invitation, and then countered with his concern about alienating organized labor and the Southern moderates. "Lowenstein is intensely disliked by the AFL-CIO people and we've been warned against any association with him," Bernhard said. On the other hand, Bernhard continued, Muskie had to have substantial liberal support in order to win the nomination. "This campaign is going to be a constant juggling act," he told me wearily. When I asked him whether he would let me present my case directly to Senator Muskie, he quickly consented.

The next day I told Muskie of the New Politics suspicion of him and of the need for him to take certain symbolic actions to convince them that he was different from Hubert Humphrey. I then described to him what I perceived to be a new balance of power in the Democratic Party. The increase in the number of open primaries, the eighteen-year-old vote, the election of New Politics-type governors in Pennsylvania (Shapp), Ohio (Gilligan), and Wisconsin (Lucey)—all showed, in my judgment, that a candidate would have great difficulty winning the nomination unless he won the support of the New Politics liberals.

Muskie listened carefully, saying very little. At one point, when I mentioned Humphrey, he interrupted and asked me: "What about Humphrey? Aren't I encouraging him to come in if I earn the enmity of people like George Meany?" Humphrey didn't represent a threat,

I countered, since he could never be nominated; I was sure the reality of a fourth party on the left, should Humphrey be nominated, would bar his ever winning the nomination.

Muskie asked me whether I really thought this was the type of forum in which he could make his best presentation. "I've spoken out against the war, and I will continue to do so. But I'm not comfortable at this kind of event. I'm not that type of public speaker." I told him Lowenstein had assured me he would be the first speaker and that his quiet style would set the tone for the rest of the rally.

In the following week, as word of the Lowenstein invitation spread, Bernhard received phone calls from the head of the Rhode Island AFL-CIO, the governor of Rhode Island, the mayor of Providence, and the AFL-CIO staff people in Washington. All of them were violently opposed to Muskie's going to Providence. Finally, after much soul searching, Muskie and Bernhard decided to accept the invitation—on the condition that Muskie would also make a campaign stop with the labor/party regular people who were boycotting the Lowenstein rally.

On April 18, 1971, Muskie went to Providence for the rally. His first stop was a reception for party leaders and organized labor. "I came to Rhode Island to try to show that it is possible to bring this party back together," he told them. "I hope that all of you will join the young people who are participating in today's rally on the steps of the state capitol now and in the future—for, together, I am sure, we will defeat this administration in 1972." He was greeted by an enthusiastic standing ovation.

About twelve thousand people, mostly college students, had turned out on the cold, darkly clouded day in front of the state capitol. Although Muskie was supposed to speak first, at the last minute a Lowenstein aide put Senator Birch Bayh on first. Bayh gave a thumping, high-pitched antiwar speech which got a relatively enthusiastic response from the young crowd. Peter Yarrow sang a seemingly endless folk song.

Finally, Muskie was warmly introduced by Lowenstein. He took the platform and spoke quietly about the tragedy of America's involvement in the war, at one point admitting his own mistake in supporting Johnson's policies. He ended the speech with his familiar plea for "all of us, of all ages and from all backgrounds within the

Democratic Party and the country, to start talking to each other, to learn to trust each other. The time for division and polarization is over." It was not the kind of speech which a public rally will interrupt with wild applause, especially where the crowd is mostly young people. At the end, Muskie got a warm, but not overly enthusiastic, response from the crowd.

As Muskie drove away, I recall thinking that there was only one man at that time in the Democratic Party who could have made two speeches to two such different audiences and gotten a good response from both of them. But in my own preoccupation with winning the New Politics constituency in the Democratic Party, I had underestimated the intense hostility the party professionals, the AFL-CIO people, and even the Southern moderate governors felt toward Lowenstein because of his Dump Johnson leadership in 1968.

Muskie was blitzed with critical phone calls. Conservative columnists announced that Muskie was chasing the left. In an interview in the Baltimore *Sun*, Muskie admitted that he had not expected the kind of vitriolic response he had received from party conservatives as a result of his Providence appearance, leaving the strong impression that he was sorry he had done it. Despite these difficulties, he insisted that he would press ahead and continue to try to talk to the warring factions of the Democratic Party.

A few days later I got a phone call from a Lowenstein aide who told me, "Al is very angry with Muskie because of the Baltimore *Sun* interview." I asked why. "He doesn't think Muskie should be apologizing for going to Providence. It looks as if he's hedging his bets, which merely reinforces the old wishy-washy image and makes it tougher for Al to convince the left that Muskie is acceptable." Muskie had managed once again to catch it from both sides—not an easy feat.

The political cross fire continued when Muskie found himself involved in the gubernatorial campaign of black civil rights leader Charles Evers, the brother of Medgar Evers, the Mississippi NAACP leader who had been assassinated in 1964. Evers, the mayor of Fayette, Mississippi, was running for governor as an independent.

In May 1971, Muskie had refused to let his name be used on a masthead as a "cochairman" of the Evers campaign, even though

Edward Kennedy, Humphrey, McGovern, Bayh, and Senator Harold Hughes of Iowa had all agreed. Muskie had a great deal of respect for Evers, but claimed he was concerned about the masthead being used in a context outside Evers' campaign. However, Muskie did promise he would personally campaign for Evers. The date of October 1 was agreed on. Muskie also made a personal contribution to the Evers campaign.

When columnists Evans and Novak got wind of the fact that Muskie had refused to go on the Evers masthead, they wrote a column "applauding" Muskie's resistance of "pressures from the left." Then James Wechsler, the widely respected liberal columnist for the New York *Post*, wrote a column questioning Muskie's motivations for avoiding political association with a black leader who held such an important place in the civil rights movement.

I called Wechsler and protested that Muskie had committed himself to campaigning in Mississippi for Evers the following fall and that the implications of his column were unfair. Wechsler responded, with some logic, that if Muskie really intended to campaign for Evers, his refusal to go on the masthead was even more inexplicable.

In August, however, Muskie was presented with a new dilemma. William Waller, who by Mississippi standards was a racial moderate, had defeated the favored racist candidate for governor in the Democratic primary. Now Bernhard, Muskie, and his national political staff found themselves in a swirl of conflicting pressures. Muskie and Bernhard were warned by Governors Scott of North Carolina, Askew of Florida, West of South Carolina, Ford of Kentucky, and Bumpers of Arkansas—all of whom had expressed great sympathy for Muskie's presidential candidacy—that to campaign against Waller would be a direct negation of the effort of Democratic moderates in the South to bring their region of the country into the mainstream of the Democratic Party. Muskie also learned that former Senator Albert Gore of Tennessee, an early Muskie supporter and a hero of the antiwar liberals, was vehemently opposed to Muskie's campaigning for Evers.

On the other hand, Muskie was under considerable pressure from liberals and black leaders to keep his October 1 commitment. Mrs. Myrlie Evers, the widow of Medgar and an early supporter of Senator Muskie, urged him to keep his campaign commitment. Muskie had also developed warm personal relationships with Walter Fauntroy, the black civil rights leader and congressional delegate from the District of Columbia, Mrs. Martin Luther King, Councilman (now Mayor) Thomas Bradley of Los Angeles, Roy Wilkins, NAACP executive director, and black labor leader Bayard Rustin. Gratified by these early signs of support from the black community, Muskie did not want to risk leaving even the slightest impression that he was retreating in the area of civil rights.

The staff tried to come up with a course of action that might somehow get Muskie off the hook with both sides. The first option was to notify Evers that Muskie had a scheduling conflict for October 1 and that the rest of the month was all booked up but that "We would try to help in other ways." The other option was to tell Evers that October 1 was impossible but that Muskie would be willing to schedule a later appearance. The risk of that option was that Evers might shift the day.

On Wednesday, September 1, Bernhard got a call from Rowland Evans of Evans and Novak. Once again—and this occurred throughout the Muskie campaign—someone [1] had tipped off these columnists to the entire debate within the Muskie campaign, and Evans told Bernhard that he intended to write a column about Muskie's planned appearance for Evers. Bernhard told Evans that a final decision hadn't been made, that it would be made within the next twenty-four hours, and Evans indicated he would hold up writing the column until the next day.

Bernhard then called Muskie. He explained to him the two options the staff had come up with, and told him that a final decision had to be made that day. Muskie told Bernhard he was going out to play golf and would give him a final decision that afternoon.

At about 2:30 P.M., Muskie called Bernhard back. "The issue is one of credibility—my word," Muskie said. "I made a statement to Charles Evers that I was going down to campaign for him. Whether it turns out by hindsight that that was a wrong decision, I cannot help now." Calling Evers and just telling him that Muskie could not keep the October 1 date was, in Muskie's words, "discourteous . . . welshing on

1. Subsequently, it was divulged at the Watergate hearings that the Nixon reelection committee had in its employ a student named Gregory Thomas, who stole documents from Muskie headquarters throughout much of 1971, and an elderly volunteer who served as a courier between the presidential headquarters and the Senate office.

a promise . . . something which I have never done in my political life. I want to treat the man with the respect to which he is entitled, and we've got to stick to that October 1 commitment."

Bernhard then pointed out to Muskie that that morning's Washington *Post* had run a picture of Governor Carter of Georgia talking about the South and its potent role in Democratic politics for the upcoming convention. Muskie responded that he was aware of all that but "I have to be able to sleep and live with myself, and that is it."

Bernhard then called Arnold Picker, the head of United Artists, who was Muskie's chief fund-raiser and financial backer. Picker had been a generous financial supporter of the civil rights movement for years and was a close friend of Evers. He had contributed generously to Evers' campaign and the previous year had purchased a fire truck for the Fayette, Mississippi, fire department. Bernhard asked Picker to call Evers and tell him that Muskie would maintain his commitment to the October 1 date.

Picker called back an hour later and told Bernhard that Evers could not get out of a fund-raiser in New Jersey which he had already scheduled for that date, and was upset that Muskie had no other open dates. Bernhard quickly responded that Evers should be told that Muskie was willing to go to Mississippi on October 1, and that if Evers really wanted him, he should reschedule his New Jersey fund-raiser. Picker called Evers back, and Evers refused to alter his plans for October 1, producing no small amount of consternation within Muskie's staff. Muskie himself couldn't understand why Evers hadn't rescheduled the fund-raiser. Some attempts were made to find another date, but at that point, given the staff's (and Muskie's) unhappiness with Evers' attitude about not changing the date of the New Jersey fund-raiser, the response was, "the hell with it."

Muskie never went to Mississippi for Evers. Evans and Novak printed a column describing Muskie's decision to adhere to his promise to Evers and then praising him for refusing to change his dates. But news of his decision to adhere to the October 1 date infuriated some Southern moderates and conservative elements of the party. On the other hand, Evers and a number of liberals criticized Muskie for not rescheduling the campaign appearance. James Wechsler of the New York *Post*, in a column entitled "Politics of Caution," wrote sadly that Muskie's "retreat" from a "rough encounter may win him some points with the old pros."

By the end of 1971, despite the increasing cross fire, Muskie's strategy for unifying the party appeared to have worked beyond his most optimistic hopes.

He and his campaign manager, Berl Bernhard, had assembled a national staff drawn almost entirely from the McCarthy and Kennedy campaigns of 1968. His political directors were Jack English from New York, who had supported Robert Kennedy in 1968, voted for McCarthy at the convention, and was elected national committeeman with the support of the McCarthy, Kennedy, and party regular forces—no easy feat; Mark Shields, a shrewd political tactician and strategist who had worked for Robert Kennedy in 1968 and won wide praise for his management of John Gilligan's successful 1970 gubernatorial campaign in Ohio; and George Mitchell, previously mentioned as a key member of the Party Reform Commission, a liberal respected by reformers and party regulars alike.

Also recruited for the political staff were Tony Podesta, Joe Duffey's deputy campaign manager; Richard Leone, who worked for Robert Kennedy in 1968 and for a short time in 1971 headed George McGovern's presidential campaign; James Johnson, a highly respected organizer for McCarthy in 1968; Harold Ickes, who had been McCarthy's campaign manager in New York; and, by the end of 1971, Anne Wexler, leader of the Connecticut McCarthy campaign and campaign manager for Joe Duffey, as head of the "citizens" organization.[2]

Muskie also won the endorsement of many of the key leaders in the 1968 McCarthy campaign, among them Don Peterson, the chairman of the Wisconsin McCarthy delegation in 1968; Senator Harold Hughes of Iowa, who had nominated McCarthy; and Joe Duffey.

Joe Duffey's explanation for his decision to support Muskie was typical. "I always resented the idea that the only New Politics people who were for Muskie were those who were only concerned about winning," he recalled. "I didn't want a Democratic candidate who was tempted by cultural demagoguery—that is, someone who would let himself get so carried away by the affluent-liberal cultural

2. It is interesting to note that nearly every top staff person in the 1970 Duffey campaign, including campaign manager Wexler and her deputy, Tony Podesta, ultimately worked for Muskie. Podesta, who, it will be recalled, had also worked for McCarthy in 1968, stated flatly that if it hadn't been for the Connecticut experience in the Duffey campaign, he would have worked for McGovern.

perspective that he would forget about addressing himself to the real problems of most of the people in this country." 𝒜 𝒜

Duffey recalled the night he decided that he couldn't endorse George McGovern and that Muskie was the superior candidate. "It was some time in December 1971, as I remember. McGovern went on television coast-to-coast for a major campaign speech. I thought to myself, 'Here's an occasion to talk about Nixon's economic policies, or government by the special interests, or the unjust manipulation of our tax laws in favor of the rich—things which remind traditional Democrats of all we have in common.' I looked forward to that speech. Instead, McGovern spent much of the time talking about amnesty. Amnesty! Of course I understood what he was up to; I remember the problems in my own campaign of keeping the purists satisfied. But, I thought to myself, the country needs something more than that . . . and so does the liberal movement."

Muskie also picked up public endorsements from the leading liberal antiwar senators and congressmen—for example, Senators Hart, Church, Gravel, Bayh, Tunney, Stevenson, Eagleton, Williams, and Symington, and Representatives Michael Harrington of Massachusetts, Morris Udall of Arizona, Sam Gibbons of Florida, Abner Mikva of Illinois; the two most important governors who had been associated with the New Politics movement in 1968—Ohio's John Gilligan, who had worked for Robert Kennedy, and Milton Shapp of Pennsylvania, who had supported McCarthy; and the leaders of the two most progressive unions—Leonard Woodcock of the UAW, and Jerry Wurf of the State, County and Municipal Employees. By the end of 1971, Muskie appeared to have consolidated his position on the left far more than he had ever hoped was possible at the start of the year.

Muskie had also managed to secure the endorsements of a broad range of moderates and conservatives and the most important party organization leaders. The Democratic boss of Philadelphia, Peter Camiel, for example, was an early Muskie supporter. Mayor Richard Daley of Chicago had left a strong impression that Muskie was his man. In addition, Muskie still commanded significant support from the most important moderate Southern leadership. Governors Robert Scott of North Carolina, Warren Hearnes of Missouri, and Wendell Ford of Kentucky were early endorsers; Governors West,

Askew, Bumpers, and Mandel all expressed their strong sympathy.

All these endorsements were significant symbolically, for they dramatized Muskie's image as a unity candidate. As it turned out, however, such symbolism had little utility when it came time to turning out votes in the primary and caucus states.

Meanwhile, in the first half of 1971, the polls showed Muskie beating Nixon by margins as large as 47 to 39 (in the May Harris Poll) and beating all other Democrats by large margins in all twenty-three of the primary states.

He was everyone's front-runner, and the air of the winner made it easy to play the role of the great unifier, for even bitter enemies are sometimes willing to jump on the same bandwagon. But the front-runner syndrome also carries a number of serious political dangers. The most obvious is that the illusion of political strength is too often mistaken for reality. Support builds on the assumption of the inevitable political victory. Once the assumption becomes shaky, support may dissipate. Another danger is that once the front-runner syndrome sets in expectations are raised which often cannot be met. Finally, in the front-runner's campaign, the candidate and his staff too often begin to believe their own press notices, ignoring contrary signals, the day-to-day evidence that things may not be as rosy as they appear.

The decision to enter the first eight primaries of the 1972 campaign—New Hampshire, Florida, Illinois, Wisconsin, Pennsylvania, Massachusetts, Ohio, and Indiana—was made in that kind of euphoric atmosphere. This primaries strategy was initially pushed by Muskie's political director, Jack English, who saw it as a way to wrap up the nomination by April 25, when English expected that Muskie would win both Pennsylvania and Massachusetts (or, at the latest, by May 1, when Muskie would win Ohio and Indiana). This strategy was perfectly consistent with Muskie's commitment to run in a way best designed to show his broad political appeal and his ability to unite the party. He would show strength in all parts of the country, and he would win the nomination in open primaries—thus convincing the party's left that he was democratically nominated and, therefore, could be supported after McGovern dropped out.

In retrospect, the political rationale for the first-eight-primaries strategy appears shortsighted. Someone should have anticipated the danger of being stretched too thin, politically and financially, as well as the disadvantage of having to run well everywhere while other candidates could choose those states where they knew they had political advantages. On the other hand, given Muskie's projection as the front-runner, any decision to duck a particular primary would itself have been fraught with political peril. Surely the political press would have had a field day interpreting Muskie's motives and speculating about the political vulnerabilities suggested by his decision (*i.e.*, "Muskie Ducks Florida—Is He Afraid of Wallace?"). Since his name would have been on the ballot of all the primaries after New Hampshire anyway, his front-runner status was sure to be damaged by a poor showing in a primary, irrespective of his decision to duck it.

But as 1971 drew to a close, who could worry about the pros and cons of the primary strategy? Everything seemed to be falling into place for Muskie—endorsements from all segments of the Democratic Party; momentum generated by the press (he was on the covers of *Life* and *Time* within a single month); and the polls holding up. Moreover, the McGovern campaign appeared to be folding. In early January, 1972 several key McGovern staffers, demoralized by the news of Senator Harold Hughes' imminent endorsement of Muskie, called friends in the Muskie campaign during this period and suggested the possibility of switching to Muskie.

Despite this general feeling of euphoria, Muskie and some of his staff were increasingly concerned about a number of troublesome political circumstances. The most important of these was the unmistakable sign that Hubert Humphrey intended to run once again for the nomination.

In the beginning of 1971, Humphrey had told friends—and, on one occasion, told Bert Bernhard directly—"I will never do anything to hurt Ed Muskie's candidacy. I had my chance in 1968. Now he deserves his chance."

At the same time, Humphrey made a number of phone calls to his old financial backers and asked them to hold off supporting Muskie for a while. This gesture hurt Muskie considerably; some major potential campaign contributions dried up.

Throughout the fall of 1971, Muskie managers Bernhard,

English, and Mitchell had done their best to exert pressure on Humphrey not to run. (One of the major incentives behind the coordinated drive to pick up political endorsements of Muskie from party leaders, elected officials, and heads of labor unions was to create such a sense of momentum in favor of Muskie that Humphrey would be discouraged from coming in.) They met with Alexander Barkan of the AFL-CIO Committee on Political Education (COPE) to urge that organized labor dissuade Humphrey from splitting up the votes of the center. Bernhard also called Humphrey financial backers to make the same argument.

But now, by the end of 1971, the old electoral compulsion reasserted itself, for Humphrey was convinced that Muskie would not run well in a multicandidate primary and that his own loyal following of organized labor, blacks, Jews, and senior citizens would hold together in enough primary states to defeat Muskie.

In retrospect, it seems that the only group that could have stopped Hubert Humphrey from running was George Meany's AFL-CIO. Muskie ate dinner with Meany on several occasions and met with his representatives throughout 1971 to solicit their early support. But, as a high official of COPE commented a few months after the November election, "There was just too much chemistry between us and Hubert to expect us to make a special effort—and that's what would've been required—to convince him not to run." "Moreover," this official continued, "it's a little much to ask us to do that while Ed Muskie seemed to be spending more time chasing after the New Politics people than anyone over here."

One little-known incident involving Humphrey is worth relating here. Toward the close of the California primary, in early June 1972, Humphrey called Muskie and asked for his support in California. "We've got to unite or else; if you don't support me, we'll split up the center and you'll be giving the nomination to George," he argued. That statement must have struck Muskie as somewhat ironic, given the history of the previous six months. Needless to say, Muskie declined Humphrey's request.

The second circumstance that hurt Muskie at the end of 1971 was that the mood of the country seemed to have changed. I began to sense that many people seemed more restless with the drift of the country than they had been earlier in 1971—more eager for strong, assertive leadership. In November 1971, a Gallup poll showed Ted Kennedy beating Muskie among Democratic voters (in a multicandidate contest which included all the other candidates). Another Gallup poll at the same time showed that Nixon was now beating Muskie 43 to 35, a major turnaround compared to the first half of the year.

A recent trip to three or four states in the Midwest and Northeast had given me some insight into why Muskie seemed to be slipping. In 1970 and the first half of 1971, I noted in a memo to Berl Bernhard, the country had looked to someone who could soothe the turmoil and polarization. "Most people responded positively to ESM's quiet passivity and did not demand any further sharpening of his identity."

Some months later, as I traveled around the country, I began to sense that more and more people were growing increasingly restless with what appeared to be a "leaderless drift" in the country. "Now, people seemed to prefer a strong leader" instead of a reconciler and a soother—and this shift was occurring "just at the time that ESM has lowered his profile and is being criticized for being 'wishy-washy.' "

It was not surprising, therefore, that Kennedy had shown movement in the polls at Muskie's expense, for he had been speaking out on controversial issues during the past few months for more than any presidential candidate. In this period, "it doesn't seem to matter that Senator Kennedy frequently takes left-wing stands," I wrote, "the ideological flavor of his speeches seems less important than the *fact* of the leadership itself." But Muskie still had no public identity beyond his generalized Abe Lincoln image. As chairman of the Senate subcommittees with jurisdiction in areas of pollution and revenue sharing, he had an outstanding record. But these issues, as Muskie's political director Mark Shields pointed out, "have the political sex appeal of a pregnant pig."

After a prolonged strategy meeting in late summer 1971, Robert Shrum, a gifted young speechwriter who had formerly worked for Mayor John Lindsay, drafted a lengthy memorandum suggesting five possible themes for the Muskie campaign: the "Democratic theme," focusing on "Ed Muskie as the Democrat who can beat Nixon in 1972"; the "economic theme," attacking the Nixon administration on bread-and-butter economic issues; the "fairness theme," emphasizing programs to bring about redistribution of corporate power, wealth, and government spending; the "insecurity theme," addressed to the problem of crime ("Muskie should not follow the Hubert Humphrey of 1968 into the trap of talking about the cliché of 'root causes,' since most people will be dead in fifty years and are not interested in crime control that will take that long;" and the "equal rights theme," aimed at the civil rights and women's rights movements.

Muskie didn't need five themes. He needed one. Moreover, the development of a public identity for a candidate who previously lacked one—or had a different one—would require careful coordination of speeches, public appearances, and media. Since Muskie often insisted on making many major decisions himself, decisions usually came too late and were sometimes left unimplemented.

Muskie continued to resist the development of a specific issue or theme throughout the campaign. He resisted, too, delivering the same speech on the same issues over and over again to build a theme for himself. Such repetition, he contended, was demeaning to himself and his audiences: "People will think I only care about one issue."

"Muskie viewed every speech as if it were a presidential speech," speechwriter Shrum would later recall. "Every question had to be answered, every pro and con had to be weighed and talked out." Shrum and the rest of Muskie's top staff privately admired this insistence on thoroughness and intellectual integrity. But there was little doubt that such qualities were often liabilities in the heat of a contested intraparty battle for a presidential nomination.

"I was always struck by the fact that Muskie's best qualities—his balance and fairness, his insistence on seeing things from the other guy's viewpoint—were better suited for a Supreme Court justice than a politician," observed Keith Haller, a Muskie youth organizer. Or, as another top Muskie aide put it, "Muskie simply lacked the instinct for the political jugular, at least in the early and middle phases of his campaign. He just couldn't bring himself to play to the galleries as effectively as someone like George McGovern was able to do on the campuses. That's why I was so devoted to him as a human being and that would have made him a great statesman-president. But in this system, at least, it's hard to get elected that way."

Muskie's resistance to politically contrived "themes" was heightened after Evans and Novak had quoted from an internal staff memorandum that urged Muskie to take his Subcommittee on Intergovernmental Relations to Southern California for field hearings on the property tax, an important issue in that area. Muskie canceled the planned hearings, angrily telling Bernhard and his legislative assistant, Dan Lewis, that in the future he would no longer consider using his Senate responsibilities to promote directly his presidential campaign.

This Evans and Novak leak was one of many examples of the effects of the sustained effort by the White House and the Committee to Re-elect the President (CREEP) to sabotage the Muskie candidacy during 1971–72. The source of this and other leaks to Evans and Novak, the Senate Watergate hearings revealed, was a paid spy who served as a courier between Muskie headquarters and the Senate office. According to the testimony of Jeb Magruder, the deputy campaign manager of CREEP, the White House had panicked after Muskie's election-eve speech put him strongly ahead of Mr. Nixon in the polls in the first half of 1971.

Elaborate espionage and sabotage plans were initiated, for the Nixon men were convinced that Muskie's broad appeal made him the most formidable Nixon opponent.

Phony stories exaggerating Muskie's alleged temper were also generated, picked up by conservative columnists, quoted and requoted in a variety of news sources. The same technique was used by the White House and CREEP to propagate a totally false story about Muskie's alleged involvement with a Maine polluter, which was also widely quoted in the press and later in Stewart Mott's anti-Muskie material.

The subversive activities of Nixon's men may have contributed to some significant negative press treatment of Muskie in the latter half of 1971. Still, Muskie's basic political problem was of his own making—he lacked a public identity associated with an issue or set of issues that people cared about. Many of Muskie's staff and political allies had hoped that, once the primaries began, his media "spots" would help develop such a public identity.

Muskie's media advisers, Robert and Jane Squier, who had been responsible for the triumphant production and setting of the 1970 election-eve speech, knew that Muskie was at his best in that quiet, personal context. They thought Muskie could reproduce that moment throughout the campaign. The Squiers helped convince Muskie and Bernhard, for example, to have Muskie announce for the presidency (in early January 1971) from the same easy chair in his cabin at Kennebunkport, Maine, in which he had delivered his election-eve speech.

The reaction to the announcement speech was generally negative, however: the setting seemed imitative of the election-eve speech, Muskie had gotten little sleep the night before, and at the time of the taping the cabin was cold and unheated. Muskie appeared somber and tense, and ended the speech by offering as his campaign theme the possibility of a "new beginning"—whatever that meant.

In planning television, radio spots and literature for the primaries, Muskie and his top aides decided to emphasize the "trust Muskie" personal character approach, rather than focusing sharply on one or two issues. The central fallacy here was that this kind of theme, while well suited for a general-election campaign against Richard Nixon, totally overlooked the political realities of winning the nomination in a multicandidate primary.

The younger members of the Muskie national staff were especially worried about the failure of Muskie's campaign managers to recognize the importance of grass-roots organization under the new party rules and to devote the resources necessary to compete with McGovern's local organization in the primary and caucus states. Many of these staffers had spent time in the field, on college campuses and at political meetings, and had returned to Washington convinced that there was a reservoir of political support for Muskie which could be tapped if the national headquarters made the necessary commitment to grass-roots political organization. The files in Washington were filled with thousands of names of people, some of them important political leaders, who had written Muskie after his 1970 election-eve speech to offer their help. Very few of them had ever been called. Most had received no answers to their offers of assistance.

When Anne Wexler joined the Muskie campaign at the end of 1971 as the director of the Citizens for Muskie effort, it was hoped that she would bring her influence to bear on Muskie and his top aides to focus their energies on grass-roots organization. But her memos and pleas fell for the most part on deaf ears. There was so much preoccupation with the day-to-day problems of the candidate—his travel schedule, his speeches, his political meetings, his demands, his moods—and with the public projection of the campaign—endorsements, the press, the polls, the television shows, the political columns—that it was difficult to get anyone to focus on the problem of long-range grass-roots organizing.

Thus by the end of 1971, despite all the signs of apparently increasing political momentum gained from his many endorsements and continued front-winner status in the polls, Muskie seemed to be in an increasingly vulnerable position as he looked ahead to the primaries. Without a clear public identity, without a grass-roots organization, and caught in the political cross fire, Senator Muskie faced inevitable difficulties in a multi-candidate primary.

seven

McGOVERN: CHASING THE PURISTS

> "How the idea gained currency that George McGovern is a radical or even an unconventional politician is a puzzle."
> —*New Republic,* May 6, 1972
> "We knew what we had to do to win the left in the Democratic Party . . . and we did it."
> —Richard Stearns, McGovern Campaign Political Coordinator, May 1973

GEORGE MCGOVERN WATCHED Ed Muskie's increasing discomfiture through 1971 with some delight and, according to some of his closest aides, some disbelief. "We just couldn't believe that Muskie was that stupid," Richard Stearns, one of McGovern's chief political organizers, recalled. "Muskie was trying to be friends with everybody and we could see from the very beginning that once the primary season began, he would have nothing left to deliver to the polls."

The conventional wisdom about George McGovern's successful strategy for winning the Democratic nomination has McGovern as the New Politics crusader, ideologically committed to an insurgent takeover of the Democratic Party by the New Politics antiwar-reformist constituency and shrewd enough to understand how the new delegate-selection procedures could be used to his and his activist constituency's advantage.

This theory is plausible enough, but it both overestimates and underestimates McGovern's political sagacity. It is an overestimation in that it implies that he had alternatives. The fact is, he did not. Despite his brief race for the Democratic nomination and his leadership in the end-the-war amendments in 1970 and 1971, McGovern was well known only to a small number of antiwar New Politics Democrats in the country. He simply could not compete with the kind of nationwide political clout and visibility both Muskie and Humphrey already had. McGovern's standing in the polls—between 3 and 6 per cent through most of 1971, a reflection of his lack of visibility—diminished even further the chances that prag-matic party professionals would support his candidacy.

If McGovern wanted to be president, and he clearly did—cer-tainly more than Muskie and perhaps, as Rick Stearns has said, more than anyone else who ran in 1972—his only chance for the Democratic nomination was to run hard for the solid backing of the New Politics constituency, who would not be bothered by his low standings in the polls. Indeed, to the more purist elements within the New Politics movement, McGovern's low standing in the polls was an important selling point.

Given these realities, McGovern understood better than most that two legacies of the 1968 campaign offered a New Politics-backed candidate important advantages. First, an extensive national network already existed, consisting of political activists who had worked in the McCarthy and Kennedy campaigns. Their political organizations had remained relatively intact since then. McGovern would not have to build from scratch a national grass-roots or-ganization to support his campaign. Second, as chairman of the Party Reform Commission, McGovern understood that the party reforms which had resulted from the turmoil of 1968 could operate to the considerable advantage of any candidate who had the backing of a well-organized and activist constituency, especially in a multican-didate contest.

McGovern also understood that there were significant advan-tages to being a 5 per cent (in the polls) candidate. He could travel around the country, taking controversial positions favored by his New Politics audiences without danger of significant exposure, since the national press was, at that time at least, totally ignoring him. Another advantage, which McGovern and his top aides masterfully exploited, was the use of the underdog image to build political sympathy. (Once the primary season began, McGovern's political director, Frank Mankiewicz, became a master at the technique of convincing the press to accept his overly pessimistic predictions and then, when the final tallies indicated a better showing than predicted, to exaggerate the political significance of the results.)

McGovern's great strategic skill—his ability to maximize the advantages of his own political circumstance—should not be confused with his having made a conscious decision to run an insurgent campaign. This commonly accepted portrait of McGovern as a New Politics ideologue grossly underestimates his basic political pragmatism and professionalism. His record through the years was undeniably liberal—but, as has already been mentioned, no more so than Muskie's and Humphrey's (except for the war issue).

Despite all the rhetoric by both supporters and detractors concerning his antiestablishment, reformist inclinations, McGovern, prior to 1970-72 at least, had always been a pragmatic politician, disdainful of political purists. As already noted above, in 1968, he refused to support Eugene McCarthy over Lyndon Johnson in the New Hampshire primary. He continued to withhold support from McCarthy after Robert Kennedy was assassinated. He chose to run himself, feeling much closer to the Kennedy-liberal coalitionists than to McCarthy's purists. After Humphrey's nomination in 1968, while McCarthy was in Grant Park telling the demonstrators he could never support Hubert Humphrey, George McGovern was standing on the platform endorsing Humphrey. Furthermore, McGovern became chairman of the Reform Commission at the suggestion of Humphrey, the party regulars, and organized labor, all of whom regarded him as far "safer" on the reform issues than the other candidate for the job, Senator Harold Hughes of Iowa.

How then did McGovern come to be so despised and feared by the party regular-labor-Southern establishment axis of the Democratic Party? As a 5 per cent candidate in the polls, with Humphrey and Muskie having first call on the party establishment, McGovern had no choice but to seek the backing of the New Politics insurgents. Once he did that, he was bound to alienate forces of the party establishment, who saw their power bases under attack at the state and local level by these New Politics activists and who would inevitably blame McGovern for this attack.

McGovern understood that he might alienate the party regulars in the course of running for the nomination, but he hoped—with hindsight, too optimistically—that, once nominated, he would be able to move to the center and unify the party. In any event, determined to run a serious race for the nomination, McGovern put these long-range concerns out of his mind and set out to do what had to be done.

The first step was to preempt all other potential purist candidates from within the New Politics movement. His earliest competition was Senator Harold Hughes of Iowa, who had nominated McCarthy at the 1968 convention and whose chairmanship of an *ad hoc* Party Reform Commission in 1968, it will be recalled, set off the chain of events that ultimately led to the creation of the Party Reform Commission. A number of New Politics leaders, among them Anne Wexler, Reform Commission counsel Eli Segal, and Iowan political organizer Alan Baron, had initially supported Hughes for the nomination.

Hughes decided relatively quickly that he could not compete successfully with McGovern for the left of the Democratic Party; more to the point, he wasn't willing to do the kinds of things which would have been necessary to "out-McGovern McGovern" among the New Politics purists. (Many McGovern supporters were shocked when Hughes ultimately endorsed Muskie over McGovern. Hughes, a former truck driver who was particularly concerned about the blue-collar vote, believed that Muskie was in a better position to build a broad coalition than McGovern.)

With Hughes out of the way, McGovern felt fairly secure that the purist elements of the New Politics constituency would be solidly for him. He had a brief scare when, during the early summer of 1971, the whimsical Senator McCarthy indicated that he would run again in 1972. It wasn't long, however, before it became clear that very few New Politics people were taking McCarthy seriously. He had disappointed even his most loyal supporters by his premature resignation of his seat on the Senate Foreign Relations Committee, then by his vote for Russell Long over Ted Kennedy for Senate whip, then by dropping out of politics completely after his decision not to run again for the Senate.

McGovern, out in front on the end-the-war amendments in 1969 and gaining increased exposure among New Politics people for his work in the Reform Commission, quickly moved in to pick up the endorsements of the New York and Massachusetts "New Democratic Coalition," composed of New Politics activists who had been assumed to favor McCarthy.

In spite of these successes among the purists, McGovern and his staff grew concerned by Muskie's inroads among the more moderate and coalitionist New Politics elements. Endorsements of Muskie by leading symbols of the 1968 McCarthy campaign—Joe Duffey and Anne Wexler, Wisconsin's Don Peterson, and especially Senator Harold Hughes—became increasingly worrisome.

McGovern's response to these Muskie gains was to do everything possible to show daylight between himself and Muskie on those issues he believed New Politics activists cared about most: foreign policy, especially the Vietnam War; and the so-called cultural issues, especially amnesty.

The most important issue for McGovern was the war in Vietnam. His campaign slogan, "Right from the start," was aimed at reminding people that he had spoken out against the war earlier than Muskie had.

Muskie's cosponsorship of McGovern's cutoff of war funds in 1969 and 1970, McGovern suggested to his campaign audiences, had been based on political expediency. McGovern attacked Muskie's vote against an amendment introduced by Senator Mike Gravel of Alaska to halt the bombing over South Vietnam as evidence that Muskie's opposition to the war was still suspect. But neither McGovern nor Stewart Mott's Accountability Project pamphlet, which accused Muskie of being a "liar" because he claimed he opposed the war and yet voted against the Gravel amendment, mentioned that most of the antiwar doves in the Senate, including Senators Hart, Fulbright, Church, Cooper, Case, and Javits, voted against the Gravel amendment as well. Muskie and these senators believed that the amendment was so loosely worded that it would give President Nixon greater freedom to continue the bombing.

In addition to attacking Muskie on the war, McGovern spent a great deal of time reminding his New Politics audiences that, while Muskie might seem as liberal by a strict reading of the Americans for Democratic Action ratings, he, George McGovern, was "right" (and Muskie was wrong) on what had come to be known as the "cultural issues." During his frequent stops on college campuses, he would discuss these issues with special emphasis: amnesty (he favored immediate amnesty for draft resisters, though not deserters, as soon as the war ended); the draft (he opposed it under any circumstances); abortion (a matter which doctor and patient ought to decide); and marijuana (he favored "decriminalization").

It didn't seem to concern McGovern that these "cultural issues" were essentially irrelevant to the concerns of the large majority of Americans and, worse, that he was taking simple stands on issues which did not easily lend themselves to simple solutions and which might come back to haunt him. The fact that McGovern stood at 5 per cent in the polls and nobody in the press seemed to be giving him much public exposure didn't encourage him to worry about the consequences of his taking these positions in a general election against Nixon.

If McGovern believed in the positions he was taking—and he did—he also understood what his New Politics audiences wanted him to talk about. He knew he needed their solid backing if he was to have a chance of winning the nomination; understandably, he addressed himself to those issues. It was that simple.

For Muskie, however, it wasn't that simple. He didn't like the draft during an unpopular war, but he also didn't like the idea of a volunteer army which depended on the poor and minorities, while the rich and the privileged were utterly protected.

On the issue of abortion, Muskie expressed his sympathy for the right of women to prevent the birth of unwanted children. He also recognized that since the wealthy would always be able to secure abortions, antiabortion laws discriminated against the poor. His political stance, however, was tempered by his own personal moral reservations about the concept of taking a human life, especially for reasons of population control.

Muskie's careful, balanced, sometimes exasperatingly lengthy discussions of these questions rarely won him any support during his college appearances in 1971. On the same issues, McGovern was scoring points with his New Politics audiences. The real problem seemed not to lie in what Muskie was saying but in how he was saying it—not an unfamiliar problem for many politicians.

As far as Muskie's amnesty position was concerned, this problem was brought home to me the day Muskie appeared on the same platform with George McGovern in the fall of 1971 for a voter-registration rally in front of Boston's City Hall. Muskie had spoken first, giving a good but not especially inspired speech about the importance of young people "participating" in the political system. The student crowd of about five thousand barely applauded when he concluded.

When George McGovern was introduced, he too was greeted by cool, indifferent applause. Even when he launched into his tirade against the war in Vietnam and the "spokesman of the old politics," there was little response. But at the end of his speech, his voice rising, McGovern declared: "If I am elected president, my first act would be to order a complete pull-out of all U.S. forces from Vietnam, and then I would declare a general amnesty for all those who avoided the draft." The crowd, suddenly electrified, roared its approval, cheering nonstop for about five minutes. McGovern, apparently surprised by the response, beamed.

After the speech I circulated through the crowd and asked a few students what they perceived to be McGovern's position on amnesty. "Immediate amnesty," I heard again and again. And Muskie? "He's against it."

One night a week or so later, I talked to Muskie in his hotel room.

"As I understand your position on amnesty," I said, "you believe that so long as there are draftees fighting in Vietnam against their will, it isn't fair to talk about amnesty for people who took another option and decided not to accept the draft."

He nodded.

"You've also said that once the war is over, you would in all likelihood follow the tradition of granting amnesty."

He nodded again.

"So," I said, "you're saying, 'I am opposed to amnesty until the war is over,' and McGovern is saying, 'First I would end the war, then I would declare amnesty.' No difference."

With some impatience, he asked: "What's your point?"

"Well, Senator, maybe what I'm suggesting is that, say, on the amnesty issue, you change the way you state your position so that it sounds more like McGovern, since it seems, substantively, you'll still be saying about the same thing. Instead of saying, 'I'm opposed to amnesty until the war is over,' say, 'I'm in favor of amnesty once the war ends.'"

"That's a helluva piece of advice," Muskie answered, not hiding his irritation. "You're suggesting to me that I should deliberately state my position in such a way that it leaves a misleading impression. I'm not for immediate amnesty. If George doesn't mind leaving the impression that he is, even though he isn't, that's his business."

McGovern understood that many New Politics people perceived themselves as more intellectual, more "issues-oriented," than any other group in the party. He knew they prided themselves on their requiring specificity from a candidate on all issues. McGovern responded with, for example, a specific welfare plan or a specific alternative military budget. Such programs were an ideal way to differentiate himself from Muskie.

For example, Muskie was in favor of defense cuts; he and McGovern had voted exactly the same way on all the Senate amendments to cut the defense budget during the past few years, including the 1971 Proxmire amendment to cut the defense budget by $11 billion. McGovern, however, came up with something much more specific.

He depended on a small academic "task force," mostly from Harvard and M.I.T., to work out the details of an alternative defense budget. In early 1971, he announced a defense budget which would result in a $31 billion cut, detailing on a line-by-line basis every item in the U.S. defense complex which he would eliminate if he could.

On the welfare issue, both Muskie and McGovern had announced their support for some form of the guaranteed-income concept. But McGovern, again wishing to go one step further than Muskie in the direction of specificity, sought to articulate a more comprehensive and fully detailed alternative to the current welfare system.

His chief aide on issues and policy, Gordon Weil, recalled that, initially, McGovern had set forth his welfare plan as a series of proposals, only one of which was the later-to-be infamous $1000-a-person grant idea. The more New Politics audiences questioned McGovern about his welfare proposals, the more he began relying on the $1,000-a-person idea until, by the late spring of 1972, it was the only proposal he used.

McGovern's prolific output of detailed programs and position papers was especially damaging to Muskie's candidacy—not just with the New Politics constituency but, more importantly, with the general public. McGovern's specificity highlighted Muskie's major political vulnerability—his tendency to come across as indecisive and vague, and his insistence on examining and reexamining many proposals, often causing him to delay addressing himself to an issue until someone else had assumed primary leadership.

The broadcast news media were especially hard on Muskie in pointing out these characteristics. During one *Face the Nation* interview program in the summer of 1971, Muskie was cross-examined by a panel of newsmen about his position on defense cuts. Muskie, citing his vote for the Proxmire $11 billion defense cut amendment, insisted that he supported "substantial" defense cuts but that he hadn't yet seen the president's new budget and therefore he wasn't yet prepared to submit a complete, detailed alternative budget. The newsmen pressed him again and again. "George McGovern knows how much he would cut. He's willing to tell everyone. Why aren't you?" By the end of the program, Muskie had grown irritable, and the overall impression he had left with the viewing public was negative and defensive. The next week, phone calls poured into Muskie headquarters, many of them from Muskie supporters, all highly critical of his performance.

"I don't accuse McGovern of being irresponsible in using this tactic," Muskie commented some time after the 1972 election. "He had to get visibility. The way to get visibility is to challenge the front-runner. It's the notion on the part of the press that I criticize: because I don't follow that strategy, therefore, that reflects a basic character weakness, an indecisiveness, a wishy-washyness.

"If George McGovern, after weeks of consideration, decided that a certain number of troops ought to be out of Vietnam by January 2 at 1:30 A.M., the minute he uttered that number, that time, I was supposed to be in a position to agree or disagree, without knowing what the basis of his rationale was. But because he decided to concentrate on making that kind of determination, I was supposed to immediately echo or challenge it, without taking a day or two days, or a week or two weeks, to make my own evaluation.

"It got to be damn frustrating," Muskie continued, "because the press insisted that you have to have a yes and a no answer to anything all the time, and you have an instant solution to any question all the time."

Obviously Muskie's reminiscences were influenced by some pretty bitter memories of the pressure and continual grilling he received from the press throughout 1971. He hadn't mentioned that, as front-runner, he had the unique opportunity to publicize programs according to his own priorities, rather than reacting to what others, especially McGovern, had presented.

There was another difference between McGovern's and Muskie's approaches to a presidential campaign. George McGovern apparently was able to distinguish in his own mind how he would conduct himself as president—for example, how he would reach a decision on proposing a particular program—and how he conducted himself as a candidate for the presidency. Muskie resisted accepting such a distinction throughout his campaign.

While Ed Muskie and the people around him were worried about political support which was a mile wide and an inch deep, George McGovern stuck gamely to his strategy of developing solid support from his own New Politics constituency—support, it might be added, which was an inch wide and a mile deep.

McGovern was helped considerably in the formulation and implementation of this strategy by a group of political pragmatists who comprised his top staff, including Gary Hart, who had worked for Kennedy in 1968 and remained convinced that grass-roots politics would surprise the pros in the primaries; Ted Van Dyke, a former Humphrey speechwriter in 1968; and especially, the prescient Frank Mankiewicz, Robert Kennedy's press secretary in 1968, who never lost an opportunity, even in early 1971, to tell you exactly why Muskie couldn't make it through the primaries and why McGovern was best positioned to win the nomination.

Another political pragmatist who came to work for McGovern in the summer of 1970 and who would play a key role in McGovern's drive for the nomination was Richard Stearns, then twenty-six years old. Stearns has since been portrayed—usually by Evans and Novak—as one of McGovern's doctrinaire radicals. Nothing could be further from the truth. In fact, as a student at Stanford and as vice president of the National Student Association, he was generally recognized by his peers as relatively conservative on most issues.

In 1967 he had come to oppose the war in Vietnam, but not out of any great moral objections. "The war just seemed to me to be a totally ludicrous enterprise," he recalled. "Not only was it quite obvious that we couldn't win over there . . . but it was pretty clear that the war was tearing the country up. Any fool should have seen that there was political disaster in keeping the war going. So my reactions were essentially on political grounds—and I knew that Johnson could be pushed out if Bobby would make the challenge."

Like so many young professionals of the New Politics, Rick Stearns was an admirer of Robert Kennedy. He went to work for McCarthy only after calling the Kennedy office in Washington and being told by one of Kennedy's aides that Kennedy had not yet made up his mind to run.

Stearns went to England on a Rhodes scholarship in 1968 and a year later, while visiting in Washington, was introduced to Senator McGovern and went on to do some work for him on the Party Reform Commission. He returned to England to write his thesis for his Ph.D. on the party-reform effort in the Democratic Party. Then, in the spring of 1970, McGovern personally wrote Stearns a short note asking him to join his presidential campaign staff, which was then in the process of being organized.

Stearns arrived in Washington in July 1970. Shortly thereafter, he wrote a thirty-four-page detailed memorandum describing the advantages McGovern would enjoy under the new rules with a well-cultivated activist constituency. The two purposes of the memo, Stearns wrote, were, first, "to show . . . that it is possible for McGovern to win the nomination"; and second, to set priorities "by determining where the delegates and potential McGovern supporters are in thickest concentration."

A state-by-state analysis of McGovern's chances followed, with Muskie serving as the chief focus of comparison. Some of Stearns' predictions were, in retrospect, uncannily accurate. For example, in weighing the advantages and disadvantages of entering the New Hampshire primary, Stearns concluded that McGovern would likely receive 35 per cent in the vote and a net of nine delegates (McGovern actually won 37 per cent and 6 delegates).[1]

Stearns also understood what most of those involved in the controversy over quotas had overlooked: McGovern's real advantage would be that his activist constituency would be easy to organize to turn out for open caucus meetings in the nonprimary states. Even in

---

1. Stearns also projected that McGovern could go into the 1972 convention with 1344 committed first-ballot votes—not very far from the 1451 final tally McGovern had counted as his after he won the credentials challenge to his California delegation.

a state like Vermont, Maine's neighbor and, on a cross-sectional basis, probably for Senator Muskie over Senator McGovern by a 90–10 per cent margin, McGovern enjoyed considerable advantages. "The open and poorly attended caucuses of Vermont," Stearns wrote, "will favor candidates with a strongly motivated following. With careful organization a good McGovern showing at the state convention can be made." (McGovern ultimately won nine of Vermont's twelve delegates.)

In Utah, hardly a liberal state, where the popular Governor Calvin Rampton had endorsed Muskie, Stearns predicted that "an active liberal-student coalition which took control of the 1970 state convention will be back in force in 1972." (McGovern ultimately won eleven of the nineteen Utah delegates to the national convention.)

Of all his political skills, George McGovern's recognition of the value of people like Stearns and other young committed grass-roots organizers proved most responsible for his successes in 1972. He had learned his lessons from the 1968 campaign well. He understood that once New Politics activists are turned on, they are self-starters—they need no further supervision, very little morale boosting, and even less support from the national headquarters in Washington. They know what small groups of people can do to get attention from the press. To such people George McGovern's apparent hopelessness as a political candidate was one of his greatest virtues.

During my travels for Muskie during 1971, I was always struck by the fact that, wherever I was, McGovern had already attracted the most committed, energetic, creative political organizers. Frequently the McGovernites would already have established their own fully staffed headquarters, put out several mailings, and sometimes—as long as six or nine months before the first primary—completed a canvass of all Democrats in their areas.

While Muskie campaigned with a large retinue of press and staff (and, by the summer of 1971, even his own campaign plane)—again, part of the glory as well as the burden of being everyone's front runner—McGovern would quietly and steadily plug away at small meetings to persuade the local leadership of the New Politics constituency that he was their man. Sometimes he would seek out a local coordinator who was not from the McCarthy or Kennedy insurgency in 1968, but who was still an ideal grass-roots organizer. This was the case with Joseph Grandmaison, a young Nashua, New Hampshire, political activist who had worked for Lyndon Johnson in 1968.

The selection of Grandmaison to head the New Hampshire campaign is a good example of McGovern's skill at political organization, and comparison to the Muskie campaign is instructive here. Muskie's primary-state campaign managers were all outsiders, brought in from the Washington national staff, and few had any significant knowledge about the state they were sent to. But McGovern had heard that Grandmaison had solid ties to the liberals and the party regulars in New Hampshire and that, once committed, he would work day and night for his candidate—the key ingredient for McGovern.

So one day Grandmaison's telephone rang, and the voice on the other end of the line said, "Joe, this is George McGovern. I'd like to eat dinner with you and talk about your helping me in my presidential campaign." That night, as Grandmaison described it, "There I was, sitting across from a United States senator who was running for president, and he was offering me the chance to run his campaign in the first and most important presidential primary of the campaign. Is there any doubt that I said yes?"

McGovern had also made a hard judgment from the beginning that he couldn't get off the ground unless he did well in two states —New Hampshire, where he needed a good enough percentage to give his campaign a morale boost, and Wisconsin, where he knew he had to come in first or a strong second in order to go on to California. (McGovern and Frank Mankiewicz had always assumed that, with Hubert Humphrey in the race—always McGovern's greatest hope for beating Muskie—he could win in a three-way contest in the California primary.)

And so McGovern spent much of his time during 1971 attending small meetings of New Politics activists in New Hampshire and Wisconsin—building organizations slowly, patiently, from the grass roots up, in ones and twos. And he sent his political organizers into the nonprimary states to do the same. In late August 1971, Rick Stearns and a young Nebraskan named Gene Pokorny, then Midwestern coordinator and later campaign manager of the Wisconsin primary, visited Iowa for the first time. Stearns recounted the experience (in an unpublished manuscript) as follows:

"Our principal organizing weapon was a list of computerized contributors gathered by our direct-mail apparatus, listing the names of some 125 Iowa Democrats. Selecting one at random in Des Moines—Chris Froisheiser, a twenty-five-year-old insurance agent—we called him, gave him a list of the other fourteen Des Moines names and asked him to organize a meeting the following night.

"We met in the basement of Froisheiser's apartment complex. Thirteen of the fourteen attended. Among them was a former precinct committeeman who had been a candidate for Polk County chairman. Deciding that this was as much experience as we were likely to find, he was named temporary state coordinator, while from the remaining thirteen, the Greater Des Moines McGovern for President Committee was created.

"That night we slept on Froisheiser's floor. The following day Pokorny and I split the remaining list by zip codes. Gene went north, I south, meeting two days later in Iowa City. By then we had a statewide organization, albeit skeletal, but with at least one contact in each major county or city. When I returned to Des Moines a month later, this time to the basement of a downtown church, 175 people were waiting."

McGovern's strategy was clear: win the New Politics left and build an activist grass-roots organization which would outwork and outproduce the other candidates in the primaries. There were some dark moments, especially in early January 1972, after Senator Harold Hughes endorsed Muskie. But McGovern's mass mailings to New Politics people continued to produce a flow of contributions: more than a million dollars was ultimately raised in the course of 1971 in this fashion.

With the news that Hubert Humphrey would declare his candidacy in early 1972, McGovern and his staff could hardly conceal their delight. "Good old Hubert," Stearns remembered. "We were all ready to concede to Muskie. And then that old Humphrey compulsion saved the day."

eight

THE YOUTH-VOTE HUSTLE

> got to the point where I was believing all those press
> releases we wrote . . . but I guess I always inwardly knew that the
> press and the foundations would believe anything you told them,
> 'cause they wanted to believe in young people, and it was all a
> happy con game."
>
> —Duane Draper, former president,
> Association of Student Governments, May 1973

BOTH George McGovern and Ed Muskie were greatly concerned
about the impact of the youth vote in the 1972 presidential campaign. But for Muskie, the youth constituency was just one group in
the overall coalition he sought to create. For McGovern, winning the
youth vote was the crux of his campaign, the linchpin of his strategy
for the nomination.

What "youth vote"? College activists from schools like Yale and
Stanford? Or the nineteen-year-old factory worker or secretary who
went to school part-time at the local community college?

Those of us from the first group were unaccustomed to making
such distinctions. In fact, we were used to only one kind of "youth"
being recognized—us. During the early sixties, we loved reading
about ourselves in the press—the "committed," "idealistic," "activist" young generation, not silent like our older brothers and sisters
who went to college in the fifties . . . not cynical and pragmatic like
our parents who went to school in the thirties and forties.

We thought that the press preoccupation with us had reached its
zenith during the 1968 McCarthy campaign, when everyone sud-

113

denly discovered the "army of idealistic young people" who "stayed clean for Gene" in the primaries. During those days we learned one of the key elements of the later youth hustle—the ability to manipulate the press and, consequently, our fellow "youths" as well.

During the early days of the McCarthy campaign in New Hampshire—in December 1967 and January 1968, when very few student volunteers were anywhere to be seen—we first experimented with a technique at which we would become very adept as time went on—the self-fulfilling press release. First we would put out press releases that we were flooded with student volunteers and couldn't find enough housing for everyone. Once that story appeared, the students would begin to arrive and, inevitably, there would come a point when the situation we had described in our early press release would become true.

When the eighteen-year-old vote was passed, the press attention—and our own sense of importance—exceeded even the glorious days of the McCarthy campaign's children's crusade. Now the cult of young people in politics reached its apotheosis. Not only were we an army of idealistic volunteers and precinct workers; now we were depicted as a political force to be reckoned with. Now it was time to flex our newly found political muscles and cash in the chips.

There was only one problem. The image of a generation of committed political activists was mostly illusion. The student on the cover of *Time* magazine in 1964 representing an entire generation was a Yale student, not a part-time student at Kenosha Technical Institute or one of those lesser types who couldn't get into an Ivy League school and ended up at a junior college, or who never went to college at all.

Those of us involved with the youth vote scene frequently referred to the number of newly eligible voters between eighteen and twenty-four—about 25 million. But too often we would leave the impression that those 25 million were liberal college-student political activists, even though we knew that, in fact, 14 million, or 56 per cent, were nonstudent young people. And even among the college students, only a small minority attended the better-known prestigious private institutions which were the scene of all the highly publicized political activities; most students attended state universities or local community colleges, and many others worked part-time and attended technical or trade schools.

But these realities of the youth-vote scene hadn't completely set in by early 1971 when the eighteen-year-old vote became effective. Instead, "youth organizers" and "youth registration directors" continued, first, to blur the distinction between the minority of us who were liberal college activists and the majority who were not and, second, to encourage the portrait of "young people" of the New Politics as being more issue-oriented and more idealistic than other interest groups from the "old politics."

Within months of the passage of the eighteen-year-old vote, both of these myths were used for all they were worth to blitz foundations and private contributors with requests for funding of elaborately structured national voter-registration organizations. The blitzers were uniformly bright young men and women from the Ivy League colleges and universities who knew their way around Washington and, most importantly, knew how to impress establishment foundation officials and businessmen with arguments about the imperative need to convince all those 25 million newly eligible voters to "stay in the system."

Foundation and corporate officials liked these "responsible young people," as they would call them—liked the idea of "investing" (to use another favorite word) funds to convince young people to join the establishment rather than confront it.

A careful study of the national organizations which resulted from this drive—their funding, their structure, their expenditures, and the actual results of their efforts in terms of the registration of young people—is beyond the scope of this book. Suffice it to say here that the two largest of such organizations—the Youth Citizenship Fund (YCF) and the National Movement for a Student Vote (Student Vote)—between them received and spent more than $1 million in less than a year's time (some of those involved with these organizations estimate that the figure may be as high as $2 million).

What all this money was spent on, what it produced, is not easy to say. The Youth Citizenship Fund ultimately became mainly a sign-making and poster-producing operation. Their signs were creative and attractive, and they probably encouraged some students to vote. The Student Vote established a national field staff all over the country, setting up "voter-registration projects" at individual campuses, which also probably contributed to the registration of some college students.

But for the most part neither organization registered many young voters. Like the best of any Washington bureaucracy, most of the staff time of both organizations was spent sending memoranda to each other, bad-mouthing their rivals in the youth-vote hustle, writing progress reports and progress reports of the progress reports, holding staff meetings, and, of course, sending out press releases claiming to have registered x number of students in x number of schools. The numbers were always on the high side but were perfectly safe since no reporter was going to take the trouble to check them out. A great deal of time was also spent on internal squabbles and power plays. Despite its huge treasury, for example, the YCF was paralyzed for a good deal of the summer and fall of 1971 while an attempt was made to oust YCF founder and director, Carol Ladt, from leadership (which succeeded at one point only to have Ladt return in a countercoup some time later).

It became increasingly apparent that the whole concept of "nonpartisan" voter-registration projects could never result in registering a large number of young people. Voter registration is probably the most time-consuming, least enjoyable political work there is. Anyone who has ever done it—many of the people involved in 1971–72 in the national youth-registration organizations never had—would know that you have to have an unusual incentive to convince people to register to vote, and an even greater incentive to get them to volunteer to help other people register. And that incentive almost always has to be a particular candidate or a specific political cause.

It also became increasingly obvious that very little money was being spent to register the invisible young people in the grade schools and junior colleges, or those who worked full time. Only two organizations did any significant work among these kinds of young people—the Alliance for Labor Action (ALA), a now defunct political arm of the UAW and the Teamsters Union, and Frontlash, an AFL-CIO-funded group.

It is difficult to measure how many newly registered young workers could be attributed to their efforts. But those who were registered were spared the elaborate bureaucracies of the Washington-based organizations. Carl Wagner, the twenty-nine-year-old youth director of Alliance for Labor Action, explained his methodology during 1971. "I just go out into the field myself," Carl Wagner would explain, "find a young shop steward, take him out for a beer, and convince him to help me get a hundred of his friends in the plant to register to vote. Then he'd take me around the plant, I'd meet his friends, and they would introduce me to their friends, and then for a week or so I'd stay on their tails and they would register."

In early 1971 after I made a number of speaking appearances before Wisconsin, Pennsylvania, and New Hampshire junior-college and technical-school audiences, I began to see through the "all-youths-are-like-us" aspect of the youth-vote hustle.

These students were entirely different from the world of antiwar liberal activists to which I was accustomed. Most of them had never heard of George McGovern, and those who had didn't like him. Muskie's name evoked some positive memories of his 1968 vice-presidential race, but not much more than that. The major issue which interested these young people was the shrinking job market. Although most didn't like the war in Vietnam, they disliked antiwar protesters even more.

On one occasion I addressed a group of young workers in a Philadelphia community called Manayunk, and then drove across town to speak to a group of University of Pennsylvania students. The cultural and values gap between the two groups was far greater, it dawned on me for the first time, than the much-publicized generation gap.

The second aspect of the youth-vote hustle—the myth that liberal student activists were the most issue-oriented, idealistic, and politically committed young people around—finally became clear to me when I attended the National Student Association Congress in Fort Collins, Colorado, in the summer of 1971. By then I was fully aware that most young people were not liberal political activists. But I still expected that an assemblage of student leaders from the nation's most elite colleges and universities would concentrate their energies on issues they claimed to care about most: the war in Vietnam, poverty and racial injustice, and, most important, the need to defeat Richard Nixon in 1972.

I sat in disbelief as the NSA Congress for five days ignored serious discussion of these issues and, instead, spent almost all its time debating whether the National Student Association should merge with another student organization, called the Association of Student Governments (ASG), a more moderate split-off from NSA, composed primarily of Southern and Southwestern schools.

Superficially the merger debate was clothed in the rhetoric of a serious philosophic split. The ASG leaders were primarily political-process oriented liberal-moderates who saw the merger as a way to dramatize student unity on the necessity of beating Richard Nixon. The president of the ASG, Duane Draper, former student-body president of the University of Oklahoma, put it very directly in his speech in support of the merger: "If you vote for the merger," he said, "you will be voting for the strategy of winning social change through the political process, not in the streets."

The NSA leadership opposed the merger. Its president, David Ifshin, claimed that Draper and his promerger supporters were "puppets of Allard Lowenstein," and antimerger forces circulated an anonymous leaflet alleging that Draper was in the employ of the Central Intelligence Agency. The antimerger speakers argued that the political system was corrupt and students should devote their energies to "community organizing" (the more radical speakers urged "trashing," *i.e.*, running through the streets and breaking windows).

On the first vote, the merger resolution passed by the required two-thirds margin, with six votes to spare. But then a funny thing happened on the way to the announcement of the results of the vote tally. The microphones mysteriously went out of commission, a group of black students took over the platform, and the meeting was adjourned.

The following morning another vote was taken. This time, with an apparent switch of four votes, the merger resolution failed.

The now-familiar phenomenon of black-bullwhipping-white-radi-cal-consciences then proceeded unabated. Three years before, at the 1969 convention, self-proclaimed leaders of the Black Students

Caucus had taken over the platform, chained all the doors shut, stationed blacks at all the doors, and threatened to "break heads" unless the NSA paid their group $50,000 in reparations. Charles Palmer, the student body president of the University of California at Berkeley, ran for president of NSA on the platform that the white students should make the payment. Once again, as he had done at the 1967 NSA Convention, Clinton Deveaux, the black student-body president from the State University of New York at Buffalo, stood up and amidst shouts of "Tom" and "traitor," denounced "this racist blackmail and these fascist tactics." Deveaux challenged Palmer for NSA president primarily on the issue of reparations and was narrowly defeated.

Now, two years later at the 1971 Congress, nothing had really changed. The blacks were still taking over the microphone and the white NSA leadership was still unwilling to challenge the coercive tactics of the Black Caucus for fear of being accused of racism. Duane Draper suggested that it didn't make sense for an organization like NSA, which had done so much over the past decade in the civil rights movement, to be forced to pay thousands of dollars in "reparations" to blacks, especially to a group of 15 or 20 black students who refused to say how the money would be used and who appeared to represent no one but themselves. But Draper was immediately denounced as a fascist pig, a racist, and a sexist dog (his wife, Cleta, a skilled and shrewd political tactician in her own right, was also denounced as a tool of male chauvinism).

When NSA president Ifshin announced that NSA had agreed to make some reparations payments, a black student, identified as the chairman of the Black Student National Voter Registration Committee (an organization which had not existed until that very moment) took the microphone and presented Ifshin with a Leadership, Service, and Distinction Award. Ifshin, who had handled a difficult situation with creditable restraint and diplomacy, thanked his benefactors. It was sometime later that I finally made the connection between the first letters of this newly created award and the world of student psychedelia. Then, the black student leader took the microphone and screamed, "Everybody stand up." And everybody stood up. "Repeat after me: We are the greatest."

And everyone shouted back, "We are the greatest."

"We are not a teepee. We're the Empire State Building."
"We are not a teepee. We're the Empire State Building."
"We are not Volkswagens. We are Rolls-Royces and Cadillacs."
"We are not Volkswagens. We are Rolls-Royces and Cadillacs."
"Student power."
"Student power."
"Student power."
"Student power."

Ifshin and the black student hugged each other in front of the microphone, as the crowd cheered ecstatically.

Duane Draper turned to me at this point and shrugged his shoulders. "We sure are the greatest, aren't we, fellow youth coordinator?"

While the NSA kids were cheering about not being Volkswagens and accepting LSD awards, George McGovern continued to worry about winning the solid support of the "youth vote."

As late as February 1972, in a Gallup poll, Muskie still led all McGovern among all college students—receiving 23 per cent, to Kennedy's 22, to McGovern's 15. However, among those students who described themselves as "left," McGovern led over Muskie by 25–19 per cent.

It's hard to know whether McGovern realized at this point that his ability to win by 80 or 90 per cent on the elite college campuses in a Democratic primary didn't necessarily mean that he would do well with the majority of young people who were *not* liberal student activists in the general election. But McGovern seemed to understand from the very beginning that these left-liberal college student activists held unusual political power in the political circumstances of 1972. Under the McGovern Commission rules and the increased number of primaries in 1972, their ability to pack party caucuses and to produce large concentrations of headquarters volunteers and canvassers in the primary and caucus states gave them political power disproportionate to their numbers.

McGovern also understood that there was great potential for a major blocking of the vote on the activist college campuses. Once the momentum for McGovern was established on college campuses, especially as the student leaders and the most prominent political activists became identified with the McGovern campaign, then it would be likely that McGovern would get margins as large as eight or ten to one in a Democratic primary. Even if the absolute numbers of student votes weren't unusually large, McGovern realized that in a multicandidate primary, or a primary in a small state such as New Hampshire, such bloc voting could make a significant difference.

By the end of 1971, after a year of campus appearances, speeches opposing the draft and suggesting sympathy with pro-marijuana and anti-abortion student sentiment (though he always stopped short of supporting legalized marijuana and abortion on demand), McGovern had good reason to expect such bloc voting in his favor on the activist campuses. His state organizations spent a good deal of their time on registration efforts on these campuses. In Wisconsin, for example, the McGovern organization registered almost ten thousand new voters from the Madison campus of the University of Wisconsin alone.

All McGovern needed for a large student turnout was some semblance of credibility as a candidate, some morale boost.

Like a good showing in the New Hampshire primary, for example.

nine

THE PRIMARIES: WHICH
WINNERS LOST
AND WHICH LOSERS WON?

"Senator Muskie has a moral commitment and his own style of idealism, but no amount of image retouching could make this quiet man sound like an angry populist or a fiery radical."
— *New York Times* editorial,
April 27, 1972

"The primaries are over. McGovern has shown himself an attractive, durable and flexible candidate. . . . Yet the question mark lingers. How much 'there' is really there in the McGovern phenomenon?"
— William V. Shannon, July 2, 1972

By April 3, the eve of the Wisconsin primary—the decisive confrontation between Muskie and McGovern, with the leadership of the liberal-New Politics wing of the Democratic Party at stake—Senator Muskie was riding high indeed.

He had beaten McGovern five out of five times during the past six weeks—in Iowa, neighbor to McGovern's South Dakota, even though McGovern's highly motivated constituency of New Politics activists had turned out for the local party caucuses in large numbers during a heavy blizzard; in Arizona, where McGovern couldn't even beat John Lindsay, who had been a Democrat for only a few weeks; in New Hampshire, where Muskie's nine-percentage-point margin would be considered under most circumstances a very good showing; in Florida, where, once again, McGovern couldn't even better Lindsay; and, most important, head-to-head in Illinois, where Muskie overwhelmed McGovern, winning sixty-two delegates to

123

McGovern's fifteen—even though McGovern, who was well organized and had waged an active campaign throughout the state, had predicted he would win twice as many delegates.

With four victories out of five over all competition (five out of five over George McGovern), and continued evidence of the broadest appeal across all factions of the Democratic Party, Muskie on the eve of the Wisconson primary was steamrollering toward the nomination precisely as expected. George McGovern's campaign was demoralized, still confined essentially to the narrow base of New Politics purists with which he had begun the year before.

Right?

Wrong. The reality was that Ed Muskie came into the Wisconsin primary as a loser, on his way down. George McGovern came in as a winner, with the air of inevitability around him.

How was reality turned on its head? And what could Muskie have done to prevent it?

We have already seen how, through the course of 1971, Muskie was exposed to a political cross fire between New Politics purists, whose support George McGovern had actively sought, and the more conservative party-regular elements, on whom Hubert Humphrey based his campaign. As long as McGovern and Humphrey could run viable campaigns, and with George Wallace winning support in Catholic, working-class neighborhoods where Muskie had expected to do well, Muskie's candidacy was doomed in a primary in which all the candidates ran at the same time. In comparison to these men, Muskie had no hard constituency he could call his own.

Party primaries often draw voters who want to express a particular grievance—to "send them a message," as George Wallace put it—rather than to judge who would make the best candidate against the opposition or, for that matter, who would make the best president. In 1956, for example, Estes Kefauver, a "message" candidate, consistently defeated Adlai Stevenson in the primaries. The party leaders, who still controlled a majority of the delegates, acknowledged Kefauver's showing by nominating him for vice president. But they still believed Stevenson had a broader appeal within the Democratic Party. Had that system prevailed in 1972, Ed Muskie, who remained the first or second choice of a substantial majority of Democrats, would probably have been nominated.

As it happened, just at a time when the "message" phenomenon was at an unprecedented high—in the form of the McGovern candidacy on the left and the Wallace candidacy on the right—the Democrats' nominating system—more precisely, the winner-take-all primary, exaggerated the political impact of "message" voters.

Under such a system, in a multicandidate primary, a candidate with a small minority of the vote could win 90 or 100 per cent of the delegates, while candidates with sizable minority votes of their own would be denied fair proportional representation.

In the past, the public and the press could look to the polls of party leaders and the results of a few key head-to-head primary contests to indicate the relative strengths of the candidates. But in 1972, with the "message" vote phenomenon, the new delegate selection procedures, and numerous winner-take-all, multicandidate primaries, the press was forced to interpret the results of a large variety of state contests.

Understandably, the press reverted to the past "keys" to political analysis—for example, headlining the winner, in absolute numbers, of a multicandidate primary, with little attention to his breadth of support among all factions of the party. Also understandably, the press drew upon Muskie's front-runner and McGovern's underdog status in the national opinion polls through much of 1971 to apply a double standard in assessing the results of the state contests. This led, for example, to the projection of Muskie's 47 per cent victory in New Hampshire as insignificant but his weak showing in Florida as significant, whereas McGovern's disastrous showing in Illinois was projected as insignificant but his 30 per cent showing in Wisconsin was depicted as impressive.

This is not to say that Muskie was in any way the victim of a press vendetta. Actually Muskie received more than his share of favorable press treatment between 1968 and 1972, and much of the negative publicity he received in 1972 was a result of the legitimate spotlighting of his weaknesses as a candidate.

Nor can the press be blamed for its failure to reassess old definitions and to grasp the full implications of the intermeshing of new political forces and new political procedures in the Democratic Party in 1972. Most of the presidential candidates were in the same boat, not least of all, Senator Muskie himself.

Arizona: The Advantages of Being a Minority

There couldn't be a better example of a system designed to maximize the impact of minority constituencies than the primary system employed by Arizona in 1972.

Arizona held its primary—the second contest of the year—on January 29.[1] Senator Muskie had accumulated the endorsements of all the state's major Democratic Party officials, past and present, including former Governor Sam Goddard and the widely respected congressman from Tucson, Morris Udall. The press understandably regarded such endorsements as evidence of political strength (though their real value in voter turnout proved minimal). Muskie was seen as an easy victor in Arizona. *Newsweek,* for example, projected Muskie as the winner of *all twenty-five* delegates.

However, what much of the press never understood was that the Arizona system had been specifically designed to make it impossible for any one candidate to sweep all the delegates. In fact, under the Arizona system, even a 50 per cent delegate win for one candidate would be an unusual show of strength.

Here's the way the Arizona system worked: A statewide primary for the state's three hundred thousand registered Democrats elected five hundred delegates to a statewide convention. The state convention would subsequently select Arizona's twenty-five delegates to a national convention. A voter had the right to cast the number of votes equal to the number of state convention delegates running

1. Iowa had held its precinct caucuses the week before, on January 24. McGovern had a number of advantages going for him in Iowa. It was a neighboring state to South Dakota; he had had an active statewide organization six months before Muskie sent his first full organizer into the state (which was less than four weeks prior to the primary). The Iowa system also made a sweep impossible for any candidate. The local caucuses elected the delegates to the state conventions on a proportional basis, thus guaranteeing some representation for minorities. Finally, the McGovern forces were blessed on election night with one of the worst blizzards in recent Iowa history, advantaging McGovern's activists, who were motivated to turn out in greater numbers than Muskie's supporters.

Despite all these disadvantages, Muskie's showing in Iowa was more than respectable. Aided by the last-minute endorsement of Senator Harold Hughes, Muskie won 39 per cent of the caucus-elected delegates compared to McGovern's 27 per cent. However, the news media had projected a Muskie landslide; and, when it didn't happen, NBC news announced: "The Muskie bandwagon has slipped off an icy Iowa road." Press reports and headlines the next day reflected the same theme.

from a particular senatorial district (the state was divided into thirty senatorial districts). The voter could allocate those votes any way he wished. For example, if a senatorial district, based on the size of its Democratic Party registrations, was entitled to elect twenty delegates to the state convention, a voter in that district could cast twenty different votes for twenty different candidates, or twenty votes all for one candidate, or ten votes for one candidate and ten votes for another. This "cumulative voting" has frequently been employed to protect the power of minority stockholders in a corporation.

Under cumulative voting systems, if every voter cast each of his votes for the same number of different candidates, then the one-man, one-vote principle remains unaffected. But as soon as anyone cumulates his votes to a greater degree than others, the one-man, one-vote principle is distorted and a minority can assume power disproportionate to their actual numbers.

Suppose, for example, in that twenty-delegate senatorial district cited above, candidate A runs twenty delegate-candidates (the delegates would be identified as "committed to candidate A") and candidate B runs ten. Suppose candidate A gets nineteen of his supporters to go to the polls, and they vote for each of his twenty delegate-candidates. Each receives nineteen votes. However, candidate B, who is not as popular as candidate A, can convince only ten of his voters to come to the polls. But he instructs those ten voters to cumulate their twenty votes for his delegates and for no others. His ten delegates will receive twenty votes each. Thus, although, in real voter turnout, candidate A beat candidate B by nearly two to one, candidate B's delegate candidates all ran ahead of candidate A's. In other words, while candidate B actually only got 34 per cent of the vote, he was able to capture 50 per cent of the delegates.

It would be instructive to relate how one young political organizer working for John Lindsay took advantage of this system in the best tradition of the New Politics mixture of brainpower, manpower, and sheer gallpower.

Arthur Kaminsky was a graduate of the Al Lowenstein school of the New Politics. He grew up in Nassau County, Long Island, and worked in Lowenstein's successful congressional campaign in 1968. After graduating from Cornell University in 1968 and Yale Law

School in 1971, Kaminsky worked for Lowenstein during the latter's tenure as chairman of the Americans for Democratic Action; it was Kaminsky who coordinated all of Lowenstein's Dump Nixon rallies around the country during 1971.

Kaminsky was sent into Arizona by the Lindsay forces in early January. He quickly understood the advantages the cumulative voting system offered a candidate who needed only a strong showing—not necessarily a win—to give his campaign a lift. His most important decision involved a realistic goal of national convention delegates Lindsay could win and running the smallest number of state convention delegates necessary to meet that goal. He set his goal at five delegates, representing 20 per cent of Arizona's twenty-five National Convention delegates, and ninety to a hundred of the five hundred state convention delegates.

"A lot of people in the press simply didn't understand that it was impossible to win more than 50 or 60 per cent of the delegates under this system, especially given the fact that the McGovern people were going to single-shot [cumulate] their votes just like us," Kaminsky recalled. "The press' expectations about Muskie's sweeping the primary simply meant they didn't understand the system."

As it happened the Muskie people also appeared to have little grasp of the realities of the system. Kaminsky recalls being utterly incredulous when he learned that the Muskie campaign people were going to run a full slate of delegates—in fact, Muskie's organization had initially filed 587 delegate candidates for only 500 places. Muskie's people had the usual problem of being too top-heavy with party officials who insisted on running as delegates. But Kaminsky dismisses that excuse out of hand, with the impatience of a hard-boiled party professional who knows how to use political muscle when it's necessary. "We had over 240 Lindsay delegates who filed initially, and we just twisted arms until we had the number down to 185, below the total of McGovern's organization" (which filed only 192 delegate candidates).

Next Kaminsky determined how many "single-shot" voters (voters who would agree to cast all their ballots for one Lindsay delegate-candidate) would be necessary to guarantee the election of a Lindsay state convention delegate. Kaminsky turned to Chuck Perry, one of the many young New Politics activists Kaminsky had recruited on short notice to work in the Arizona campaign. Perry, twenty-seven years old, a shrewd political organizer who had formerly worked at the Democratic National Committee, used a rented electronic calculator to calculate what he called a "universal single-shot number"—the number of "single-shot" voters necessary to elect at least one state convention delegate. The "universal single-shot number" would vary proportionally according to the vote turnout, that is, the higher the turnout, the higher the number of "single shots" necessary to assure the election of a state convention delegate. Assuming a turnout of about 10 per cent, Perry calculated a "universal single-shot number" of thirty. All of Lindsay's delegate-candidates would win if each of them could find thirty friends who would agree to "single-shot" all their votes.

Among the delegates Kaminsky recruited were the police chief of a small mining town in Southwest Arizona and the student-body presidents of all three state universities and three other junior colleges. "A lot of people forget," Kaminsky observed some months later, "that student-body presidents usually have the best political organization around on campus, and sometimes off campus as well."

In addition, Kaminsky ran as delegate-candidates fourteen members of the Phoenix Chicano organization named Nosotros. This organization had previously been committed to Muskie's candidacy. By the time Kaminsky arrived in Arizona, the Nosotros leaders had become so irritated at the failure of the Muskie managers to give them much attention, especially financial, that Kaminsky was able to take full advantage of the situation. He made the same pitch to the Chicanos as he had to the Muskie-leaning student-body presidents: "Muskie has too many heavies in his campaign who are going to have the first shot at going to the national convention. You guys are going to get shafted by Muskie. If you endorse Lindsay, we'll guarantee you financial help and a slot as a delegate or alternate to the national convention."

Central to Kaminsky's system was an election-day operation efficient enough to keep track of how many votes were being cast for Lindsay delegates throughout the day and disciplined enough to control specific votes at any particular time. Once the totals for a particular candidate reached Chuck Perry's "universal single-shot number," thus ensuring his election, Kaminsky's poll captains would inform subsequent voters to switch their votes to another Lindsay delegate who needed help. Kaminsky printed a set of three-by-five cards instructing voters how they should allocate their votes. Another set of cards had blank spaces to permit Kaminsky and his staff to write in different vote allocation numbers as the day progressed. A table in front of each polling place was manned by Lindsay workers with a sign: "All Lindsay voters report here for instructions before voting."

Kaminsky also distributed to each of the thirty senatorial district coordinators an election-day staff sheet, listing the job responsibilities which had to be filled for the election day operation. These included the "single-shot scribe," responsible for keeping track of the turnout of "single-shot" voters; the "voter adviser," who would "cordially explain how we would like voters to distribute votes"; and a "guide-card noodge," who would hand out the three-by-five-card instructions and, where possible, direct "strays (Lindsay voters who happened to show up at the polls but weren't on anyone's single-shot list) to voter adviser for instruction." An added instruction to the "guide-card noodge" advised, "At all times be as inoffensive as possible."

One of Kaminsky's more creative young staff people, Curt Mead, installed telephones at all of his polling places to keep a running tally of how the votes were coming in and to permit him to make sudden switches in vote allocations. In one instance, when a polling official refused to permit Mead to set up his telephone and table at the polling place, Mead had a telephone installed in a tree. One Lindsay staffer picked up students from Arizona State in buses well supplied with beer and marijuana. Meanwhile, out in the barren wilds of southwest Arizona, another Kaminsky-recruited activist, Mitch Goldman, visited every bar and ranch in sight. It was a tough assignment for a young Jewish boy from Long Island, but somehow Goldman managed to plead, cajole, and bully leading local Democrats and civic leaders to support Lindsay.

The results of the primary more than vindicated Kaminsky's skillful combination of old politics muscle and grease and New Politics activism and creativity. One good example of the operation of the cumulative voting system was senatorial district 23, a wealthy residential area in downtown Phoenix which had thirteen state convention delegates up for election. Muskie ran thirteen candidates, Lindsay and McGovern nine delegates each. One of Muskie's delegates, a candidate for Congress, spent a considerable amount of money on his delegate campaign. He came in first by three times as many votes as he needed; this overkill was a serious hindrance to Muskie, because it deprived other Muskie delegates of votes they needed. The results dramatically show the effects of cumulative voting. Overall (votes cast), Muskie came in first by a large margin, winning 7559 cumulative votes to 4314 for the "uncommitteds," 3883 for McGovern and running last was Lindsay, with 3796 cumulative votes. Yet out of the thirteen state convention delegates in that district, Muskie won only five, Lindsay came in *second* with four, and McGovern won three (the uncommitteds won only a single delegate).

In addition to Kaminsky's organizational techniques, his use of money and media was also important to Lindsay's strong showing in Arizona. Kaminsky spent about $4400 on billboards throughout Phoenix and Tuscon, giving Lindsay, for a modest sum of money, instant visibility and the appearance of an extensive, highly financed political operation. Kaminsky spent about $12,000 on TV and radio ads, which he described as "frosting on the cake." Despite charges by embittered Muskie and McGovern staffers about Lindsay's having spent as much as $50,000 to $75,000 in Arizona, in fact that total was about $20,000 to $25,000, and, as Kaminsky put it, "If all our single-shot voters had showed up, we could have done without most of the media and still done just as well."

The final delegate vote totals statewide gave Muskie 188 delegates (out of 489 candidates); Lindsay, 120 (out of 185); and McGovern, 102 (out of 192). On a proportional basis, Muskie ultimately received nine delegates (out of 25) to the national convention; Lindsay won six (one more than Kaminsky's initial goal); and McGovern, following the same limited strategy as Lindsay, won five delegates.

The McGovern showing in Arizona struck some as disappointing, since it was assumed that McGovern should have beaten at least Lindsay. Actually, McGovern's totals should have been an impressive signal of the kind of grass-roots organization which he and his staff could put together with minimal resources and maximum polit-

ical handicaps. With Rick Stearns in charge, the Arizona McGovernites, quietly and almost invisibly—without media or billboards,
without the high-powered endorsements of the Muskie campaign
and the computerized complexity of the Kaminsky operation—held
their loyalists together, analyzed the workings of the cumulative
voting system accurately, concentrated their votes on each other,
and somehow managed to elect five delegates, all, according to
Stearns, with a budget of less than $5000.

As in the Iowa caucuses the week before, the results in Arizona
bore out the disadvantages of entering the primary season as a
front-runner. Expectations that the front-runner will do well lead to
expectations by the press that he *must* do well. If he then does less
well than predicted, that is news: the front-runner might be slipping. Once a campaign is depicted in the press as "slipping," the
description can become a self-fulfilling prophecy, for at a time when
presidential campaigns require huge sums of money to remain viable, any reversal in momentum can be fatal.

After the Arizona primary, the press emphasized that Muskie's
showing was "disappointing." Some of the political press, such as R.
W. Apple of *The New York Times,* misleadingly referred to a combined "44 per cent" delegate total for Lindsay and McGovern as
evidence of a "potent" bloc of liberal-New Politics Democrats in the
Arizona Democratic Party. In the first place, only 15 per cent of all
registered Arizona Democrats voted.

In addition, subsequent opinion surveys by Harris and Yankelovich indicated that most Lindsay voters preferred Muskie over
McGovern.

Given all of Muskie's organizational mistakes, Muskie's
showing—winning nearly 40 per cent of the delegates—was, as
Kaminsky himself pointed out, "quite extraordinary."

New Hampshire: Chasing the 50 Per Cent Phantom

Muskie's momentum may have been somewhat deflected by his
showing in Arizona, but New Hampshire in March was the real
beginning of his rapid fall from front-runner status. It was also in
New Hampshire that the sabotage activities of the Committee to

Re-elect the President had their most significant impact on the Democratic presidential race.

New Hampshire gave George McGovern a morale and credibility boost without which he could not have been nominated. McGovern's winning 37 per cent of the popular vote, while a good showing, should not have been very surprising to anyone who understood New Hampshire politics. There is a relatively automatic 20 to 30 per cent "peace-liberal" vote in any New Hampshire Democratic primary; McCarthy got it in 1968, and McGovern got it in 1972.

This isn't to denigrate McGovern's campaign. He was able to expand the relatively automatic 20 to 30 per cent vote to 37 per cent. At least two to three percentage points of this excess over the 1968 liberal vote were due to a heavy student vote in his favor. For example, he carried Hanover, New Hampshire (the home of Dartmouth College), by almost four to one over Muskie, largely as a result of student voting. He also gained several percentage points by the sheer force of his long hours and days of campaigning. After all, if you shake eight hundred hands in New Hampshire, you are reaching about 1 per cent of the vote in a Democratic primary. McGovern spent considerably more campaign time in New Hampshire than Muskie did. His organization of New Politics activists and student canvassers managed to maximize every possible source of support in the state. Finally, McGovern gained several percentage points as a result of the Manchester *Union Leader*'s campaign against Senator Muskie.

Whether or not McGovern's 37 per cent showing should have been treated as "surprising" by the press, the question remains: Why didn't Muskie win the other 63 per cent, or, more realistically, why didn't he at least win a majority of the vote? Didn't the press have a right to expect a fellow New Englander from a neighboring state to win 50 per cent or more of the vote in a contest against the mayor of Los Angeles and an unknown and apparently leftist senator from South Dakota?

The 50 per cent target is a classic example of the kind of double standard to which Muskie was apparently subjected. Although Muskie's campaign workers raised expectations by speaking too loosely to the press about the need for Muskie to win at least 50 per cent of the vote, the 50 per cent-neighboring state standard was never applied to any other candidate in any other primary in the 1972 campaign. For example, George Wallace's 42 per cent in the Florida primary was not described as a "disappointing" showing in a "neighboring state"; nor was McGovern's 27 per cent in his neighboring state of Iowa (compared to Muskie's 39 per cent); nor was Humphrey's 21 per cent in his neighboring state of Wisconsin.

Since Muskie's final 47 per cent margin was so close to the 50 per cent target which the press had set, it is important to isolate some of his strategic mistakes in the New Hampshire campaign which might have made a three- or four-percentage-point difference. One was a late start at grass-roots organization. The state campaign director, Tony Podesta, a veteran of the McCarthy campaign and former deputy campaign manager of the 1970 Duffey campaign, didn't arrive in he state until the fall of 1971—some nine months after McGovern's Joe Grandmaison had begun active grass-roots organizing around the state. "With a few extra months of organizing," Podesta claims, "I think we would have gotten over 50 per cent."

Muskie was also hurt by his inability to spend as much time in the state as McGovern in the closing days of the campaign. Muskie, increasingly worried about Humphrey's apparent strength in Florida, was committed to an active campaign in that state's primary, scheduled for the week after New Hampshire. He found himself in the familiar crossfire, with Humphrey accusing him of not caring about the people of Florida because he spent too much time in New Hampshire and McGovern denouncing him for spending too much time in Florida and "taking the people of New Hampshire for granted."

Muskie damaged himself, especially among the college and high school voters and some liberal-moderates, by his refusal to debate McGovern and the other candidates until the very end of the campaign and by his early refusal to disclose his financial contributors until after the April 7 date of the campaign disclosure law.

On the disclosure issue, it is hard to understand why Muskie resisted so long. He gave McGovern an ideal opportunity to contrast his own "open" New Politics with Muskie's "old-politics secrecy." Stewart Mott wasted no time running full-page ads in big-city newspapers of the major primary states condemning Muskie's failure to disclose his contributors. Not until the second week in March—a few days before the Florida primary—did Muskie announce that he would disclose—only after he learned that Hubert Humphrey was about to do so.

Muskie always insisted that disclosure was a phony issue, that he had voluntarily disclosed in 1970 but no one else had. But neither he nor his top advisers, who were constantly warning him about the financial perils of disclosure (on the theory that there was some Republican money which would not come in if there was disclosure), fully understood that the issue was especially damaging for a candidate who had based his campaign on the slogan "Trust Muskie."

An analysis of the returns of the primary vote make it clear that these strategic errors by Muskie were not, in the end, the crucial factors in his submajority showing. Nor was the relative effectiveness of the campaigns of any of his competitors a crucial variable. A study of the town-by-town, county-by-county results of the New Hampshire primary shows that the determinative factor was the impact of William Loeb's systematic campaign of slander and distortion in his newspaper, the Manchester *Union Leader*.

Compare, for example, the results of the primary vote in the city of Nashua with those from the city of Manchester. Nashua is in the southern portion of the state, near the Massachusetts border, about a ninety-minute drive to Boston and under the liberal influences of the Boston media. Nashua also has its own relatively liberal city newspaper. McCarthy had run neck-and-neck with Johnson in 1968 in Nashua and McGovern had expected to do well there. McGovern did do well, with 35 per cent of the vote (compared to McCarthy's 38 per cent). Muskie won with a total vote exceeding 58 per cent.

Thirty miles north of Nashua is the city of Manchester, slightly more working-class, a little more conservative, and therefore expected to be for Muskie by a larger margin than Nashua. (In 1968 Johnson had beaten McCarthy soundly in Manchester and surrounding towns.) McGovern campaigned actively in Manchester, and his student volunteers canvassed every household two or three times, writing personal letters to each voter. Yet he managed to win the same 35 per cent in Manchester that he had won in Nashua—a good showing but no better than McCarthy's showing in 1968. Yet Muskie received only 38 per cent of the vote—a full *twenty points*

lower than his showing in Nashua, despite the fact that he should
have run stronger in Manchester.

Take a map and draw a line around the city of Manchester and
those suburbs where the circulation of the Manchester *Union Leader*
is most concentrated—and you will find Muskie running fifteen to
twenty points behind his showing in comparable cities outside that
area.

Or compare Muskie's and McGovern's showing in comparable
working-class, French-Canadian neighborhoods in the state.
McGovern's energetic campaign in the blue-collar neighborhoods
and factories of Manchester—largely the result of the arrival of
Steven Robbins, a young Yale Law School graduate who had been
chief of advance and scheduling in the 1970 Duffey campaign in
Connecticut—paid off. Robbins had insisted that McGovern stop
wasting his time on long drives into the small rural towns and,
instead, concentrate his campaigning in the cities where most of the
votes were. When the election returns came in showing McGovern's
respectable showing against Muskie in these Manchester working-
class districts, the press immediately trumpeted the "McGovern
phenomenon" of popularity among working-class people.

The description of McGovern's "impressive" strength in
working-class neighborhoods in New Hampshire was, quite frankly,
an exaggeration. For example, McGovern carried ward 14 in
Manchester, a French-Canadian, blue-collar ward that went heavily
for Johnson in 1968, with 35 per cent of the vote (the same percentage he got statewide). Muskie received only 34 per cent (thirteen
points lower than his statewide total). The result startled the press.

However, in Ward 7 of Nashua—composed of the same kinds of
French-Canadian working-class Democrats as in Manchester's ward
14—Muskie swamped McGovern by a margin exceeding two to one,
winning 66 per cent of the vote to McGovern's 28 per cent. Again,
McGovern surprised the press by beating Muskie in several small
working-class towns just outside the city of Manchester—by 42 to 38
per cent in Goffstown and 43 to 34 per cent in Bedford. Yet Muskie
consistently overwhelmed McGovern in other, similar, blue-collar
towns and neighborhoods in all other sections of the state—winning
Somersworth, in the northeast, by 69 per cent, swamping McGovern

in the heavily French-Canadian working-class Ward 4 of Berlin by a margin of almost three to one.

These contrasts in Muskie's and McGovern's showings in towns and neighborhoods of nearly identical ethnic and economic makeup (with organizational and campaign efforts being relatively comparable) is not explicable by anything George McGovern did right or Ed Muskie did wrong. The critical factor which explains the markedly differing results is not hard to isolate: Ward 14 of Manchester and the towns of Goffstown and Bedford were all exposed to the diatribes of Loeb's *Union Leader;* Ward 7 of Nashua, ward 4 of Berlin, and the city of Somersworth were not.

Even in the places where Muskie had been subjected to the *Union Leader* attacks, McGovern's totals remained fairly close to his statewide totals. In fact, it is clear that the chief beneficiaries of Loeb's attacks were Mayor Sam Yorty of Los Angeles, Representative Wilbur Mills of Arkansas, and Senator Vance Hartke of Indiana. The significance of the candidacies of these three is another example of the news media's failure to understand the political realities in a state primary campaign.

In general, the press totally neglected the possible impact of Yorty, Mills, and Hartke in the race. This can be seen by the news media's repeated references to the fall 1971 Boston *Globe* poll, showing Muskie ahead by 65 per cent, as a benchmark with which to measure Muskie's relative political strength. The poll had been taken before the Loeb campaign against Muskie had heated up, before Yorty had begun heavy campaigning, and before Mills and Hartke had entered the contest. When Mills and Hartke began to spend huge sums of money in a very small state—they spent more than an estimated $75,000 in the last two weeks—the press barely took notice.

Meanwhile, by January and February 1972, Sam Yorty, Loeb's favorite, was receiving lavish attention on the front pages of the *Union Leader.* Washington *Post* (then Los Angeles *Times*) reporter Jules Witcover, in a study published in the June 1972 *Columbia Journalism Review*, reported that Yorty had received 870 inches of coverage by Loeb, as compared to Muskie's 420 inches, and 17 pictures to Muskie's 10. Apart from the difference in space and numbers of pictures, Yorty stories were always favorable, Muskie stories always negative.[2]

Outside of the *Union Leader* circulation, Yorty, Mills, and Hartke accumulated only a negligible number of votes—for example, 7 per cent total for all three in Nashua, 8 per cent total in Somersworth, and 10 per cent total in Berlin. However, within the area covered by the *Union Leader*, they received a total of 22 per cent of the vote in Goffstown, 27 per cent in the city of Manchester, and in Ward 14 of Manchester, Yorty received 15 per cent of the vote, Mills 11, and Hartke 6 per cent—a total of 32 per cent of the vote, or 18 percentage points higher than their combined statewide totals.

A concerted sabotage campaign by the Committee to Re-elect the President contributed to Muskie's weak showing in the Manchester area. The full extent of the Segretti sabotage operation in New Hampshire may never be known. But the one tactic which the Muskie campaign knew about, because it produced a stream of complaining phone calls and letters, was what must have been thousands of telephone calls to Manchester voters by Nixon campaign operatives at 2 or 3 A.M.[3] The caller announced that he was a representative of the "Harlem for Muskie Committee" and urged the sleepy New Hampshireite on the other end of the line to "support Ed Muskie because he's for us blacks."

William Loeb's daily diatribes against Muskie were, however, most responsible for his weak showing within the ambit of the *Union Leader*'s circulation. All fall and winter Loeb had filled the paper with front-page editorials entitled "Moscow Muskie Is a Phony," "Sportsmen, Beware of 'Flip-Flop' Muskie," and "Muskie's a Left-Winger." On February 24, 1972, under the headline "Muskie Insults Franco-Americans," Loeb reprinted a letter on the front page by a

2. Another favorite Loeb tactic, aimed exclusively against Muskie, was to run a continuing stream of anti-Muskie columns by conservative columnists, some of them a year or more old, in banner headlines, giving them the appearance of news stories. Witcover cites the example of a column written by David Lawrence on January 14, 1971, criticizing Muskie's trip to Moscow. The *Union Leader* ran the column on February 16, 1972, under banner headlines about "Moscow Muskie." Another conservative columnist, Holmes Alexander, had written a column a year earlier critical of Muskie's endorsement of an April 1971 antiwar march. On February 11, 1972, Alexander's column was reprinted under the headline "Senator Muskie and the Freaks."

3. These phone calls were admitted to by Herbert Porter, CREEP scheduler, during his Watergate hearings testimony.

person identified as "Paul Morrison" from Fort Lauderdale, Florida. Morrison accused Muskie of having laughed during a Florida campaign stop after hearing someone say that, while Maine didn't have many blacks, "we have Cannocks [sic]." In a front-page editorial, Loeb wrote, "We have always known that Senator Muskie was a hypocrite. But we never expected to have it so clearly revealed as in this letter sent to us from Florida."

Muskie's campaign manager, Tony Podesta, recalls that for the remainder of the campaign, the Manchester headquarters was blitzed with telephone calls from French-Canadian citizens expressing their outrage at Muskie. Several French-Canadian Democratic Party officials withdrew their endorsement of Muskie. The "Canuck letter" was clearly responsible for Muskie's significantly weaker showing in the French-Canadian neighborhoods in Manchester and surrounding towns.

The most damaging long-term consequence of the so-called Canuck letter was Muskie's emotional display in front of the Manchester *Union Leader*. The original idea was to do what John Kennedy had done in 1960—to win some points by standing up to William Loeb. State coordinator Tony Podesta, concerned about the impact of the Canuck letter in the French-Canadian wards, convinced Muskie that he should do it. He flew into Manchester from Florida late on Friday night, February 25. Podesta picked him up at the airport.

On the drive in to Manchester's Sheraton-Park Hotel, Muskie was silent, obviously exhausted from the rigors of two major primary campaigns, Florida and New Hampshire. Just before the car arrived at the hotel, Muskie turned to Podesta and said: "You know, I've been waiting for this for twenty-five years. Tomorrow morning, one of us is going to be destroyed."

The following morning, Saturday, Muskie climbed onto the back of a flatbed truck and, with snow falling very heavily, called Loeb a "gutless coward" and a "liar." After introducing some French-Canadians from New Hampshire and Maine, who testified to the fact that some of Ed Muskie's best friends were French-Canadians, Muskie resumed by denouncing Loeb's reprinting of a *Newsweek* article which had excerpted from a magazine interview a few salty quotations of his wife, Jane. Muskie, growing increasingly angry, spoke haltingly: "This man doesn't walk, he crawls . . . [pause] . . . He's talking about my wife . . . [longer pause] It's fortunate for him he's not on this platform beside me."

One of the most respected political journalists in the country, David Broder of the Washington *Post*, filed a story which was picked up in newspapers and news broadcasts all over the country. It began:

> MANCHESTER, N.H.—With tears streaming down his face and his voice choked with emotion, Senator Edmund S. Muskie (D., Maine) stood in the snow outside the Manchester Union Leader this morning and accused its publisher of making vicious attacks on him and his wife, Jane.

Some reporters covering the scene filed stories which did not highlight Muskie's emotional breakdown as much as Broder's story did. But one TV news network ran the entire episode on Saturday night's news, and repeated it several times the following week.

Muskie still insists that he hadn't cried. "It would have been an impossible thing for me to try to prove to the press because they had already accepted the fact that I had cried," he said some months after the November 1972 elections. "I was goddamned mad. I was so mad that I choked up, but I was not crying." Muskie paused for a moment, then added, "Not that I think it is wrong for a man to cry about the right things."

Muskie admitted, however, that it was a mistake to go in front of the *Union Leader* in the first place. "It was a piece of bad judgment."

In analyzing his receptivity to the idea, Muskie recalled, "I guess one of the reasons I made the decision was that the press kept harping on the fact that I didn't care about anything . . . this cool profile . . . that I was unemotional. This was something that did get me angry—those lies . . . the attack on my wife. I thought it was the place to show there was something I cared about, and, I thought, maybe it would do something about this image that I don't have the capacity to care about anything very deeply."

He paused. "It's pretty difficult to expect—in an effort which must be sustained over a two- or three-year period—you're never going to make a mistake. You have to hope, I guess, that it isn't going to be a mortal mistake. That's all you can do."

Muskie's show of emotion hurt him to some extent in New

Hampshire—again, exclusively within the circulation area of the *Union Leader*. But it dealt his candidacy a damaging blow around the rest of the country. And once again, press coverage of this incident must bear some responsibility for the seriousness of the damage.

It is difficult to dispute David Broder's or the TV network's judgment that Muskie's emotional breakdown was a politically significant event that deserved commensurate news treatment. What can be questioned is the failure of Broder or any other journalist to report Muskie's actions in the full context of Loeb's six-month effort to discredit him. Even in the two or three weeks prior to the primary, when the press corps spent a good deal of time in New Hampshire, there was almost total neglect of the story of what Loeb was doing to Muskie every day on the pages of the *Union Leader*. Instead, press coverage of the Muskie campaign was largely confined to projections of his "slippage."

The American public, which read Broder's story the morning after the incident, could only assume that Ed Muskie had gotten a little heat from some unimportant hick New Hampshire newspaper editor and had reacted totally out of proportion.

There is also the press's failure to expose fully the fraudulent source of the "Canuck letter." Some news organizations tried unsuccessfully to locate the "Paul Morrison" who had allegedly written the Canuck letter. Nor was anyone able to locate the "Harold W. Eldredge," also allegedly from Fort Lauderdale, who wrote a letter a few days after the Morrison letter allegedly corroborating Muskie's "Canuck" slur. Nevertheless, the question of the authenticity of these letters—much less the possibility that they were the handiwork of Richard Nixon's saboteurs—was totally neglected in the national press coverage of the incident both immediately after the incident and in the weeks following.

Florida: Who Lost Worse?

Prior to New Hampshire, Ed Muskie had two major advantages: the national polls showed him to be the front-runner, so he had the air of a winner about him; and the public impression of him remained that of the quiet-spoken, calm, stable man from Maine whose demeanor and style reminded people of Abraham Lincoln.

The newspaper headlines which resulted from the New Hampshire primary destroyed the first advantage, and the Manchester *Union Leader* "crying" incident destroyed the second.

During the week before the New Hampshire primary, Florida newspapers headlined that Muskie was "slipping" and his campaign "deteriorating." Over and over again, headlines bannered Muskie's "sobbing breakdown" and his "emotional display" in front of the *Union Leader*. The day after the New Hampshire primary—March 8—the Florida newspapers described Muskie's 47 per cent vote as a severe setback to his campaign.

The quickness of the fall was dizzying for Muskie and his organization. Just two weeks before, Muskie had appeared to be the party's inevitable nominee. Almost overnight, everything seemed to be falling apart. "You had this oppressive sensation of being in the middle of a slide, and you couldn't get out of it," recalls Keith Haller, a Muskie national staff political organizer who was in Florida during the primary. "Once the press gets negative, the people you canvass get negative, then the staff gets negative, then you feel it sagging all around you, and you begin to feel utterly helpless to do anything about it."

The New Hampshire publicity only added to Muskie's formidable problems in Florida. Underlying all of them was the cross-fire phenomenon. George Wallace, running hard on the busing issue, was clearly far out in front. Senator Henry Jackson of Washington picked up strength by attacking Muskie not only on his pro-busing stand but, in the central Florida area, where the aerospace industry is strong, for his announced opposition to the space shuttle.

Meanwhile, the liberal-New Politics forces, largely centered around the Miami area in the south and the Gainesville (University of Florida) area in the north, continued to attack Muskie from the left. At an appearance at the University of Florida in Gainesville, Muskie was cross-examined by a small group of McGovern supporters for close to an hour on his positions on amnesty, abortion, and marijuana.

Muskie's positions on the issues may have been sharply defined—to his detriment—as far as the conservatives in Florida were concerned. But, for the large number of middle-of-the-road, less issue-oriented voters in Florida, Muskie's inability during 1971 to develop a personal identity associated with some important issue proved to be very damaging.

The beneficiary of that fudgy Muskie image was Hubert Humphrey. Ironically, Humphrey's position on the issues was far less defined than Muskie's. He seemed to be both for and against busing, depending on which audience he was talking to. He was in favor of the space shuttle, but he was in favor of "reordering our priorities." However, where Humphrey stood on the issues was less important than the intense loyalty felt toward him among his constituents—blacks, Jews, senior citizens, and labor. All of these groups—especially the first three—were concentrated in significant numbers in many of Florida's cities, especially Miami, Tampa, St. Petersburg, and Jacksonville. As soon as Humphrey declared his candidacy, these middle-of-the-road voters were in his corner, blocked off from Muskie.

Meanwhile, John Lindsay was waging what his strategists thought was a classic New Politics campaign—combining hard, tough stands on the issues with a sophisticated blitz of television and radio spots which sold Lindsay's shirt-sleeved, blond-haired charisma. The Lindsay Florida managers kept leaking stories to the press that Lindsay would "surprise" everyone, that he was "moving fast and might even win it all." In mid-January *The New York Times* ran a news analysis which concluded that Lindsay was the man to watch in Florida.

The Lindsay Florida campaign was a classic case of the "advance man" mentality which afflicted all of us in the New Politics more than we cared to admit. Two key Lindsay aides, Jeff Greenfield and Jerry Bruno, had coauthored a book entitled *The Advance Man* and had written a last chapter entitled "Lindsay Will Beat Nixon in 1972." The theory was that Lindsay's charisma would carry him over the top. "The press sees crowds ... [and] the crowds sense that they're part of something exciting and important," Greenfield and Bruno wrote. "And that's what goes on the TV and in the press while the intellectuals debate the last sentence on the first page of the speech. But the average voter, he sees excitement and enthusiasm, and *that's* what he wants to be part of."

Lindsay's campaign, both in Florida and later on in Wisconsin, showed that most voters needed more than that to be won over. Lindsay had two major political problems in Florida which neither he nor his advisers understood until the end of his campaign. First, people thought his probusing stand was not only wrong but hypocritical. "It burns me up to see that man come down to Florida and tell me to bus my kids while he's put his own kids in private schools back in New York," one lady from the Miami area told me in late January, echoing a comment I must have heard fifteen or twenty times. One also heard repeated references to the effect that "Lindsay can't even run New York City. How's he going to run the country?" [4]

Meanwhile, George McGovern had told the press that he didn't consider Florida important, thereby wisely discounting from the beginning the effects of a poor showing. He spent one or two campaign days in the state in the week before the primary, but concentrated his energies in Illinois and Wisconsin. The McGovern organization in Florida, meanwhile, was frantically organizing the small bloc of liberal activists who, they hoped, would at least be large enough to come in ahead of John Lindsay.

The final results on March 14 had Muskie running a weak fourth, with 9 per cent—behind Wallace's 42 per cent, Humphrey's 18, and Senator Henry Jackson, who ran strongly in military and aerospace areas, coming in third with 13 per cent. Lindsay's weak fifth-place showing—at 7 per cent—was at least larger than McGovern's sixth-place showing of less than 6 per cent.

Understandably the press zeroed in on Muskie as the big loser, and totally ignored McGovern. And why not? Muskie's people had been projecting Florida as an easy win through 1971. After Wallace came in, they increased their efforts and talked about a strong second-place finish. When the returns were in, the press reported

4. Some Lindsay workers toward the end of the campaign, to combat the discouraging reactions they were getting in their telephone canvass, created the following suggested telephone conversation for breaking the monotony: "Hi ... My name is _____. I'm a volunteer for Mayor Lindsay and, believe it or not, I don't work in the New York City government. I'm calling to remind you that there is a very important election next Tuesday. As you know, George Wallace is running for president and is supporting a special vote which could turn into the most dangerous piece of legislation since the notorious Granahan Bill. Do you know who opposed the Granahan Bill? (If yes, express amazement and hang up. If no, proceed.)

"Well, gee, I'm sorry to hear that. Muskie was silent, Humphrey backed down, but John Lindsay stood up for obscene mail. Do you enjoy obscene mail? (If no, thank callee and hang up. If yes, thank callee. Record number. Call back between midnight and 2 A.M. and breathe deeply into phone. Whisper, "Lindsay, Lindsay, Lindsay," and hang up.)

Muskie's "lack of political appeal," and more and more journalists projected his imminent demise.

The day after the Florida primary, *The New York Times* published a poll taken by Daniel Yankelovich Associates as voters were leaving the election booths throughout the state. Each voter was asked to vote for president in a series of contests between Richard Nixon and each of the Democratic candidates. The results should have stunned the news media: *The only candidate who beat Richard Nixon in the poll was Ed Muskie!* The meaning was clear: In a multicandidate primary, where voters could "message" vote their personal preferences, Muskie ran poorly; but when it came time to vote for president, Muskie had far more support against Richard Nixon among the supporters of the other candidates than anyone else.

Muskie's speech denouncing the Wallace victory on the evening of the Florida primary added a third negative impression of him in the mind of the general public: not only was he overly emotional and a loser, he was also an overly emotional sore loser. Before Muskie went down to face the television cameras, one of his top aides, Mark Shields, urged him to be magnanimous and to focus everyone's attention on the Illinois primary the following week. As Muskie recalls it, as he walked up to the microphone he still didn't know what he was going to say. But, the more he spoke, the angrier he seemed to get. "What disturbs me," he said, "is that Wallace's victory reveals to a greater extent than I had imagined that some of the worst instincts of which human beings are capable have too strong an influence on our elections."

It was not only a petulant remark; it was an arrogant one—for it said that 42 per cent of the people who had voted in the Democratic primary had done so for racist reasons. And it totally misread the deeper issues of alienation and voter frustration with establishment politics which gave Wallace an appeal far beyond the racial issue.

In retrospect, Muskie regretted the speech. "It probably was too harsh an attack," he said glumly some time later. "It presented too one-sided a characterization of the Wallace campaign. His campaign in Florida had a broader ideological base than just the race question. He was talking about the tax issue, the responsiveness-of-government issue, as well as the busing issue."

Interestingly, Muskie's explanation of why he made the speech was strikingly similar to the one offered concerning the *Union Leader* incident: his sensitivity to assertions by New Politics liberals and the press that he lacked passion, that he was unwilling to "break a lance" on an issue.

Illinois and Wisconsin: From One-on-one to the Cross Fire

By March 15, the day after the Florida primary, Muskie headed for the March 21 Illinois primary, a totally debilitated candidate. His campaign seemed to be falling apart, with squabbling among his top political staff, money running out, and a stream of negative commentary about him in the national and local press. To add to the atmosphere of deterioration and disarray, Berl Bernhard, the campaign manager, announced the day after the Florida primary that the staff would be going off the payroll indefinitely.

A comparison between Muskie's showing in the March 21 Illinois primary and in the April 4 Wisconsin primary, and the contrasting treatment accorded by the news media to these two primaries, holds the key to an understanding of why Muskie lost the nomination in 1972.

In the Illinois primary, Muskie defeated George McGovern overwhelmingly, winning 62 delegates to McGovern's 15, despite the fact that McGovern had predicted he would win at least 30 delegates.[5] Two weeks later, in Wisconsin, Muskie came in a weak fourth, winning just nine per cent of the vote.

The same Muskie ran in both primaries. The difference was that in Illinois Muskie was running against only one candidate, while in Wisconsin, he was in the political cross fire of a multicandidate winner-take-all primary.

Of course, all of the mistakes which Muskie and his political organization had made in the course of the campaign contributed to his early downfall—his lack of identity or association with an issue or set of issues; the overemphasis on political endorsements and a

5. Muskie's 62 delegates did *not* include the large bloc of delegates elected in Chicago on a slate headed by Mayor Daley, most of which, it was assumed, favored Muskie.

top-heavy Washington national staff at the expense of grass-roots state organizations; his failure to be more selective about which states should be emphasized; and, especially, the decision to go in front of the *Union Leader* and the anti-Wallace speech after the Florida primary. But these mistakes hurt his candidacy in Illinois just as they did in Wisconsin.

First, a few words about the Illinois system for selecting national convention delegates. Here, delegates ran in each congressional district directly in an open primary. Their names—and the names of the candidates they supported—were listed directly on the ballot (or they were listed as "uncommitted," if that was the case). The top vote-getters were elected, up to the number of delegates to which that district was entitled. There was also a statewide nonbinding presidential "preference" primary in which voters could cast their ballots directly for a presidential candidate. There is simply no justification for this dual system of electing delegates directly plus a nonbinding preferential contest, for it permits one candidate to run in the congressional districts and not in the preference contest. This is actually what happened in Illinois. McGovern, not wanting to split up the liberal vote with Eugene McCarthy, who was committed to run on the preference line, had at least an implicit agreement with McCarthy: McGovern ran delegates in the congressional districts and McCarthy ran only in the preference contest, supporting McGovern's delegates.

I arrived in Illinois about four weeks before the primary to coordinate Muskie's campaign for the 21st Congressional District. At that point, Muskie had absolutely no local political organization. Few people knew where he stood on any issue, and after the *Union Leader* incident, the voters we canvassed asked, "How come he cried like that up there in New Hampshire?"

Meanwhile, McGovern had had a functioning grass-roots organization for at least six months and had completed a full canvass of Democratic voters in Champaign-Urbana, the largest city in the district, with twice as many Democratic votes as any other city.

In Illinois, however, Humphrey, Jackson, Wallace and Lindsay voters were supporting Muskie over McGovern. We had no trouble building a political organization for Muskie in a very short time. A week after we arrived in Champaign-Urbana, we had published full-page advertisements in the Champaign and Bloomington newspapers of a "Citizens Committee" for Muskie which included representatives of every major interest group in the district: students, party regulars, reformers, farmers, businessmen, lawyers, organized labor. A week later we sent out a personal letter from Muskie to all registered Democrats in the district asking them to vote for all six of his delegates.

In Champaign, the Democratic Party was split, with a "reform" organization in power that had defeated the party regulars the previous year. At meetings of both the reform organization and the regulars, I found considerable support for the Muskie campaign. Meanwhile, the McGovern organization was totally confined to the academic-student constituencies surrounding the University of Illinois and Illinois State University. The McGovern organizer in Champaign rarely even showed up at the meetings of the party regulars or of local farm groups.

In Decatur, the third largest city of the district, with a large population of blue-collar workers and no major college or university, the McGovern campaign had almost no organization at all. After a few days of negotiations, the Decatur Democratic organization agreed to support four Muskie delegates out of a total of six running in the district. This meant that the party precinct workers would distribute sample ballots with four Muskie delegates marked off as endorsed by the organization. The other two delegates supported by the Decatur regulars were two uncommitted labor leaders who leaned to Humphrey. We agreed not to open a separate campaign headquarters in Decatur and, while we insisted on the right to do a mailing pushing all six Muskie delegates, we agreed not to "oppose" the two uncommitted candidates in speeches and campaign literature.

The McGovern Illinois campaign manager had predicted that their only safe district was this particular congressional district—the 21st—on the assumption that the heavy student population at the University of Illinois and Illinois State would turn out heavily for McGovern and put his six delegates over. The McGovern campaign had registered more than 3500 students at the University of Illinois alone and, as it happened, turned out almost all of them to vote for McGovern in margins as high as ten to one.

Despite that vote margin, the Muskie campaign organization did make an extensive effort on the campuses to challenge McGovern's student support. We spoke in classes, at fraternities, and at sororities, wrote articles for the campus newspaper, debated leaders of the McGovern organization on all-night student radio programs. And for the first time since I had been in the Muskie campaign, we put out anti-McGovern literature, citing McGovern's past votes in favor of the war (the Gulf of Tonkin resolution and war appropriations) and asking whether McGovern had the right to say he was "right from the start."

The McGovern organizers were livid at the literature. When McGovern appeared at the University of Illinois a few days before the primary, he also denounced any criticisms of his record on the war and went on to assert that Muskie's foreign-policy views were indistinguishable from those of the then hawkish Senator Jackson.

McGovern denounced Muskie throughout Illinois for failing to meet the quotas on young people, women, and minorities which, he said, were required by the Reform Commission. McGovern never reminded people about the footnote which he himself had inserted in the Reform Commission report forswearing the imposition of quotas. Nor did he point out that in Illinois the candidate has no control over the makeup of the individual congressional district delegation.

The returns on election night in Illinois's 21st C.D. showed McGovern with a 3000 to 4000 vote margin in Champaign County —a direct result of the heavy student vote from the University of Illinois. But Muskie delegates carried the other five counties of the district—including McClean, which included Bloomington, the site of Illinois State University (Muskie ran even with McGovern among the students at Illinois State, who were largely from blue-collar and farming families). When I went to bed on election night, I assumed that McGovern had won all six delegates in the district. I couldn't conceive that Muskie would be able to make up the margin he had lost to McGovern in Champaign County. The next morning at six o'clock, I got a call from the local McGovern campaign director. "I still can't believe it, but Muskie's won two delegates and he's not far from winning four."

In fact, the two Muskie delegates who ran seventh and eighth —just out of the money—were fewer than 500 and 1000 votes, respectively, behind the last two elected McGovern delegates. And, as it turned out, if the Decatur Democratic organization hadn't spread its votes for six delegates among eight candidates (the six Muskie delegates plus the two uncommitteds), Muskie would probably have won all six delegates handily.

Throughout the rest of Illinois, Muskie's delegates swept McGovern slates by wide margins, with the same phenomenon repeating itself: McGovern won the hard core of New Politics activists and liberal intellectuals, and Muskie picked up all the rest of the Democratic vote. Although McGovern hadn't run in the separate preference primary—a direct vote for president that had no legally binding effect on the delegates—Eugene McCarthy had. There was almost a direct one-to-one correlation between people who voted for McGovern delegates and people who voted for McCarthy over Muskie, as can be seen by comparing McGovern's local delegate totals to McCarthy's popular vote totals in the same district. Muskie's margin over McCarthy—65 to 35—probably represented a relatively accurate breakdown of a Muskie-McGovern popular vote contest, had it taken place.

Despite this impressive win by Muskie in the Illinois primary, much of the news media gave it scant attention in the next day's newspapers. In fact, the Illinois primary was the great nonevent of the 1972 campaign. One explanation once again relates to the expectations associated with a front-runner. It was widely assumed that Muskie would have no trouble beating McGovern in Illinois. This sentiment was apparently shared by McGovern's staffers. Frank Mankiewicz began to suspect Illinois would be a disaster and, a few days before the primary, made excessively pessimistic predictions and dismissed the importance of the primary. Given these expectations, Muskie's victory could hardly have been treated as important news.

Another explanation for the downplaying of the Illinois results was that, as in Arizona, much of the press simply didn't understand the new realities and procedures within the Democratic Party. Most reporters viewed the Illinois primary as a contest between Muskie and McCarthy; and, of course, McCarthy couldn't be taken seriously. There were two serious fallacies in that analysis. First, as indicated above, there was just about a one-to-one correlation between McCarthy's preference votes and McGovern's delegate votes; second, there was in fact little distinction, as a test of political strength, between delegate contests, where the delegates are clearly labeled on the ballots as committed to their respective candidates, and the Wisconsin type of primary, where voters vote for the candidates directly. Moreover, few in the press seemed to appreciate fully that the McGovern organization had conducted an active, energetic grass-roots effort and that McGovern had spent at least as much—and probably more—campaign time in Illinois as Muskie. Yet, he could do no better than to win fifteen delegates.

A crucial misconception of the news media which hurt Muskie more than the other candidates was that, somehow, a multicandidate primary was a better test of strength than a one-on-one contest. Thus, a lot of reporters dismissed Illinois because the other candidates, like Humphrey and Wallace, weren't competing. In fact, a head-to-head contest gives a clear indication of the relative strength of each candidate across a broad cross section of the party and hence, a much better indication about relative political strength in the general election. In that sense, one could argue that the news media should have focused on Illinois as a crucial contest between McGovern and Muskie, with the leadership of the liberal wing of the party at stake.

Despite Muskie's impressive Illinois win, he didn't find himself with that kind of unified liberal backing in the state of Wisconsin. In fact, he found George McGovern more determined than ever to win his first primary. From the start of his campaign, McGovern had regarded the Wisconsin primary as the linchpin of his nomination campaign—and he went to great pains to depict it as such to the press. If the New Hampshire primary had to bring him back to life—which it did—then the Wisconsin primary had to save him from political death.

He knew that Wisconsin gave him some important political advantages—geographical proximity, a large student population, a progressive political history, and extensive anti-Vietnam War public sentiment. If McGovern couldn't win or come in a strong second in Wisconsin, he knew his campaign could not go on.

I arrived in Madison, Wisconsin, the state capital and home of the University of Wisconsin's largest campus, the day after the

March 21 Illinois primary. I was picked up at the airport by Muskie political coordinator Gregory Craig. Craig was glum. When I asked him about the status of the campaign in light of Muskie's great victory in Illinois, Craig responded: "Illinois? As far as Wisconsin is concerned, Illinois never happened."

That afternoon I went out canvassing in a blue-collar neighborhood on Madison's east side (the west side contained the University of Wisconsin's largest campus, with more than 30,000 students, and most of the academic and administrative personnel connected with the university). If there was a neighborhood where Muskie should have had strength, the east side was it. Nevertheless, over and over voters described Muskie as a "crybaby," a "sore loser," or, typically, "kind of wishy-washy"—the same kinds of comments I had heard in Illinois.

Of course the comments about McGovern seemed just as bad: "He's a radical," "He chases the longhairs all over the place," "He doesn't have the stuff to be president." But the McGovern organization had already door-to-door canvassed this neighborhood twice, and McGovern was picking up about 30 to 35 per cent of the votes, just as in Illinois. But, unlike in Illinois, the other 65 to 70 per cent were not going to Muskie.

Instead, Wallace was picking up a number of blue-collar workers, who liked his denunciation of politicians who tax too much and return too little. Jackson was picking up the hawkish conservatives by speaking out on his support of the Pentagon. But the critical difference between Illinois and Wisconsin, as far as Muskie's candidacy was concerned, was Hubert Humphrey. In two weeks of canvassing, handing out Muskie literature with Greg Craig at five degrees above zero at five in the morning in front of the Oscar Mayer plant in Madison, or leafleting the lines of people every night who were waiting to get in to see *The Godfather*, the comment I heard most was, "I would have been for Muskie, but with Humphrey in the race, I'm for Humphrey."

Polls showed that even John Lindsay was taking more votes from Muskie than McGovern was (largely, those liberals who didn't like McGovern). But Lindsay couldn't find many votes to steal. If Florida had seriously undermined the notion that "Muskie's a winner," it had utterly destroyed the notion that "Lindsay's charisma can win."

By the Wisconsin primary, McGovern had already locked up the left. And Lindsay, like Muskie, had no constituency of his own to turn to in a multicandidate primary.

The final results—Muskie running fourth with 10 per cent, Lindsay fifth with 7 per cent—eliminated Lindsay from the campaign.

Muskie met with his campaign advisers and financial backers and promised them that he would go to Massachusetts and Pennsylvania two weeks ahead. But most—including Muskie—realized by then that the same cross fire, organization, and image problems lay ahead, and that his campaign couldn't hold together very much longer.

Meanwhile, McGovern's win in Wisconsin projected him overnight into a strong position to win the nomination. He had won five out of seven congressional districts and, hence, 54 of Wisconsin's 67 delegates. Hubert Humphrey had captured the other two congressional districts—the Fifth District, encompassing the heavily pro-Humphrey black neighborhoods in Milwaukee, and the Seventh District in northwest Wisconsin, close to his native state of Minnesota. Once again George Wallace had taken advantage of a divided field and captured 22 per cent of the vote, good for a second-place finish one point ahead of Humphrey.

Conventional wisdom then and now has it otherwise, but the fact is that McGovern's showing in Wisconsin was strikingly similar—in terms of political base and even in the percentage of vote he received—to his showing in (for him) a disastrous Illinois primary. Again, the major difference was that in Illinois, where no one else but Muskie was running against him, 35 per cent of the popular vote [6] (or, more accurately, a 62-to-15 delegate margin) was a landslide defeat. But in Wisconsin, where there were five other candidates, 30 per cent was enough to win.

Wisconsin provided another example of the news media's misreading of the results of a primary. Having written off Muskie's win in Illinois as insignificant, the media now hyperbolically discovered the "McGovern phenomenon," as Evans and Novak described it—the theory that McGovern's vote included significant support among blue-collar voters (similar to the "blue-collar appeal"

6. I am correlating the McCarthy and the McGovern vote—again, based on Illinois polls and my own impressions.

stories which followed McGovern's showing in New Hampshire). An analysis in the Washington *Post* the day after the Wisconsin primary was typical. After discussing the heavy Republican crossover vote, a large portion of which had apparently gone to McGovern, the article continued: "Stunning as the crossover was, it was hardly more dramatic than the evidence of McGovern's ... inroads into the bedrock blue-collar, white working class that is the key to Democratic election victories and that was supposed to be the base of the Humphrey and Muskie strength." The article then cited the lakefront industrial cities of Kenosha and Racine, in which McGovern had run first and second, respectively. What the *Post* report failed to mention, however, was that McGovern had received only 27 per cent of the vote in Racine and 26 per cent of the vote in Kenosha.

The voting sheets of the Wisconsin primary show that McGovern's pattern of voter support was essentially the same as it was in Illinois—basically liberal-student-intellectual-upper-class professionals; in other words, the New Politics constituency—though his underdog image, his emphasis on the tax issue, and his highly effective grass-roots organization gave him his most impressive showing to date among blue-collar workers. Even so, his percentages in blue-collar neighborhoods throughout the state rarely went over 35 or 40 per cent, and were usually in the low and mid-twenties.

In the city of Madison, for example, where McGovern had the best organization, McGovern carried two student-university wards by 70 and 76 per cent, respectively. In these two wards alone he piled up a margin of more than 2000 votes over his nearest competitor, bearing out the advantage of winning a solid voting bloc in a primary. In contrast to these percentages, in wards 17 and 12, two predominantly working-class wards, McGovern received 35 and 37 per cent of the vote, respectively—respectable showings but hardly overwhelming.

McGovern supporters also liked to cite as evidence of McGovern's blue-collar appeal his ability to carry the Fourth Congressional District, which encompasses part of Milwaukee. McGovern "won" that district with only 27 per cent of the vote, and a substantial portion of that percentage was accumulated in the liberal-professional neighborhoods in the suburbs and villages that were part of that district. In fact, in most of the ethnic working-class wards of Milwaukee, McGovern was rarely able to get more than 20 to 25 per cent of the vote. In Ward 12, for example, the heavily Polish-Germanic-Slavic working-class neighborhood, McGovern received only 20 per cent of the vote, a weak fourth behind Muskie, who won the ward, Humphrey, and Wallace.

The importance of these results is that there was substantial evidence that McGovern's vote totals were a *ceiling* of his popularity in a multicandidate situation. That is, the polling evidence by Yankelovich and others, as well as the experiences of many Muskie and McGovern canvassers, showed that a large bulk of the non-McGovern votes in these blue-collar neighborhoods—for Humphrey, Wallace, Muskie, Lindsay, and Jackson—would not have gone to McGovern as second choices (or, in many instances, as third or fourth choices).

As early as the Wisconsin primary, there was significant evidence that McGovern's pattern of support in blue-collar neighborhoods, far from signaling dramatic political breakthroughs, instead suggested a dangerous weakness among traditional working-class Democrats —one which would come back to haunt McGovern after he won the Democratic nomination.

The news media exaggerated not only McGovern's blue-collar appeal in Wisconsin but also the significance of his statewide totals. Having written off McGovern for more than a year as a candidate who couldn't get more than 5 per cent in the national polls, the press understandably seized upon McGovern's 30 per cent win in Wisconsin as an impressive showing. In fact, many members of the press corps—and many of the post-Wisconsin headlines—treated McGovern as if he were the new front-runner.

McGovern's 30 per cent vote total in Wisconsin may have been a surprise, but it was not by any means very impressive. In fact, for anyone who understood Wisconsin politics, that total should not have come as very much of a surprise. The Wisconsin Democratic Party had a proud tradition of progressive insurgencies throughout the twentieth century, from the days of Robert LaFollette's Progressive Party to the 1968 primary in which Eugene McCarthy overwhelmingly defeated Lyndon Johnson.

Moreover, from the outset of his candidacy, McGovern had set his sights on Wisconsin as the make-or-break place for his candidacy. He had spent more campaign days in Wisconsin and had invested more organizational energy there than all the other candidates put together. McGovern also knew that Wisconsin's heavy concentration of college students, particularly on the various University of Wisconsin campuses, would offer him special advantages for campaign manpower and, with the passage of the eighteen-year-old vote, a reservoir of votes unavailable to Eugene McCarthy in 1968.

Given these advantages, if anyone had told me when McGovern first announced in 1971 that he would not be able to manage more than 30 per cent of the Wisconsin vote in a Democratic primary, I would have been skeptical. As it was, even the 30 per cent figure exaggerated McGovern's strength among rank-and-file Wisconsin Democrats. According to the Daniel Yankelovich poll, McGovern's percentage of Democratic votes was actually about 21 per cent; the other 9 per cent were Republican crossovers.[7] In other words, if the Wisconsin Democratic primary had been confined to Democrats, McGovern would have run in a dead heat with Hubert Humphrey.

Yankelovich also found that about 10 per cent of McGovern's total vote—or 3 per cent of his statewide vote—was from the youth vote (the University of Wisconsin, Madison campus, gave McGovern about an 8000-vote *margin* over the next nearest candidate). If McGovern had not had the benefit of the eighteen-year-old-vote amendment, and if there had been no Republican crossovers, he would have received a mere 18 per cent of the Democratic vote in one of the most liberal state Democratic parties in the nation.

While it is now obvious that McGovern's win in Wisconsin gave him a momentum disproportionate to his actual strength in the Democratic Party, this is not to denigrate the extraordinary political campaign which McGovern built for himself in Wisconsin. McGovern's skill as a politician was his ability to measure his own strengths and weaknesses, and those of his opponents, and then take advantage of that knowledge. He knew that he would have no chance in Wisconsin unless he got solid backing from the college-

7. George Wallace's 22 per cent totals in Wisconsin would also have been considerably lower without Republican crossovers. Estimates were that almost half of Wallace's votes were Republican crossovers.

student vote, and so he spent most of 1971 in low profile, touring Wisconsin's college campuses, talking about the "cultural" issues of marijuana, abortion, and amnesty, as well as the war in Vietnam, encouraging his student audiences to perceive him as *their* candidate.

Just as he had done in New Hampshire, McGovern turned to a young, unknown political organizer—this time, a Nebraskan named Gene Pokorny—to organize his effort in Wisconsin. By the end of 1971, Pokorny had mobilized the extensive network of antiwar liberals and student activists, of necessity mostly from the purist side of the New Politics movement, who had been active in the Dump Johnson movement and the 1968 McCarthy campaign. Once McGovern's campaign got a morale boost in the national press as a result of the New Hampshire primary, Pokorny had the dose of candidate viability he needed to turn out the winning 30 per cent vote.

The press can hardly be blamed for focusing so much attention on the Wisconsin primary and on McGovern's win. Wisconsin had always been an important primary (the most recent examples were John Kennedy's win over Humphrey in 1960 and McCarthy's win over Johnson in 1968). Furthermore, the fact that a candidate running at 5 per cent in the national polls, who just six weeks before no one had taken seriously, could come out of nowhere and whip Ed Muskie and Hubert Humphrey on the wave of what seemed to be a fresh, entirely new kind of political movement not only made good copy, but might well have signaled the beginning of a truly historic political watershed in the country's history. Without the benefit of hindsight, that press assessment did not seem totally apocryphal to me and most other people at the time.

The understandable problem for the news media was that they were using old "keys" to political analysis and that circumstances did not permit the development of a set of new definitions of political strength under the new delegate-selection procedures in 1972. In 1960 there was no doubt that the Wisconsin Democratic primary was significant because the primary was confined to two candidates, and if John Kennedy beat Hubert Humphrey head-to-head in Humphrey's own back yard, that showed something important about Kennedy's political appeal. In 1968, when McCarthy beat Johnson head-to-head, there was no doubt that the results indicated that the incumbent President had serious political problems in his own party—in Wisconsin and elsewhere.

Once again, the problem was that the news media had made no distinction between assessment of political strength resulting from a head-to-head contest and that of a multicandidate contest. In other words, the press defined the "winner" of a multicandidate primary in precisely the same way as the winner of a head-to-head contest: The candidate who came in first, regardless of the percentage of his vote or the quality and pattern of his support.

In a multicandidate primary, the major "key" to assess overall political strength of a candidate is an analysis of his ability to garner support from the other candidates' supporters. With such an analysis Muskie's poor fourth-place showing in Wisconsin would not have hurt his candidacy as much as it did. As in Florida, postelection surveys found that Muskie had more second-choice support than any other candidate. Another way of stating this is that Muskie still seemed to be the only candidate in the Wisconsin primary who would win head-to-head against any other candidate.

Another aspect of a new analysis of the results of multicandidate primaries would be to put a candidate's vote percentage in a larger context than merely the order in which he finished in the primary. It has already been pointed out that, while McGovern came in first in Kenosha, Wisconsin, in fact, the pattern of his vote indicated future weakness among traditional working-class Democrats. George Wallace's strength was exaggerated by the press in much the same way. Like McGovern's percentages, Wallace's votes were essentially ceilings of support within the Democratic Party. Even in Florida, the scene of Wallace's most important triumph, it is quite possible that Humphrey, Jackson, or Muskie, running head-to-head against Wallace, might have given him a close contest.

Thus, the 1972 Democratic contest raises provocative questions about the role of the press in influencing the outcome of the nominating process. Presidential campaigns have become so large and complex, the demands for money and people are so great, that more than ever they have come to be dependent on the public's perception of their momentum and morale. And that perception is, of course, almost totally dependent on the interpretations of the news media, especially the political columnists and the network news shows.

The self-fulfilling prophecy is especially applicable here. Once the press turns sour on a candidate, the switch in mood and loss of momentum can occur very quickly. The deterioration of the candidate himself can follow just as quickly, witness George Romney in 1968. The question arises, how can a front-runner survive the kind of scrutiny he can expect to receive by the national press? Even if he gets nominated, what will be the costs of such scrutiny when he has to run in the national election?

The 1972 nominating race also highlights the difficulties faced by the press in accurately interpreting the results of a complex and confusing nominating system. Can the news media be expected to engage in sophisticated political research and analysis to correct the deficiencies of that system and convey an accurate picture of the relative political strengths of the candidates? In other words, was the problem in 1972 the press coverage of the Democrats' nominating system, or the system itself?

Muskie: The Final Fall

As Ed Muskie sat in a hotel suite on Tuesday night, April 25, there was a strange kind of serenity about him. Milton Shapp, the governor of Pennsylvania, who had supported McCarthy in 1968 and had won the nomination and election for governor as an insurgent Democrat in 1970, sat on one side of him. On the other side was Peter Camiel, the boss of the Philadelphia Democratic Party machine who had been an arch-foe of Shapp during the 1970 campaign. Ed Muskie had brought them together in that hotel room that night.

Muskie sat in an easy chair puffing on a cigar, listening to the bad news come in over the television. He had been beaten by Humphrey in both the preference poll and the delegate-election contests in Pennsylvania. McGovern had won by a substantial margin in Massachusetts (where he had run essentially unopposed) and had narrowly beaten Muskie in the Pennsylvania preference voting, running third with 20 per cent of the vote, with Wallace once again surprising everyone by placing second in the preference balloting. Muskie realized that he wouldn't be helped by the fact that he had come in a strong second in Massachusetts even though his campaign had come to a complete standstill almost three weeks before the primary.

Muskie understood by now that his position as a front-runner had created a set of now-unfulfilled expectations, and that it didn't matter that one set of expectations had been applied to him and another to McGovern. What mattered was that his candidacy, more than most, depended on momentum for sustenance—political and financial—and that he had lost his momentum.

At one point that night, one of Governor Shapp's aides kidded Philadelphia boss Pete Camiel about reports that Muskie's name had been removed from the ballots circulated by Camiel's precinct captains on election day. Camiel's face reddened, but Muskie only laughed, patting him on the knee. "Don't worry, Pete, at this point in my life I'm not bothered by the thought that I help you more by removing my name from the ballot than by putting it on."

There was an air of unreality in the hotel room. I thought, Less than eight weeks before, very few people could have imagined anyone other than Ed Muskie winning the Democratic nomination. His fall had happened so fast, it was still hard to believe. Senator Philip Hart of Michigan, a close personal friend of Muskie's who had supported him from the very beginning and was there, appropriately, at the end, pulled me aside and asked, "How did it happen? You've been out in the field from the very beginning. Where did he lose it? How could he have lost it?"

We talked about the fact that Muskie had never defined himself as a candidate, never given people a sense of who he was or what hard, pressing concern he could speak to better than anyone else. I told Senator Hart of my experience running Muskie's campaign in a Philadelphia suburb, the canvassing in which people would constantly say, "Aside from his crying in New Hampshire, I don't know much about him." But Hart shook his head. "Still, that identity thing can't be the whole explanation. John Kennedy didn't have much of a hard identity in 1960 and he won."

Then we talked about the failure to allocate adequate resources to field organization. He had a high-priced Washington payroll but he let George McGovern and John Lindsay recruit the lower-priced young people who understood grass-roots organizing and the importance of the youth-activist constituency under the new rules. "But Humphrey had no grass-roots organization in Pennsylvania either, and he didn't have the activists, but he still won the primary," Hart observed.

Then we talked about some of Muskie's personal weaknesses as a candidate, his soft-spoken, cautious style, which, in comparison to George McGovern, Hubert Humphrey, and George Wallace, sometimes came across as indecisiveness and lack of passion. "But his balance, his restraint, his moderation—these qualities were the source of his wide appeal after the 1968 vice-presidential campaign and, especially, the 1970 election-eve speech," Hart said.

We then talked about Muskie's mistake of entering the first eight primaries and spreading himself too thin, and about a different primary strategy which might have changed the outcome. The most advantageous Muskie scenario for the primaries we could come up with, in hindsight, was to have had Muskie run hard in New Hampshire, omit Florida, go on to Illinois, omit Wisconsin, and then on to Pennsylvania. Such a strategy might have put Muskie in a better position; but, still, we realized, it wouldn't have affected the outcome. Sooner or later, Muskie would have been faced with the same fatal cross fire between Humphrey and McGovern.

At the end of all this analysis, one is struck by a certain inevitability in Muskie's demise in 1972. Of course, there were serious mistakes made by Muskie and his managers. But the central reason for Muskie's demise—beyond any mistakes—was the presence in the race, at the same time, of George McGovern and Hubert Humphrey. If either one had dropped out early, or had not run, it is probable that Muskie, despite all his mistakes, would have been the nominee.

The question arises, could Muskie have done anything to prevent McGovern and Humphrey from being viable candidates? Muskie made extensive efforts to cut into both McGovern's New Politics support and Humphrey's support among the party regulars, and he did make considerable inroads in both directions. But it didn't work. Both McGovern and Humphrey believed their natural base of support within the party would hold together in the primaries, and they were right.

The postmortem about the Muskie campaign I have heard most often is that Muskie's best strategy would have been to decide early on which way he wanted to go in the Democratic Party, and then stick to it. That is, he might have decided in early 1971 to move as far left as necessary to wipe out George McGovern completely—to wait, if need be, until after the convention to try to reconcile the party regulars, labor leaders, and Southerners in the party. Or he might have turned his attention to the party establishment, moved to the center or even right of center, pleased George Meany and other Hubert Humphrey friends, and thus made it practically impossible for Humphrey to make a run of it. He might have permitted a coalescence of the New Politics constituency around George McGovern's or John Lindsay's candidacies, believing that, after the nomination, he could do a better job of reconciling this group than Humphrey had been able to do in 1968.

The best strategy for Muskie, it seems, would have made it most difficult for him to reunify the Democratic Party after the convention and run a strong race against Nixon in the general election.

Again and again Muskie resisted this strategy. He insisted that a nomination won at the expense of alienating the New Politics young people and reformers, on the one hand, or traditional working-class people and moderate Democrats on the other, would not be worth much. But beyond such pragmatic considerations, Muskie rebelled at the thought of having to chase a political constituency in order to get nominated, especially when to do so would place him in a divisive role within the Democratic Party. Such a role was contrary to his own sense of what the country needed, of what a president needed to govern; and it was contrary to his own sense of himself.

A few months after the November 1972 elections, Muskie tried to explain the roots of his coalitionist philosophy.

"I knew that the primary game is something different," he recalled. "Maybe, in retrospect, I should have been realistic enough, and cold-blooded enough, to recognize it and distinguish what I had to do to get nominated and what I had to do to ensure I could beat Nixon and govern the country afterward.

"But I felt that the task of healing that would face the candidate after the convention was a very important objective to bear in mind through the primaries, that I had the best chance of doing that."

We talked a bit about what he would have had to do to "win the left" and "win the right" and, in the middle of a question on this issue, Muskie interrupted me with a flash of impatience. "Look, what the hell, it's academic. I didn't have it *in me* to contrive such a strategy."

Maybe, Muskie ruminated introspectively, the critical factor in his demise was not that he remained faithful to his coalitionist philosophy but that he gave in to pressures from both sides to say and do things which were not really in character.

"You remember two or three years ago," he said, "I told all of you that I would not let myself be twisted out of shape. And yet, to a certain degree, I guess I was twisted out of shape, reacting to the perceptions of the press that I was trying to correct.

"In other words, maybe I should have been just myself."

Given the factionalism in the Democratic Party, the delegate-selection system, the constant scrutiny and pressures from the news media, the political and financial magnitude of any race for the presidency—given the realities of running for president, I asked, was it possible to just be yourself, from the beginning of the campaign through the end?

"I don't know," he said after a brief silence. "I really don't know."

One immediate result of Muskie's string of setbacks in Florida, Wisconsin, and Pennsylvania was the rapid deterioration of support for his candidacy among New Politics coalitionists. They became increasingly doubtful that Muskie could build the kind of broad, progressive coalition which they believed was so urgently needed in 1972. "I still believe he's the best man of all of them," said former Joe Duffey campaign manager Anne Wexler at the time. "But it's obvious that he just can't pull it together at this point."

Not surprisingly, most of the leading New Politics coalitionists from the Muskie campaign quickly gravitated to George McGovern. Shortly after the Pennsylvania primary, when Muskie had withdrawn from "active" candidacy, most of Muskie's top political staff signed up with the McGovern campaign, including Anne Wexler, Tony Podesta (Muskie's New Hampshire campaign manager), Alan Baron (Florida), Jim Johnson (Iowa, Illinois), and some time later, Joe Duffey. Art Kaminsky, Lindsay's Arizona manager, also signed up with McGovern's California campaign.

They did so with some reluctance, however, for most strongly suspected that McGovern's purist constituents, and the positions he had had to take in order to please them, would make coalition building very difficult. On the other hand, even the most politically sophisticated New Politics coalitionists had begun to think that perhaps this McGovern "phenomenon" was the real thing.

In the aftermath of the Wisconsin, Pennsylvania, and Massachusetts primaries, McGovern reached the zenith of his political appeal. The May 1972 Gallup poll had him within seven points of President Nixon—48 to 41. He had the best of both worlds. To the New Politics constituency, he was a candidate with sharply defined positions on a wide variety of issues, including the "cultural" issues, such as amnesty, abortion, and marijuana. To the general public, most of his past positions were totally unknown, but his image as a political Horatio Alger successfully challenging the establishment gave him some general voter appeal. This was the combination which carried McGovern within a hair's breadth of defeating Hubert Humphrey in the April 2 Ohio primary.

Once Senator Muskie had dropped out of contention after the April 25 Pennsylvania primary, McGovern also enjoyed the political advantages of running against Hubert Humphrey as his chief opposition. Not only did the threat of Humphrey's candidacy produce an unprecedented unity in the New Politics ranks, but, while Humphrey had a loyal constituency within the Democratic Party, he also had a negative image among wide segments of the general public, stemming primarily from the sense that he was "old hat," a loser who had been around for too long and had run for office too many times. McGovern was able to gain a number of votes in Ohio from those who had a vaguely positive impression of himself and a generally negative impression of Senator Humphrey.

Notwithstanding the euphoria inside the McGovern campaign at this time, Rick Stearns had no illusions about the realities of McGovern's popular appeal, or the strategy McGovern had to pursue in order to win delegates in the nonprimary states. Stearns understood that, despite press reports in the aftermath of the Wisconsin primary about the "McGovern phenomenon," McGovern's appeal was still limited. On a perfectly cross-sectional, one-man, one-vote procedure for selecting delegates, McGovern could not, at least at this point, win a majority of the delegates and, perhaps, not even a significant plurality.

However, Stearns also understood that the new rules offered a New Politics candidate two advantages in the nonprimary states. First, the reforms would require state party regulars to change, to learn new habits and techniques. The candidate who had political leadership and a political constituency, who could take the necessary time to understand the new procedures and plan how to use them, had the advantage.

"We managed our nominating campaign from a flow chart that covered an entire wall of my Washington office," Stearns wrote in an unpublished account of his organizing efforts in this period. "Based on a construction diagram that I had once seen for a Polaris submarine, the chart showed in schematic fashion what was happening in any given state on any given day that had relevance to the nomination of a presidential candidate."

The second advantage was the bias of the new reforms in favor of political activists. The requirement of "public participation" in the delegate-selection process, based upon the reformist effort to democratize party procedures, offered the greatest opportunity for distorting the one-man, one-vote principle. Since party primaries normally attract a low voter turnout, a well-organized activist constituency could be turned out to attend "public" party caucuses in the nonprimary states and thus be able to wield a political impact disproportionate to their actual numbers in the party as a whole.

Stearns' use of both of these advantages is highlighted by his organizing efforts in Kansas in April 1972. The new Kansas rules, adopted only three months before, provided for public party caucuses at the precinct level in each county. Delegates elected at these caucuses would then meet at the congressional-district level and choose delegates to the national convention. A state convention of all delegates would subsequently be held to select a small number of at-large delegates.

Stearns' basic strategy for McGovern's Kansas campaign (or any other nonprimary state effort) was to avoid doing anything which would encourage a large voter turnout. He says he deliberately held off any organizing drive in Kansas until late March, just a few weeks prior to the party caucuses, because he didn't want to stir up the party regulars to prepare adequately for the party caucuses.

Stearns decided to use techniques that maintained low organizational profile. After studying the 1970 precinct primaries in
Wichita, for example, he determined that a turnout of seventy-five
McGovern supporters in each precinct caucus would easily
dominate the district. To turn out this number, however, he decided
to use the telephone rather than a foot canvass because, as he wrote,
"our strategy banked on a low turnout of interested voters. It was to
our advantage to be as quiet and unobtrusive as we could. Canvassers
attract attention, telephone surveys do not. A canvasser has to
explain why he is there. With a candidate at 5 per cent in the polls,
the net effect of a canvass is to turn out three of his opponents to
every supporter identified by a canvass. On the telephone, however,
the voter's preference can be ascertained, and then a decision made
whether to complete the message."

Not surprisingly, Stearns' first list of telephone calls in the district
was to the readily identified New Politics constituency in town. "We
... collected every sympathetic list we could—student directories,
the Women's Caucus, the ACLU, Unitarians, the New Democratic
Coalition, Methodist Church voters, and so on." The positive response from this list was, as expected, quite high—Stearns estimates
about 40 or 50 per cent.

Once that list was completed, Stearns' telephoners turned to the
Democratic precinct lists, calling all the names randomly. Here they
found their positive response to be about 10 per cent—undoubtedly
an accurate measurement of McGovern's political support among a
cross section of Democrats in Wichita, and probably not far from his
total statewide support. Yet, as Stearns relates, this lower positive
response percentage meant only that more people had to be called.
With enough hard work and persistence, the McGovern telephoners
were able to rally enough people to carry 80 per cent of the caucuses
with about 10 per cent or so of rank-and-file support.

Statewide, McGovern wound up with 18 of Kansas' 35 delegates.
In other words, Stearns was able to win a percentage of delegates in
Kansas which represented four or five times the percentage of
McGovern's actual political support among a cross section of Kansas
Democrats. Sterns later estimated the total cost of the campaign for
McGovern as $1100.

Stearns applied the same strategy and techniques in the other nonprimary states. In Georgia, he claims he spent $2000, mostly, he writes, "to pay for chartered buses to move students and blacks to caucus sites in two key congressional districts." The result: seven delegates. In Vermont, Stearns claims he spent only $200 for a statewide telephone toll line and, in two weeks' time, turned out enough liberals and student activists to win nine delegates, despite the fact that, on a strictly one-man, one-vote basis, Vermont Democrats would overwhelmingly have favored their New England neighbor, Ed Muskie, over McGovern.

Ironically, such results were inconsistent with a basic philosophic premise underlying the McGovern Commission reforms—that national convention state delegations must be representative of the preferences of rank-and-file Democrats. It might be argued that political sentiment in a democracy can only be measured among those who participate. It is obvious, however, that some McGovern New Politics activists were determined to do whatever was necessary to nominate George McGovern. Thus, even where a state primary had resulted in a democratically arrived at preference among Democrats who chose to participate, they saw no philosophic problem with raiding the postprimary caucuses of other candidates who had won the primary and winning election as national convention delegates.[8]

This occurred in Indiana, which Humphrey had won, and North Carolina and Tennessee, which Wallace had won. Most of these McGovern supporters who got elected on Wallace or Humphrey delegations cast their votes at the national convention according to the mandate of the preference vote. But on the procedural questions—which, in the case of the California challenge and several other credentials fights, were more crucial to McGovern's nomination than the actual nomination roll call—these delegates supported the position favorable to Senator McGovern. Moreover, several McGovern delegates from Tennessee refused to cast their ballots for Wallace and, instead, voted for Senator McGovern at the convention. No one in the McGovern organization did very much to dissuade these delegates from violating the democratically expressed

8. In some primary states, the actual selection of national convention delegates took place *after* the preference poll. Once the results were in, each candidate who had won delegates would have to call a public meeting, which anyone could attend, and select delegates to attend the national convention.

preferences of the overwhelming majority of Democratic voters in Tennessee. And even if McGovern and his top staff had expressed their disapproval, it is not likely that anyone would have listened.

The full story of McGovern's defeat of Hubert Humphrey in the post-Pennsylvania primaries and at the Democratic National Convention is outside the scope of this narrative. It should be pointed out, however, that none of McGovern's primary victories in May (in Nebraska, Rhode Island, and Oregon) and in June (in California, New Jersey, and New York) were inconsistent with the political reality that his appeal was narrowly based and still largely confined to the New Politics constituency of upper-middle-class reformers and youth activists.

His victories in Rhode Island, Oregon, New Jersey, and New York were due to the total lack of any opposition and an incredibly small voter turnout—less than 10 per cent of eligible registered Democrats in Rhode Island and New York, and less than 15 per cent in New Jersey and Oregon. In Nebraska, in which McGovern beat Humphrey narrowly, as in Ohio the week before, McGovern once again had the advantage because of sharp definition on the issues among his New Politics supporters (who turned out heavily in and around Lincoln, home of the University of Nebraska) and lack of issues definition among ordinary Nebraskan voters, many of whom were still attracted to his underdog image and, especially, to his image as a "prairie Populist" in the William Jennings Bryan tradition.

McGovern's primary campaign in California represented a high point of the New Politics political movement, the confluence of all the forces and people and techniques the New Politics had developed since 1967. New Politics activists converged on California from all over the country to help organize one of the most effective grass-roots political organizations in the history of American presidential campaigns. The McGovern campaign claimed that an incredible four million registered Democrats were personally canvassed.

The final returns more than vindicated McGovern and other New Politics leaders' emphasis on the importance of the youth vote. McGovern managed to win 425,000 out of an estimated 580,000 youth votes—providing him with his margin of victory over

Humphrey (just as the youth vote had done for him in the Wisconsin primary).

Nevertheless, it was in the latter days of the California primary that McGovern and his top staff began to understand the price they would have to pay for his earlier campaign to win the New Politics constituency. A week before the primary, McGovern had led Humphrey by twenty points in the respected California Field poll. But Humphrey's persistent attacks on McGovern's $1000-per-person welfare program and his $31 billion defense-cut proposal began to get through to the general public, especially during the televised debates. The substance of these positions was bad enough from a political standpoint; what made matters immeasurably worse was that McGovern had clearly not thought them through.

Both of these proposals, it will be recalled, had been very useful in McGovern's campaign to discredit Muskie among the New Politics constituency. Then, the press had chosen to ignore the details of what McGovern was saying and, instead, to focus on the fact that Muskie was not saying anything with comparable specificity. Now, with McGovern as the seeming front-runner, for the first time he had to justify his positions to a larger audience than New Politics purists. Nothing in the previous fifteen months of campaigning had prepared him or his staff for that kind of effort.

On the so-called cultural issues, McGovern was also unprepared for close scrutiny of his past statements before all-student audiences. When Humphrey criticized McGovern during the debates for past statements on the issues of amnesty, abortion, and marijuana, McGovern insisted that "there's not a dime's worth of difference between us on those issues." In fact, this was essentially true—McGovern favored amnesty only after the war was over, and only for draft resisters, not deserters; he didn't favor abortion on demand; and he favored "decriminalizing" marijuana possession, which, he explained, was not synonymous with legalization.

But the denial didn't ring true, especially because most people remembered McGovern as the candidate who had energetically courted the New Politics constituency, which was most identified with those very issues. Also, McGovern had obviously done little or nothing to discourage his student supporters from continually asserting that McGovern favored amnesty for all, abortions on demand, and legalized pot.

McGovern's narrow margin of victory over Humphrey in California, 45 to 40 per cent, was a severe disappointment to him and his campaign organization. He had dropped fifteen points in less than a week. Even more ominously, *The New York Times* pollster, Daniel Yankelovich, had found that 40 per cent of the Humphrey vote in the California primary would defect to Nixon in November. McGovern realized that he had better begin putting some daylight between himself and his New Politics constituency if he was to have any chance of winning the presidency.

The challenge to McGovern's California delegation, organized by an anti-McGovern coalition composed largely of Humphrey and Jackson supporters, halted McGovern's efforts to build a broader political coalition. He was forced to consolidate his forces and to muscle his way through to the very end, rather than to spend the month of June seeking to reconcile the party regulars and organized labor. Nevertheless, McGovern—again reflecting his new concern about the general election campaign—still felt obliged to renege on prior commitments to his New Politics backers at the convention. He succeeded in defusing most of the major controversial issues on the Platform Committee; and on several credentials challenges —especially the Women's Political Caucus challenge to the South Carolina delegation—he withdrew the support he had earlier promised to his New Politics activist supporters.

The New Politics movement seemed to have come full circle: from the small group of visionary insurgents in the Dump Johnson movement; to the small group of reformers who had fundamentally altered the Democratic Party presidential nominating process; to the formidable political constituency George McGovern and Ed Muskie had devoted so much time and energy to win. Now, at the moment of its greatest triumph—the takeover of the Democratic Party and the nomination of its own candidate for president—the New Politics movement found that candidate doing his best to disassociate himself from it as much and as quickly as possible.

Within the next four months, it became clear to McGovern and his campaign organization that mastering the intricacies of the new party rules was not the same as winning a majority of the electoral vote in the general election . . . that winning the New Politics constituency of student activists and liberal reformers was not the same as winning America.

PART IV

The Emerging Democratic Majority

Both George McGovern and Richard Nixon seemed to agree that their contest for the presidency in 1972 represented a choice, not an echo. But they couldn't seem to agree on precisely what the choices were.

McGovern saw his candidacy as an opportunity for the country to vote up or down on a clear-cut ideological choice: a liberal-populist Democrat versus a conservative-big business-oriented Republican. It was Roosevelt and Hoover all over again. Nixon, articulated the alternatives differently. He portrayed himself as a pragmatist who believed in "change that works," while George McGovern was depicted as a man who stood for disorderly, ill-thought-out schemes and who represented a narrow cultural clique, out of step with the mainstream of American politics.

Most postelection analyses, on the left as well as the right, concluded that Mr. Nixon's victory was a mandate for his Republican conservatism and a defeat for McGovern's Democratic liberalism. Kevin Phillips, author of *The Emerging Republican Majority*, saw the 1972 presidential returns as a complete vindication of his prediction, after the 1968 elections, of a Republican-Wallaceite conservative majority coalition. Gary Hart, in his chronicle of the McGovern campaign, *Right from the Start*, argued that once Wallace had been shot and thus removed as a third-party candidate, McGovern was doomed to lose. The thrust of both men's

171

analyses is that American politics has become increasingly polarized and that the political center and coalition politics are no longer the central reality of the American political system.

There is an important fallacy throughout such an analysis: the assumption that most voters supported Nixon over McGovern on the basis of a perceived conservative *v.* liberal choice. In fact, the evidence strongly suggests that most voters adopted not Mr. McGovern's definitions of the alternatives but Mr. Nixon's. Pollster Lou Harris persuasively argues that most voters came to perceive Nixon not as an antichange conservative but as someone who stood for "change that works"; and, more importantly, they came to perceive George McGovern not as a candidate who supported traditional liberal social and economic programs but as an erratic, unreliable and somewhat incompetent man who couldn't be trusted with the presidency.

If this latter, non-ideological interpretation is correct, then two important and related political trends which seem to be contradicted by the Nixon victory become explicable—trends which were established well before the Watergate and related scandals hit the front pages in 1973. First is the increasingly positive response of American voters to programs aimed at alleviating racial and economic injustice and solving basic social problems in the country today—in short, the traditional liberal-populist philosophy. Second is the emergence of a new Democratic majority coalition, combining the New Politics constituency, significant portions of which include formerly Republican college-educated, upper-middle-class neighborhoods, with the traditional minorities and blue-collar voters of the old FDR coalition, including many Wallace voters. That new Democratic coalition could be seen in operation in numerous House, Senate, and gubernatorial contests from 1968 to 1973 in all regions of the country.

The Nixon landslide must be viewed far more as a repudiation of McGovern personally—of the image of incompetence and instability which he acquired in the course of his campaign—than as a repudiation of McGovern's liberal program or a mandate in favor of conservative Republicanism.

ten

THE DECENCY VOTE

"I don't believe the American people are moving to the right. Nor do I believe that the Democratic Party has moved too far to the left.... I have not given up on the basic decency of the American people. I believe you can still rally a majority in this country around an ideal."

—Jerry Wurf, president, American
Federation of State, County and
Municipal Employees, March 1973

EVER SINCE FRANKLIN ROOSEVELT's landslide victory over Herbert Hoover in 1932, conservative Republicans have become accustomed to minority political status in the country. Even during the Eisenhower years, they could feel little ideological gratification. Their own candidate had been Senator Robert Taft, and Eisenhower's grandfatherly nonideology hardly altered their own sense of being a political minority. The 1964 Goldwater debacle only confirmed what they had known for more than a generation: a conservative of necessity had to prefer being right to being president.

Suddenly, in 1972, a political watershed appeared to have occurred. For the first time since Herbert Hoover and Calvin Coolidge, conservatives believed they could denounce traditional liberal social programs in the name of a political majority.

The issues dividing conservatives and liberals during the days of Hoover and Roosevelt haven't changed much up to the present day. The basic philosophic split continues to be the responsibility of the federal government to help solve problems in the society. Traditional conservatives believe that governmental interference with the natural workings of the social and economic marketplace is not only an unjust infringement of individual property rights but counterproductive in actually solving these problems. Traditional liberals, on the other hand, believe that government in general, and the federal government in particular, has the responsibility to correct economic and racial injustice, and thus to set spending priorities which benefit those who, historically, have failed to receive a fair share of the country's wealth and political power.

Understanding that these definitions are overly simplistic, that both parties contain elements of conservative and liberal philosophies, and that a number of problems and programs do not easily divide up in this kind of simple dichotomy, the fact is that most people perceive the Democratic Party—from Jackson to Wilson, from FDR to Truman, Kennedy, and Johnson—as the party of liberalism, identified with those middle- and lower-income people who are the most in need of governmental aid and social change. The Republican Party—from McKinley to Taft to Hoover to Eisenhower—is generally perceived as the party of conservatism, responsive to upper-middle-class and upper-class interests who have the greatest stake in maintaining the status quo.[1]

Thus, when Richard Nixon turned his attention a few weeks after the November election to dismantling Lyndon Johnson's Office of Economic Opportunity (OEO)—the agency which most symbolized the traditional liberal Democratic approach to solving social problems—he saw himself as the carrier of a traditional conservative ethic which now, he believed, represented a new political majority in the country. He appointed Howard Phillips, a former head of the conservative youth group Young Americans for Freedom, to take charge of the destruction of OEO.

Phillips, after so many years in the political desert, took great public delight in his new job. In a July 1973 interview in the

1. A postelection study by the University of Michigan's Center for Political Studies entitled *A Party in Disarray: Policy Polarization in the 1972 Election,* by Arthur H. Miller, Warren E. Miller, Alden S. Raine, and Thad A. Brown (hereafter referred to as "CPS study"), confirms that voters perceive the Democratic Party as a whole to be to the left of the Republican Party on all the major issues. (See figure 1, p. 14, and p. 16.)

Washington *Post*, Phillips, who had recently stepped down as acting director of OEO, expressed gratification at his success in blocking a bill that would have strengthened the OEO Legal Services Program. He described the dismantling of OEO in terms of traditional conservative philosophy—"government must get out of the business of trying to solve social problems"—and in terms of political pragmatism. Opposing legal services was not only right philosophically, it was good politics. "If the President will stick to his own script," Phillips told the Washington *Post*'s David Broder, "endorsed by 60 per cent of the American people, and force the issue to the Congress in ways that the social and political ethic of the New American Majority comes into play, as it did on the legal services bill, we can prevail."

The problem with all this conventional wisdom about a prevailing conservative ethic in the country is that all the major opinion surveys indicate that, under the traditional definitions of conservatism and liberalism set forth above, the American people are on most issues more liberal now than they have ever been before. After a detailed study of voter preferences on fourteen major issues between 1968 and 1972, the University of Michigan Center for Political Studies (CPS) concluded that the general population had "noticeably shift[ed] leftward on the issues," as part of what the authors concluded was a "liberalizing trend occurring not only in the ranks of the Democrats but in the population as a whole." [2] In fact, this "liberalizing" trend is reflected not on isolated issues by some pollsters but on a wide variety of issues in national surveys conducted by every major opinion pollster in the nation today.

Notwithstanding Howard Phillips' rhetoric about a conservative "New American Majority" supporting his dismantling of the anti-poverty programs, the Harris poll taken in February 1973 reported that overall, the public opposed the decision to eliminate OEO by 46

2. CPS study, *op. cit.*, pp. 13–17. The authors depict a graph of voters' views on two of the most volatile issues in the 1968–72 period—the Vietnam War and urban unrest. On the war, the authors asked voters to place themselves on a left *v.* right spectrum (with furthest left being unilateral withdrawal and furthest right, military victory). On the urban unrest issue, the parameters were "focusing on solving problems of poverty and unemployment as a means of ending urban unrest" (the left position) and "increasing the use of police force" (the right position). The study found a "steady progression in a dovish direction" on the war issue, and a "noticeably leftward direction" on the urban unrest issue.

to 39 per cent. The margins were enormous when asked about specific programs. By 62 to 25 per cent, the public opposed an end to Head Start, a compensatory education program aimed particularly at black children; 64 per cent disagreed with the disbanding of the Job Corps, compared to 29 per cent in agreement.

On the philosophic question as to the role of the federal government in solving economic and social problems, the liberal-conservative split isn't even close. Pollsters Gallup and Albert Cantril reported in January 1973 that nearly three out of four Americans—72 per cent—agreed with the statement "The federal government has a responsibility to do away with poverty in this country." Even the business community—the traditional bastion of governmental laissez-faire conservatism—has become increasingly liberal. A Daniel Yankelovich survey of 300 top executives from the *Fortune* magazine "500" list—the 500 largest and most important corporations and banks in America—found that 57 per cent favored a "step-up" of federal regulatory activity, and another 27 per cent supported federal regulatory activity at the current levels, while only 8 per cent believed that federal regulation of business affairs should be cut back.

There can also be little doubt that the American people overwhelmingly support increased governmental spending on a broad range of social problems. A June 1972 Gallup poll showed that 77 per cent of the public favored increased spending for crime control; 74 per cent, increased spending for aid to the elderly; 74 per cent for drug-addiction programs; 62 per cent for educating low-income children; 61 per cent, to reduce air pollution; 54 per cent for college education for young people; 52 per cent for increased "medicaid" for low-income families; and 51 per cent to rebuild the nation's cities. In September 1972 Gallup reported that 69 per cent of the public would be more likely to vote for a candidate who stood for a national health-insurance program, and only 18 per cent would be less likely.

Louis Harris found that, by early 1973, the constituency in favor of the federal government's taking an active role in solving these problems was not only greater than ever, but the priority of expenditures followed traditional liberal philosophic lines. According to Harris, the public endorsed an increase in Social Security by 70 to 25 per cent; federal aid for new hospital construction (70 to 24); free milk for the school lunch program (79 to 18); and raising the amount which the elderly received under Medicare, by 92 to 5 per cent. On the other hand, 55 per cent of Harris's sample was opposed to increased spending for research and development; 50 per cent opposed increases in funding to improve highways; and 69 per cent opposed larger subsidies for farmers. The *Fortune* 500 survey reported that two-thirds of the 300 top executives believed that defense expenditures were unduly high and filled with waste. Even among President Nixon's supporters, a majority stated that they would be "more likely" to vote for someone who favored a cut in defense expenditures than someone who supported defense spending at current levels.[3]

The American people also exhibit a strong antiestablishment populism, a general resentment and distrust of the wealthy, corporate interests of the country. Cantril found in February 1973 that 78 per cent of the public agreed that "the big special interests in this country have too much power and pretty much get their own way."

This is a part of what seems to be a growing class consciousness in the country in recent years. As Harris pointed out in a November 1972 survey, the percentage of people who believe that the rich are getting richer and the poor poorer has significantly increased from 48 per cent in 1966 to 61 per cent in 1972. When the public was asked in the same poll to choose between a crackdown on young protesters and militant blacks or a crackdown on corporate polluters, the public preferred a crackdown on corporate polluters by a margin of 58 to 30 per cent. In addition, an overwhelming 91 per cent of the public expressed a desire for changes in the tax laws which "ease the burden on moderate-and-low income families but increases taxes on higher-income people and corporations."

If there is a public ambivalence on the subject of traditional liberal social programs, it occurs when the issue is articulated in a way which challenges the deeply ingrained "work ethic" of blue-collar and middle-income Americans. That is why the welfare issue aroused so much hostility among such people in 1972. People saw their taxes and living costs rising and believed Nixon's charges that

3. Gallup poll, reported September 1972.

most of the expenditures for welfare were undeserved, that most people on welfare could work but preferred taking money from the government instead.

But the broad opposition to the symbolized issue of welfare—meaning *undeserved* welfare—does not mean, as Nixon and other conservatives have suggested, that there is public opposition to special financial aid to help the poor. A December 1972 Harris poll dramatically bore this out. By a margin of 69 to 22 per cent, the public expressed its opposition to spending more money for welfare. But the same cross section of people, by a margin of 62 to 31 per cent, supported increased spending to "help the poor."

What this means is that while most people will not support a generalized philosophy of government spending, those same people *will* support liberal social programs aimed at solving *specific* problems. In a national survey just prior to the 1964 elections, pollster and political analyst Lloyd Free sought public reaction to two types of statements on the role of the federal government. One set couched the role in generalized ideological terms: "the federal government is interfering too much in state and local matters" or "we should rely more on individual initiative and ability and not so much on governmental welfare programs." The response was substantial opposition to an extensive role for the federal government. The same cross section of people was then asked to react to statements referring to *specific* federal programs: for example, "a broad program of federal aid to education," or "a compulsory medical insurance program covering hospital and nursing care for the elderly." The reaction was overwhelmingly in favor of an extensive federal responsibility.[4]

In other words, most people will resist an ideological position—that all government programs are good *per se*, that all poor people have the right to special government financial and social support—for such a position calls forth a host of negative associations, images of government waste, of working people supporting lazy people, of naive liberal do-goodism. On the other hand, when the issue is framed in terms of a specific program—with the implica-

4. This analysis of the Free Study is based on a privately commissioned postelection study by Albert H. Cantril, done for Jerry Wurf and the State, County and Municipal Employees Union (dated February 15, 1973).

tion that not all government programs are necessarily good but this one is—this job-training bill or this aid-to-education measure deserves special consideration—the response is more positive.

On another front—the race question—there seems to be nearly unanimous agreement, from the architects of the Nixon "Southern strategy" to the New Politics theorists who explain the 1972 election results in terms of racism in America, that most whites no longer support special governmental attention to the problems of blacks who suffer from race discrimination and who live in poverty.

This is simply untrue. For one thing, more people than ever before recognize that there is discrimination against blacks in key areas of American life. In January 1973, Harris reported that there had been a significant increase in awareness by whites of discrimination against blacks over the past four years in the following problem areas—getting decent housing (from 46 per cent in 1969 to 51 per cent in 1972); getting white-collar jobs (from 38 to 40 per cent); getting skilled-labor jobs (from 35 to 40 per cent); "way treated as human beings" (from 35 to 38 per cent); getting quality education in public schools (from 23 to 29 per cent); getting into labor unions (from 22 to 28 per cent); "way treated by police" (from 19 to 25 per cent).

The same survey also refutes the generally accepted notion that racial polarization in the country is as bad as ever. Although blacks in higher percentage than whites report an awareness of discrimination in these areas, the trend is down—that is, more blacks see less discrimination in American life than ever before.

The Michigan CPS study confirmed these Harris findings, concluding that, from 1968 to 1972, there had been a "diminution in the salience and potency of racial issues." The CPS authors found that, during this period, the number of whites who believed the civil rights movement was "pushing too fast" had declined, as had the number who believed that blacks resorted to violence to get what they wanted, while white preferences for desegregation had increased.[5]

Some of the more pessimistic analysis of the race issue have focused on adverse white reaction to ideologically phrased questions

5. CPS study, *op. cit.*, pp. 21–22.

on race in order to prove white America's continuing racist inclinations. A March 1973 *Harper's* magazine analysis of public sentiment on the race question, based on an Oliver Quayle survey of the influence of the race issue on a Ted Kennedy–Spiro Agnew (prior to his legal difficulties and resignation) presidential contest in the state of Illinois, led off with the dramatic subheadline: "According to a new *Harper's*/Quayle poll, the easiest way for a liberal Democrat to lose in 1976 would be to advocate justice—racial justice." To support that statement, the magazine cited the fact that 46 per cent of all U.S. voters agree that "America has *gone far enough* in helping blacks achieve equality" (Quayle defines that attitude as "slightly prejudiced") 19 per cent agreed that the nation has *gone too far* ("strongly prejudiced"); and 35 per cent believe that it has *not gone far enough* ("liberal"). However, omitted from the *Harper's*/Quayle analysis is that the *trend* of people who believe that *more* must be done for blacks has steadily gone up over the years—a trend which Harris called "measurable and significant." [6]

The *Harper's* analysis went on to claim that, while Kennedy would defeat Agnew in the Quayle poll by a 60 to 40 per cent margin in Illinois (Nixon beat McGovern in Illinois in 1972 by 59 to 41 per cent), he would face "massive defections" unless he stuck to "bland programs" for blacks. To support that statement, the magazine cited a Quayle survey of Illinois voters who were asked how their choice between Ted Kennedy and Spiro Agnew would be affected if Kennedy took certain problack positions. Quayle found that if Kennedy supported a law requiring every labor union to admit a minimum percentage of black members—the controversial job-quotas issue—he would lose only two points to Agnew; if he supported a federal housing program to eliminate black city ghettos by building more low-income housing outside big-city ghettos—the inflammatory issue of forced integration of black, low-income housing in the white suburbs—Kennedy's vote totals against Agnew would remain the same; and if Kennedy supported a "welfare program with work incentives that would give every family in the poverty class, whites and blacks, a guaranteed income of $5000 a year"—a guaranteed-income position more radical even than George McGovern's $1000-

6. Harris poll, published in the New York *Post*, January 15, 1973.

per-person plan—Kennedy's vote totals against Agnew actually would go up two points. These are hardly "bland" programs; nor would Kennedy suffer anything resembling "massive" voter defections for endorsing them. Quite the contrary. A Kennedy position favoring a "large federal program to give special and extra aid to schools in the nation's black ghettos" would increase his vote totals in Illinois in a contest with Agnew by *twelve points;* and a position favoring "an intensive job-training program to give poor black Americans the opportunity to learn skills and gain useful employment" would bring Kennedy an incredible *twenty-four-point* increase in his vote totals.

Other national opinion surveys demonstrate that a substantial majority of the American people—in all regions of the country, of all ages and income groups, and of all ideological and political loyalties—recognize the need for special governmental efforts to help blacks and other minorities. A September 1972 Gallup poll is worth citing in full. The responses to the question, "Would you be *more* or *less likely* to vote for a candidate who favors improving the opportunities of minorities," are shown in the table on page 182.

Blue-collar "manual" workers, whom many liberals would dismiss as Archie Bunker racists, support opportunities for minorities at the same level as the nation as a whole. Clerical people are thirteen points above the national average, the $5000 to $15,000 per-year middle-income people only five points below. Pro-equal-opportunities candidates are supported by large margins in all regions of the countries—including more than three out of five voters in the South. Also striking here is that the next generation of voters seems even more committed to equality of racial opportunity—the eighteen-to-thirty group runs nine points above the national average. And at least three out of five Nixon voters and people who call themselves Republicans prefer a candidate who stands for improving the opportunities of minorities.

This support among traditional Republicans is also reflected in the September 1969 *Fortune* 500 survey of largely Republican business executives. Asked to choose from a list of problems which merited the highest priority, more than half selected "insuring minority equality" and employing the hard-core unemployed. A Harris poll, published in the New York *Post* in January 1971 under

FAVORS IMPROVING OPPORTUNITIES OF MINORITIES

	"More Likely"	"Less Likely"
Nat'l	67%	21%
White	64%	23%
Nonwhite	93%	0%
Coll/Prof'l	74%	16%
Clerical	80%	10%
Manual	67%	20%
18–30	76%	15%
30+	64%	23%
Rep	63%	24%
Dem	70%	17%
Indep	66%	23%
East	71%	17%
Midwest	67%	20%
South	61%	23%
West	68%	23%
$15,000+/yr	73%	18%
$5–15,000/yr	62%	25%
Under $5000/yr	58%	22%
Nixon voters	60%	27%
McGov voters	82%	11%

the headline "Rich Getting a Bit Radical," also found that in the more Republican, allegedly more conservative upper-income brackets—$15,000 and above—the proposition that blacks should be helped to "move faster to achieve racial equality" was supported by a margin of 58 to 30 per cent.

The only exception to this pattern of public support for programs to undo the effects of past discrimination is in the area of busing to achieve integration. Compare, for example, the results of the same September 1972 Gallup poll cited above, when voters were asked whether they would be *more* or *less* likely to vote for a candidate who supported racial busing to achieve integration.

The national public would be "less likely" to support a candidate who favored busing for school integration by almost the identical margin as it indicated it would be "more likely" to favor a candidate

SUPPORTS RACIAL BUSING TO ACHIEVE INTEGRATION

	"More Likely"	*"Less Likely"*
Nat'l	22%	66%
White	19%	70%
Nonwhite	52%	32%
Coll/Prof'l	21%	69%
Clerical	27%	61%
Manual	25%	66%
18–30	28%	62%
30+	18%	67%
Rep	13%	75%
Dem	26%	59%
Indep	25%	68%
East	24%	66%
Midwest	22%	65%
South	22%	64%
West	20%	69%
$15,000/yr	21%	71%
$5–15,000/yr	26%	58%
Under $5000/yr	16%	71%
Nixon voters	16%	75%
McGov voters	37%	59%

who supported improving the "opportunities" of minorities. The opposition to busing for integration is so deep that even among nonwhites, who are the only group in this survey expressing support for busing, a substantial minority—one out of three of all of those asked, almost 40 per cent of those who expressed an opinion—would favor an antibusing candidate over a probusing one.

Despite the effort of some New Politics liberals to portray the anti-McGovern vote as primarily racist, in fact the New Politics constituency—the college graduates and professionals, young people, Democrats, Easterners—all indicate fairly overwhelming preference for an antibusing position by a candidate. Even self-identified McGovern voters in the poll indicate they would favor an antibusing candidate by a substantial margin of 59 to 37 per cent. These voter preferences are uniform throughout the country—in fact, slightly more voters in the East and Midwest would be "less likely" to support a candidate who took a probusing position than in the South.

According to a September 1973 Gallup poll, a substantial majority favors school integration throughout the country and a variety of means to achieve integration. Only busing across school district lines arouses significant opposition, among black as well as white parents. Gallup found that 76 per cent of his national sample favored school integration, as opposed to 18 per cent who opposed it. Of the 76 per cent who favored school integration, 27 per cent favored changing school boundaries to allow more persons from different economic and racial groups to attend the same schools, 22 per cent favored the creation of more housing for low-income people in middle-income neighborhoods as a means to achieve it, and only 5 per cent favored busing from one school district to another (with 22 per cent favoring some other integration solution). Among black parents, the favored solution was building low-income housing in middle-class neighborhoods (32 per cent), and only 9 per cent—less than one out of ten—favored the interschool-district busing solution.

It is crucial for those who are committed to school integration to understand antibusing sentiments and their implications on the future of racial integration. Even if the Supreme Court defuses the busing issue, George Wallace's victory in the Michigan primary in 1972, as well as the massive opposition to busing among all segments of the population, should make it clear that any candidate who can be labeled as indiscriminately probusing will find himself in considerable political difficulty. At any time the busing issue could heat up, polarizing the political process and leading otherwise progressive people to support reactionary candidates for high public office.

Antibusing sentiment cannot be adequately attributed to racist-based opposition to the cause of racial equality; nor can it be interpreted as a "code word"—to use a favorite liberal term—for the alleged resentment by whites of special governmental programs aimed at helping poor blacks. The opinion surveys refute such an interpretation. Rather, whites are willing to support a wide variety of programs to help equalize economic and social opportunities for blacks, but they are not willing to have their children bused from a good neighborhood to a bad one, from a good school to a poor one, or over long distances, as a means of achieving an integrated school system.

All this leads to another important insight concerning the busing issue—that all busing is not the same, either politically or substantively. Most people appear to be willing to support the necessity of busing to correct *de jure* school segregation, where, for example, school district lines have deliberately been drawn to ensure a dual school system. There is simply no way to justify such blatantly racist and illegal actions by school boards.

However, the major opposition to busing has arisen from widespread fears that busing will be used to correct *de facto* segregated school systems, in which neighborhood residential patterns alone have led to racial imbalances within or between school districts. This is the circumstance which raises the specter of good school–bad school, good neighborhood–bad neighborhood busing. Fears soared in 1970 and 1971 when decisions were handed down by Richmond and Detroit federal district courts requiring consolidation of school districts between white suburbs and largely black inner cities.

Civil rights lawyer Joseph Rauh points out that such fears are unjustified, since in the large majority of school busing cases, busing plans were implemented as a means of dismantling *de jure* segregated school systems, established through gerrymandered school district lines. Nevertheless, most people fear the possibility that their kids may be sent into a bad neighborhood and a bad school, and it doesn't help to tell them the possibility is remote.

William Raspberry, a black columnist for the Washington *Post*, in a column in late February 1972 emphasized the need to consider the *political* costs of forced busing. Busing, he wrote, has "scared hell out of an awful lot of white Americans whom it is useless to call racists." He continued, "More and more white people who would not object to black neighbors or black schoolmates for their children when they have reason to believe that they and their black neighbors share the same general values will head for the hills, the courts and the state legislature, rather than face the prospect of 'busing.' "

Raspberry also agreed that there are legitimate substantive

questions about the value of some busing plans. How much do black children in run-down, ghetto schools really benefit by going to the same schools with white middle-class kids from the suburbs?

Some liberals have argued that the only way to get increased aid for the inner-city schools is to force white parents, whose children have been bused, to fight for the funds. That argument assumes it is necessary to risk the backlash and polarization which might result from a busing plan in order to win white backing for increased aid to inner-city schools. The surveys cited in this chapter demonstrate that that assumption is inaccurate; white support for such increased aid for ghetto schools, job training, special tutoring programs and income guarantees is considerable. However, a busing plan which forces white parents to bus their kids to a school they perceive to be inferior is likely to lead them to vote for candidates who oppose such aid.

Another frequent liberal argument in favor of uncompromising support for busing is that it injures liberal credibility to retreat from long-standing support of integration. Many liberal Democratic candidates in 1972 who tried to run as antibusing candidates ended up injuring their own credibility—and still were perceived by many voters as probusing. However, the argument is circular: one must take a wrong position on an issue because he did so in the past. The question remains, What is the right position on busing for a prointegrationist to take?

No matter how justified a reassessment of the liberal probusing stand is on substantive or pragmatic grounds, many blacks might regard even the suggestion of a turnabout as a serious symbolic retreat of traditional liberal support for integration and civil rights, perhaps increasing a sense of isolation and despair in the black community about the possibility of achieving racial justice. Perhaps the only credible liberal argument is that one can be prointegrationist and still oppose busing orders in *de facto* situations, which might result in the busing of children from good to poor school systems.

The question is not whether there ought to be school integration, but rather, by what route? The prointegrationist can argue that a more rapid route to a fully integrated society is through the building of a majority coalition, based on common class interests, between low- and middle-income blacks and white. Such a coalition could elect a president and a Congress which is committed to the kinds of economic and social programs which will help the poor and those who have suffered from racial discrimination, rebuild and reinvigorate the urban centers, bring about integrated residential living patterns in city and suburbs and, ultimately, achieve fully integrated school systems.

One concern I had when I began writing this chapter was that, whatever disclaimers I attempted, I would still be accused of advocating that the public leaders in general and the Democratic Party in particular take positions on the issues on the basis of what the public-opinion surveys indicated.

That has not been my intention. In fact, I have tried to show that liberal Democrats can follow their instincts and support programs which they perceive as dealing with problems of poverty and social inequities without necessarily risking public disfavor.

Even on the race question—specifically, the question of busing—I am not arguing that liberals should reassess their traditional support for all kinds of busing plans simply because there is such overwhelming opposition by the public to some forms of busing. There are serious substantive questions about the social and educational benefits of some types of busing which have not, in my judgment, been satisfactorily answered.

I must admit to certain mixed feelings, however, about the relevance of public-opinion surveys on the busing issue. This may well be one of the rare occasions when substance and politics intersect. There may simply be a limit to which a majority of people can be pushed in a democratic society in order to achieve a particular social goal. Sometimes that limit must be tested and the social goals pressed notwithstanding the political opposition. Sometimes, despite such opposition at the outset, the public may learn to adapt and public opinion may change. There are more than enough previous examples of such adaptation and shift in public opinion, including communities which initially resisted busing plans and then learned to accept them. However, one must wonder whether at some point, on some issues, the continued resistance of a large majority of people in a community to a particular social goal must be respected, at least for a period of time. This might be wise from a tactical point of view, even when the substantive case is clear. It is even more so when serious substantive questions remain, or when many people who support the particular social goal involved—*i.e.*, integrated schools —are unconvinced that the particular mechanism causing the controversy—*i.e.*, busing—is the best one for achieving the goal.

In any event, whatever disagreement there may be about various tactics and strategies for mobilizing a political majority, there should be no ambiguity about the inherent decency of a majority of American voters—a decency which, according to numerous polls and issue analyses, will opt for a government committed to solving the problems of the poor over one which is blatantly indifferent to such problems and, indeed, which exploits the fears of voters rather than their better instincts.

But in order for a candidate to win such a decency vote, he must show that he also cares about the needs of middle-income people as well as the poor. Most important, he must convey the qualities of character and political sensitivity to bring about changes in the society which are well thought out, ordered, and fair.

And that leads us to the enigma of the 1972 presidential campaign: If, in 1972, public sentiment was as liberal on the issues as opinion samplings seem to indicate, why did the American people vote overwhelmingly *against* a man whose views were largely in accord with theirs and *for* a man whose positions and philosophy, for the most part, were not?

eleven

McGOVERN v. NIXON: PAYING THE PRICE OF PURISM

> "He was right, but they weren't listening. All the rightness in the
> world means little unless a politician can take his views to the
> people, can relate them in the way they experience the problem,
> and can persuade them that his solution fits their needs."
> —Jeremy Larner, writing about Senator
> Eugene McCarthy in the 1968 campaign

WITH SENATOR MCGOVERN AND President Nixon both insisting that
the 1972 election offered voters an unprecedented opportunity to
make an ideological choice, it is not surprising that so many people
concluded that that's precisely what the country did. When the
results were in, Nixon's supporters lost no time in proclaiming that
the Nixon landslide constituted a historical mandate to reverse the
liberal social and economic programs of the past decade.

This thesis rests on the assumption that voters in 1972 were most
influenced by their perceptions of where the two candidates stood on
the issues. There is some evidence of this in a postelection study of
McGovern and Nixon voters by the Michigan Center for Political
Studies to support this contention. The CPS data showed that voters
perceived McGovern to be substantially to the left not only of
themselves but of the Democratic Party as a whole. By the same
token, Nixon's more conservative positions on some so-called cultural or social issues—amnesty, abortion, and busing—were more in

189

tune with the prevailing sentiment than were McGovern's more liberal positions.[1]

Nevertheless, the margin of Nixon's victory—and perhaps the victory itself—cannot be satisfactorily explained as a mandate for conservatism over liberalism. For one thing, those "cultural" issues on which McGovern was especially vulnerable, such as amnesty or abortion, were (and are) essentially peripheral to the major domestic and foreign-policy issues that have traditionally divided liberals and conservatives. In fact, Nixon had acquired his greatest advantages on these major issues—for example, his trips to Peking and Moscow, his imposition of a wage-price program—by moving not to the right but considerably to the left of his 1968 platform.

The conservative-mandate theory also fails to explain why millions of voters, including Wallace voters, were supporting Nixon over McGovern but then switched over to vote for liberal Democratic candidates for governor, the House, and the Senate over conservative Republicans in state campaigns which revolved around the same national liberal v. conservative issues as the presidential race.

The fact is, the most important element in George McGovern's demise related not to his liberal positions on the issues but to a severely critical judgment which voters had made about his personal qualities—judgments that he was erratic, unreliable, even incompetent. In other words, McGovern's defeat was more a personal than an ideological failure.[2]

The extent of that personal image deterioration is apparent from a wide variety of surveys. Albert Cantril's postelection study cited a *Newsweek* poll, conducted by the Gallup organization in mid-August 1972, in which only 17 per cent of those questioned saw McGovern as a man who stuck to his principles, compared to Nixon's 40 per cent. Another 17 per cent saw McGovern as "strong and forceful," compared to Nixon's 34 per cent, while a mere 11 per cent thought he had good judgment, compared to Nixon's 30. McGovern

---

1. CPS study, *op. cit.*, at pp. 10 (table 1), 11, 13, and 16.

2. Despite some inflated rhetoric about the importance of ideology in the McGovern-Nixon contest, the CPS authors ultimately conclude that the personal "assessments" of McGovern were more "potent" an influence on voter decisions than issues. (CPS study, *op. cit.*, pp. 67, 68, *et seq.*)

also received a high percentage on the most politically damaging voter perceptions of all, especially in the arena of presidential politics. Twenty per cent of those questioned saw him as an "extremist," compared to Nixon's 3 per cent, and 18 per cent felt he made "snap decisions" (v. 9 per cent for Nixon). In other words, on the personal qualities which most people deem most essential in a president—integrity, strength, good judgment, and moderation—Nixon trounced McGovern each time.

Given these kinds of negative personal voter judgments about McGovern, it is not surprising that he was unable to exploit what was actually a large number of issues on which the Nixon administration was particularly vulnerable.

On a wide variety of issues relating to social welfare programs——in education, health, employment, and special efforts to help the poor and minorities—surveys indicated that a majority of the public agreed with McGovern's positions over Nixon's. Although Nixon's turnaround on the economy had helped him to some extent, the public remained overwhelmingly negative about his handling of the economy in general and, in particular, the president's wage-price control program. Cantril found that, as late as mid-October, the public believed, by a margin of 57 to 29 per cent, that the wage-price controls had failed "because they are not tough enough on profits of corporations." ✓

Polls taken just before the election also indicated that Nixon was increasingly vulnerable on the issue of "corruption": not only the Watergate break-in, but successive incidents which smelled of loose money and shady dealing, including ITT, the Russian wheat deal, the dairy price hike a few days after a $300,000 campaign contribution from the various dairymen's associations, and so on.

Even on the war, the public seemed to be growing increasingly restless. Nixon rallied public opinion after he mined and blockaded the port of Haiphong in the summer of 1972. The hopes for peace, sent soaring by Henry Kissinger in mid-October, also helped Nixon considerably. Nevertheless, according to Harris, by mid-October, the Vietnam issue was beginning to cut against Nixon and, by the end of the month, there was clear slippage as more and more of the public began to suspect that the "peace is at hand" statement was a politically contrived fraud.

But McGovern was unable to exploit Nixon's vulnerabilities, nor could he take advantage of those traditional liberal-populist issues on which he had based his entire campaign. Cantril cites an August 1972 survey which found that the public believed by 59 to 35 per cent that Nixon would do a better job reducing unemployment; by 61 to 43 per cent that Nixon would more likely to "pay attention to the problems of the working man"; and, despite McGovern's eloquent plea in his nominating acceptance speech that America should "come home" from the "entrenchment of special privilege," the public believed by a 52 to 35 per cent margin that Nixon would do a better job of "keeping the big interests from having too much influence over government." ✓

George McGovern did his best to raise these issues. His speeches were hard-hitting and, at times, eloquent. But somehow, between the speechwriter's typewriter and the voter's mind, something was lost, something very fundamental to the political process. A barrier had been created which blocked the pathways of communication between George McGovern and large segments of the American people. By the end of the campaign, it didn't seem to matter what McGovern said or did. Millions of voters had apparently tuned him out—completely.

Nothing dramatizes McGovern's problems in personal image and communications with the public better than the black voter statistics. Surely no other voter bloc had more incentive—after four years of Nixon's Southern/strategy, including a slowdown on civil rights, the attempted emasculation of the Voting Rights Act, and the Carswell and Haynesworth nominations—to turn out heavily and solidly against Richard Nixon. Moreover, McGovern had, at great political sacrifice, identified himself with a wide variety of programs aimed especially at the problems of low-income blacks, especially his $1000-per-person welfare plan. Yet, according to Harris, the black vote approximately doubled from 10 to 20 per cent for Nixon in 1972 as compared to 1968, accounting by itself for a 2 per cent net shift in the final vote. And, throughout the country, black turnout was significantly down. According to the Joint Center for Political Studies, 58 per cent of registered black city voters went to the polls; four years before, the turnout of black voters, with Hubert Humphrey on the Democratic ticket, was 87 per cent.

Black labor leader Bayard Rustin, writing about the apathy which blacks felt toward the McGovern candidacy, cited as further evidence the 27 per cent turnout of all voters in predominantly black Washington, D.C., representing the poorest voter-participation rate since the district won the franchise. Despite all of McGovern's speeches and position papers on problems directly relevant to blacks, Rustin pointed out, there was "a surprising level of discontent with his campaign" by such black leaders as Jesse Jackson, Mayor Richard Hatcher of Gary, Indiana, and Vernon Jordan of the Urban League, who perceived McGovern as lacking in concern and attention to black needs.

Here again is an obvious example of perception being sometimes more important than reality in the political arena, of the style and context of the articulation of issues being more important, in some circumstances, than substance. It is certainly further proof that McGovern's political problem was not the substance of his views but his inability to persuade people—in this case, black people—that he was a man who deserved to be listened to.

Nixon's vulnerabilities in 1972 and McGovern's inability to exploit them were best highlighted by another Albert Cantril national poll, taken shortly after the November election. Cantril divided the Nixon and McGovern vote totals into pro-Nixon and anti-McGovern segments. For those who like to cite Mr. Nixon's 62 per cent total as the "new Republican majority," the findings are hardly reassuring. In fact, out of that 62 per cent total, only 37 per cent said they voted for Nixon because they liked him or agreed with his policies—essentially, Nixon's loyal Republican base which he still had from 1968; but *16 per cent* said they voted for him because they disliked McGovern.

Meanwhile, among McGovern's 38 per cent vote totals, only 18 per cent would say that they liked him, with 12 per cent explaining their support because they disliked Nixon. In other words, according to this poll, among all voters casting their ballots in the presidential race, there was not much more pro-McGovern sentiment (18 per cent) than anti-McGovern sentiment (16 per cent). Concludes Cantril: "For the most part, Richard Nixon's New American Majority was the creation of George McGovern."

Why did George McGovern develop these kinds of personal

difficulties with the voters? For ten years his political career had been a series of successes. He had won wide respect among professional politicians for his brief 1968 presidential campaign. Why, and when, did his communications barrier develop?

Most analyses of the election focus on various McGovern campaign mistakes. He has generally been portrayed as an unusually inept candidate with an unusually inept staff. The consensus seems to be that (a) McGovern "divided" the Democratic Party; (b) he and his supporters came across as an elitist group, indifferent to the problems of working people; and (c) he took a number of positions, such as his $1000-per-person welfare plan, which led voters to perceive him as "radical" and, worse, irresponsible.

All of these were elements in McGovern's downfall. But still, merely citing them begs the issue. They are effects rather than causes. The fact is, most of the major problems of communication which McGovern faced during the campaign were the *result* of his doing what was necessary to win the nomination—meaning, what was necessary to win the purist elements of the New Politics constituency and to keep them satisfied during his campaign.

When I first presented this thesis to some friends, they argued that the candidate usually makes the constituency, not the other way around. That may have been true in 1960 in the case of John Kennedy, or in 1952 and 1956 in the case of Dwight Eisenhower. But in 1972, a network of political activists already existed—with shared values and experiences, molded in the McCarthy and Kennedy campaigns of 1968; with a common political purpose, the nomination of one of its own in 1972; and with the potential, given the right kind of candidate, for rapid conversion into a national fund-raising apparatus and a political organization. If McGovern was serious about winning the nomination—and he was—he had no choice but to seek the backing of the purist elements of this New Politics constituency. During the barren months of 1971, with Muskie's steamroller tying up all the major powers in the liberal and moderate factions of the party, McGovern had nowhere else to go. Party reforms also made that strategy the most pragmatic one to follow. Having taken that course, however, McGovern then had to pay the price.

We have already seen how Joe Duffey had to pay a similar price in his Connecticut general election campaign. Despite all his efforts to build a broadly based coalition encompassing working-class families, Duffey's dependence on the backing of the New Politics constituency for the Senate nomination meant that, in the general election, he was never able to escape fully from a public perception that he was a candidate of a narrow culture of affluent professionals and radical activists.

A comparison between the McGovern and Goldwater campaigns is also instructive on this point. Although McGovern was more politically pragmatic and coalitionist than the more ideological and doctrinaire Goldwater, both men viewed politics as a means to build an ideologically pure social-political movement to radically transform the country's basic institutions. Both abhorred the coalition-building process, with its necessary emphasis on diversity and compromise.

Dependence on a purist constituency to win a nomination means that, once the nomination is won, it becomes very difficult to reunite the party for the general election. Goldwater discovered that he had to pay heavily for the abusive tactics of his right-wing supporters against moderate and liberal Republicans. The scene of Nelson Rockefeller being shouted down at the 1964 Republican convention would reverberate in the Republican Party—and the public mind—for the remainder of the Goldwater campaign.

So would the scene of a McGovern delegation representing Cook County (Chicago), Illinois—unelected, containing only one Italian and three Poles, totally unrepresentative of voter sentiment as expressed in an open primary—replacing Mayor Daley's elected delegation at the Miami convention. Whatever McGovern's own intentions—and he announced as early as a day after the Wisconsin primary that he did not intend to let the "purists" prevent him, if he were the nominee, from bringing about party unity—the reality in politics is more often judged by the actions of the candidate's supporters at the local level than by his own actions in the national campaign.

Again and again, McGovern and his staff would be dismayed to learn that his local purist supporters were more involved in warring with the local party regulars than in nominating George McGovern. Not infrequently McGovern's state and local campaign leaders would ignore his and his staff's instructions. In Missouri, for example, the McGovernites insisted on blocking a resolution at the state convention which offered some general and relatively lukewarm praise to Democratic Governor Warren Hearnes.[3]

McGovern aide Rick Stearns recalled with utter contempt his experiences with the McGovern leadership in Connecticut. The head of the Hartford, Connecticut, McGovern drive, Dr. Bernard Sorokin (also national chairman of the New Democratic Coalition, a New Politics organization), refused to accept a compromise on delegate representation that Stearns had worked out with Democratic state chairman John Bailey.

There were seven spots on the national delegation slotted for Hartford. Stearns and Bailey had worked out a formula whereby the McGovernites would get two delegates and two alternates, plus Senator Abraham Ribicoff, an early McGovern endorser—a total of three delegates. Sorokin and the McGovern organization insisted on five out of seven and decided to press a primary challenge against the Ribicoff-headed slate. When Stearns told the McGovern organization that they were acting contrary to McGovern's best interests, he was told to mind his own business. The result of the primary: the McGovernites were defeated by a seven-to-one margin, and they left behind more open wounds.

McGovern himself contributed to the difficulties of reuniting the party by his actions and statements immediately preceding the California challenge vote at the Democratic National Convention. He was legitimately outraged when he saw the "anyone-but-McGovern" coalition of supporters of Humphrey, Jackson, and some Muskie people, plus organized labor, attempt to deprive McGovern of 40 per cent of his California delegates by a division of the delegation along proportional lines, even though McGovern had won 100 per cent of the delegates under the rules which prevailed at the time of the primary. That was changing the rules after the game was over, McGovern complained. Realizing he was fighting for his political life, and under intense pressure from his purist backers to

3. In all fairness, the reaction of the McGovernites was not exactly unprovoked. Hearnes had refused to give the McGovernites any of the thirteen at-large delegates to the national convention, offering instead merely a spot on the presidential elector slate. In any event, a few months later, McGovern tried to tell Hearnes he did not approve of the actions of his supporters at the state convention, but Hearnes insisted on holding him accountable.

portray the anti-McGovern coalition as composed of reactionary political hacks, McGovern overreacted. He told *Life* magazine:

If a bunch of old established politicians gang up to prevent me from getting the nomination because I didn't come to them for help—just a negative, spiteful movement that subverts the democratic process—if I feel that has happened, then I will not let them get away with it. There's been so much hard work and emotion poured into this campaign by so many thousands of people—it would be such an infuriating, disillusioning experience for them all—that I would repudiate the whole process. I would run as an independent or support somebody else on an independent ticket.

The statement reeked of a self-righteous double standard. It was common knowledge that, had McGovern lost the primary to Humphrey in California, there would have been a challenge to Humphrey's delegation on the same grounds—whether by McGovern's supporters in California or by Kenneth Bode, whose Center for Political Reform had pressed lawsuits around the country to enforce the reforms. Bode had, in fact, taken some preliminary steps prior to the California primary to enforce a proportional system in California; he gave up his attempts only after McGovern had won the primary.

After the convention, McGovern, having threatened to bolt the party ticket if he lost the nomination due to the California challenge, was not in a very good position to ask party loyalty from Democrats who were preparing to sign up for Democrats for Nixon.

A second result of a nomination campaign dependent on a purist political constituency is that the candidate comes to be perceived in terms of the worst caricature of the values and culture of that constituency—indeed, as a captive of that constituency. Goldwater was seen by many people as the candidate of the atomic bomb-dropping, Communist-under-every-bed John Birchers of the far right. Likewise, many saw McGovern as the candidate of the long-haired, arrogant, pot-smoking hippies of the far left. Each man adopted a campaign slogan that appealed to the moralistic and self-righteous attitudes of his constituency: "Goldwater—In your heart you know he's right"; "McGovern—Right from the start."

That McGovern seemed to represent an elitist, moralistic constituency [4] was responsible for alienating white working-class and Middle American voters. Expressions of hostility from blue-collar workers uniformly tended to lump McGovern together with the worst caricature of this constituency. Richard Krickus, in a Washington *Post* article entitled "Why McGovern Turns Off the Ethnics," written shortly before the election, quoted an insurance claims adjuster's response when he was asked why he disliked McGovern so much:

> You know, what bothers me about McGovern and people like Bella Abzug, the student militants and others like them is that they know everything: What to do in Vietnam, what's wrong with America, how you should raise your kids, amnesty, abortion, everything. . . . If you don't agree with them, you're stupid. Well, . . . I'm not the smartest guy in the world, but I know what's right and wrong and I know that I don't like them or anything about them.

The cultural and value gap between the New Politics activists and the blue-collar Middle American communities can be seen in various McGovern-Nixon voting patterns throughout the country. The pattern of the youth vote is a good example. It will be recalled that McGovern had always viewed the youth vote as a key to his nomination and election. One of his closest advisers, a former aide to Robert Kennedy, Fred Dutton, had written a book, *Changing Sources of Power,* which had argued that the eighteen-year-old vote would give a momentous political advantage to progressive candidates in the future. Dutton authored the campaign memorandum recommending that McGovern devote almost $2 million to a massive voter-registration effort, much of it aimed at young people.

The problem was that McGovern or Dutton apparently didn't

4. The Michigan CPS study argues that McGovern's primary supporters were in fact "not very dissimilar from the traditional Democratic coalition," since "they were more likely to have an urban background, to live in the Northeast, to be Catholic, and to come from a union household" (p. 79). However, the CPS authors also point out that McGovern's primary voters were "more likely" to be young and college-educated and to have a relatively high family income—fitting precisely the image of the elitist New Politics constituency held by most people in 1972. Also, once again, what is important here is voter perception, and whatever the exact statistics about McGovern's primary voters, there is little doubt that he was generally perceived as the candidate of a narrow, rather elitist political base.

fully understand that winning liberal activist students in the prenomination phase was not the same as winning the votes of the rest of the youth population in the postnomination phase. In California, for example, McGovern won on the liberal campuses of the state university and private institutions by margins ranging from 70.2 per cent (UCLA student precincts) to 94.5 per cent (University of California, Santa Cruz). But Nixon won a majority of the student vote at California Polytechnic, San Luis Obispo and Cal Poly, Pomona, whose student bodies came predominantly from working-class families. McGovern won the national college student vote by a margin of 53 to 40 per cent, but lost the overall eighteen- to twenty-four-year-old vote by a margin of 46 to 43 per cent. In other words, the technical-school kids and young workers seemed to be as turned off as their parents were by what they perceived to be the arrogant snobbery of the New Politics culture.

The disparity between the standards of political purity he had set for himself and other candidates prior to the nomination and his own conduct after the convention made matters worse. If Richard Nixon, Lyndon Johnson, or even John Kennedy, had kicked his vice-presidential running mate off the ticket less than a week after indicating "1000 per cent" support, most people would have shrugged and said, "That's a politician for you." But when George McGovern did it—the man who had based his entire campaign on running against (to use his words) "a bunch of old established politicians"—it was like catching the stern fundamentalist preacher sinning behind the barn with the farmer's daughter. After one speech I delivered on behalf of McGovern during the fall, a middle-aged man stood up and said, "It gives me a lot of pleasure to see that that great moralistic preacher who says he was 'right from the start' is as dirty as the rest of us mortals—except he's a little bit more hypocritical." Garry Wills, a formerly pro-McGovern newspaper columnist, wrote bitterly in a similar vein of McGovern's handling of the Eagleton matter:

> The trouble with McGovern is that he had decreed an end to conventional politics. . . . But McGovern's campaign prides itself on being squeaky clean. Purity looks to issues, not mere "personalities." That is why purity takes so quickly to the knife. . . . It's not one for all

and all for one around McGovern; just one for one and all for one—a
code that leads, rapidly, to political loneliness and Lonesome George
will soon find that out.

Unlike Goldwater, McGovern tried his best to undo the damage
of the divisive prenomination campaign and to reconcile some of the
party regulars. He withdrew his $1000-per-person proposal,
modified his tax reform proposals, soft-pedaled his earlier statements
on marijuana and abortions. He even went so far as to endorse the
Cook County state's attorney, Edward Hanrahan (then under in-
dictment for murder), and Representative Louise Day Hicks of Boston, and to visit Lyndon Johnson and declare that the Vietnam War
wasn't really his fault—"he didn't get in there in the first place."

But these efforts to pull back from his prenomination purist-
oriented campaign, not surprisingly, only made matters worse. To
the general public, vaguely recalling his earlier image of public
purity, McGovern appeared to be opportunistic and somewhat
hypocritical. And to his own New Politics constituency, especially
the more purist elements, his actions constituted nothing less than a
betrayal, leading some to some rather extreme personal attacks.

McGovern's efforts to recoup from the days of the nominating
campaign also were bound to produce tensions within the campaign
organization. Those internal squabbles in August and September
1972, were publicized by the national press and were especially
damaging, for they reinforced the image of McGovern as a man who
was not competent to run his own campaign, much less the executive
branch of the U.S. government.

Still another consequence of McGovern's nomination effort was
that positions he had to take to win his purist constituency came
back to haunt him in the general election. McGovern was especially
damaged by the $1000-per-person proposal, which pollster Lou
Harris has shown to be a crucial error and turning point in his
candidacy. The proposal itself was rejected by the substantial margin
of 73 to 15 per cent of the public. Having earlier made an effective
pitch in favor of tax reform, says Harris, "McGovern in one fell
swoop went clear past the rank-and-file of voters . . . [and] alienated
nearly every family with an income of $12,000 or over." But more
damaging to McGovern's public image than the substance of the

proposal—and central to subsequent voter judgments that he lacked the competence or stature to be president—was his nationally televised response when Humphrey challenged the proposal as too costly. "I don't know how you're able to make that statement," McGovern said, "since even I don't know the actual cost."

In fact, a good argument could be made that McGovern lost the general election during this period, the California primary, well before the Eagleton episode. In May 1972—about the time of the Ohio primary—McGovern was within striking distance of President Nixon. As Harris points out, he was behind only seven points overall—48 to 41 per cent—and led in the East, in the big cities, among the young, and was only a single point behind Nixon among the crucial independent voters and a few points behind in the suburbs. As noted above, McGovern had the best of both worlds: The New Politics constituency knew where he stood on the most controversial issues, while the general public knew little about him at this point. Many in fact were attracted to his underdog image.

However, reports Harris, immediately after the California primary and the extensive public exposure to a variety of McGovern's past statements and positions—not only the $1000-per-person plan, but also, the $31 billion defense-cut proposal, which under Humphrey's skillful cross-examination, seemed to be rash and ill thought out as well as politically unrealistic—McGovern's 7-point deficit more than doubled. He was now losing to Nixon by 16 percentage points. By the end of June, the margin had dropped to 20 points.[5] After the Eagleton episode, the margin dropped to 24 points, where it stayed for the remainder of the campaign.

The key ingredient in the communication barrier between George McGovern and the voting public was the voter perception of him as a man who spoke too quickly, proposed ill-thought-out schemes, and stood for "radical" change. As the general election campaign progressed, it became increasingly apparent that even on those issues on which, substantively, McGovern could have had the edge, he had

5. Yankelovich found that, with each primary, as McGovern's campaign gained public exposure, an increasing number of Democratic voters indicated that they would bolt to Richard Nixon if McGovern were the nominee. After the Florida primary, Yankelovich found, 25 per cent of Humphrey's voters said they would prefer Nixon over McGovern; after Wisconsin, 24 per cent, after Pennsylvania, 34 per cent. And after California, the figure had reached 40 per cent.

articulated them in such a way to give Nixon the advantage. The war is a good example. Surveys indicated, as mentioned above, that voters had begun to turn against Nixon in mid-October on the war issue. But, as Louis Harris pointed out shortly after the 1972 election, "Instead of letting the quicksand run out on President Nixon on the issue, as it did on President Johnson, McGovern overkilled and . . . communicated to the nation that America should feel a terrible guilt about Vietnam, on the one hand, and that he was willing to accept peace at any price, on the other." [6]

But a purist constituency demands simple answers on a wide variety of issues. For Goldwater, who had no conservative opposition for the nomination, there was still intense pressure from the right to show his pure conservatism on the issues, irrespective of political consequences—resulting in talk about ending social security, defoliating Vietnamese jungles through atomic weapons, or dismantling the TVA.

For McGovern, the pressure from the purists of the New Politics constituency to take moralistic stances and to pronounce a series of detailed positions on complicated issues was even more intense than that which Goldwater faced. McGovern may not have ever endorsed immediate amnesty, legalized marijuana or abortion on demand. Throughout 1971, however, he visited college campuses and was repeatedly asked to take positions on these three issues. He couldn't avoid leaving some kind of track record of favorable responses. During these appearances it was never enough, as Muskie had previously discovered, to say merely that he favored substantial defense cuts. McGovern had to go further: set an exact figure, $31 billion, and outline a detailed program. Merely saying he supported welfare reform was not enough. He had to suggest a specific new program: $1000 per person, as untested and ill thought out as it might be. Pressures were always intense to appear as uncompromising on the issues as possible, to avoid at all costs any suggestion of centrism or moderation.

McGovern's personal-image problems, then, were largely the result of his doing what was necessary to win the Democratic

6. Address by Louis Harris, delivered on November 10, 1972, before the National Press Club in Washington, D. C.

nomination. While brilliantly winning the battle for the Democratic Party in 1972, he had developed a communications barrier between himself and the public—and ensured the loss of the war in the general election.

Focusing on the results of the Nixon-McGovern clash to predict either future ideological trends in the country or the future of the Democratic Party is, therefore, terribly misleading. It ignores the basically nonsubstantive roots of the Nixon landslide. It suggests the exception as the rule.

It will be much more useful to ascertain whether there has been any new coalescing of voter constituencies within the Democratic Party which, while submerged in the 1972 presidential balloting, might have already emerged in the balloting for the Senate, the House, and the state houses during the past few years.

twelve

THE EMERGING NEW DEMOCRATIC COALITION

> "Those who like to see themselves as preferring morality to victory will point to the [1972] election as proof that a liberal coalition which includes the mainstream of the labor movement is no longer viable. . . . [But] if this election proved anything, it was that coalition politics as traditionally defined is not dead, but rather essential to the future health of liberalism."
>
> —Bayard Rustin, black civil rights leader, February 1973

KEVIN PHILLIPS's book, *The Emerging Republican Majority*, published shortly after the 1968 elections, predicted a new Republican majority coalition of Wallace voters in the North and South plus traditional Republican Middle Americans. In the aftermath of the 1972 elections, Phillips' thesis seemed to have been vindicated. Moreover, the ideological direction of things seemed clearly to have shifted rightward—some, including Senator McGovern himself, believed rather sharply. And that too seemed to be the wave of the political future.

Then came Watergate, the Senate hearings, John Dean, the White House tapes, the Agnew resignation, the Saturday-night massacre of Cox, Richardson, and Ruckelshaus, and the calls for Mr. Nixon's resignation or impeachment. The theory now seemed to be that, while the country was still conservative (as seen by the results of the Nixon-McGovern contest), the Watergate and related scandals

205

had reversed the Democratic Party's decline.[1] The 1973 state and local elections, in which Democrats scored dramatic victories throughout the nation, including many places which were former Republican strongholds, were seen as the best evidence of the impact of Watergate.

The problem with this new conventional wisdom is that it is based on all the faulty premises of the older one. The so-called new Republican majority has not been dismantled by Watergate and related events because, simply, the new Republican majority never existed in the first place. There is no doubt that Watergate helped the Democrats in the 1973 elections and will strengthen some candidates in the 1974 congressional elections. But the trend toward a reconstituted Democratic majority coalition had gained significant momentum long before Mr. Nixon's men got caught bugging the Democrats or Spiro Agnew got caught with his hands in the cookie jar. Roots of that trend can be traced to the early days of the antiwar movement and the McCarthy campaign of 1968 and through the 1970 and 1972 congressional and gubernatorial results in all parts of the country. In this context, the 1973 local elections can be viewed as a part of an ongoing process, not as a sudden reversal caused solely by Mr. Nixon's and Mr. Agnew's difficulties.

Those who predicted the birth of a "new Republican majority" after the 1968 elections and the death of the majority Democratic coalition after the 1972 elections based their projections on three major premises:

(1) The public is growing increasingly conservative—meaning, increasingly hostile to traditional liberal concepts of aid to minorities, the poor, and strong governmental action to solve basic social problems.

(2) This conservatism was manifested in George Wallace's 14 per cent vote totals in 1968, which included a large number of blue-collar voters who had formerly voted Democratic, and which was based primarily on the race issue. By this reasoning, Nixon's 1968 vote of 43 per cent can be combined with Wallace's 14 per cent to

---

1. The headline in the Washington *Post* of December 9, 1973, proclaimed the new conventional wisdom: "New Majority Seen Drifting to Democrats."

give a 57 per cent Republican majority in a one-on-one contest against a liberal Democratic presidential candidate—essentially what happened in the 1972 presidential election. In other words, political trends indicate that the Democratic base is shrinking among many parts of the old New Deal coalition without commensurate broadening of the party's base into formerly Republican and independent voter constituencies.

(3) Finally, in light of this perceived increased polarization in the country, the 1972 presidential elections showed that the political center—and coalition politics—was no longer operative. Thus, the Democratic Party faced one of two alternatives: write the insurgent New Politics liberals out of the party, inviting the formation of a left-wing third or fourth party; or break up the old coalition by writing off the South and the "Archie Bunker" vote in the North and, instead, building a "top-bottom" coalition of New Politics upper-middle-class liberals and the poor and minorities.

There is, I suggest, a third alternative available to the Democratic Party: the building of a new Democratic Party majority coalition, a new center, uniting the forces of the New Politics, with its new areas of political support in formerly Republican and independent voter constituencies, with the traditional Democratic base of working-class and middle-class-income people, of all races and in all regions of the country.

The viability of that new Democratic coalition—of which there is already considerable evidence—renders invalid each of the three premises set forth.

The perception of the general public as hostile to traditional liberal federal aid programs which help the poor and minorities is simply inaccurate. Kevin Phillips assumed this public conservatism throughout *The Emerging Republican Majority*. Even those who saw a dramatic rise in the Democratic Party's fortunes due to Watergate still perceived the electorate as conservative on the issues. But a study of the opinion surveys on issues taken throughout 1972 and 1973 demonstrates that most traditional liberal economic and social programs—including specific programs associated with Lyndon Johnson's Great Society, such as Head Start or the Job Corps—still hold majority support in the country, as above in Chapter Ten.

As to the second premise—that the Wallace voters and the

Republican voters will combine to give a conservative presidential candidate a majority—there are two major fallacies: first, it seriously overestimates the number of Wallace voters who will defect to the Republicans; and second, it underestimates the Democratic Party's significant inroads into formerly traditional Republican and independent-voter constituencies.

The Wallace Vote

The University of Michigan postelection study presents the view that any liberal Democrat would have been faced with the solid transference of the Wallace vote to the Republicans. The authors of this study suggest that the McGovern coalition was strikingly similar to the Humphrey coalition and, by the same token, both Democratic candidates experienced similar problems with the Wallace voter. The authors then conclude that "there is little evidence to suggest that [a slightly more centrist Democratic candidate than McGovern] would have done significantly better in absolute vote-winning terms than Humphrey did in 1968 with 43 per cent of the total vote." [2]

The obvious fallacy here is that every opinion survey indicated that Wallace voters would have split for Nixon over Humphrey nationwide by less than a two-to-one margin. Thus, with Wallace out of the race in 1968, Humphrey's percentage would have been 47.5, not 43, and Nixon's would have been 52.4—a far cry from the 57 per cent so frequently mentioned in Kevin Phillips' *Emerging Republican Majority*, or the 62 per cent which Nixon received against McGovern in the 1972 election. Moreover, if the split was less than two to one among Wallace voters nationwide in favor of Nixon over Humphrey, then among Wallace voters in the Northern states, the margin was clearly much narrower, since the nationwide totals include an eight- or ten-to-one Nixon advantage over Humphrey among southern Wallace voters. This is borne out by surveys which have shown that in some Northern states, Humphrey would have won more Wallace voters than Nixon in 1968. Without Wallace in the race, Humphrey might have carried some of the Northern states he narrowly lost.

2. CPS study, *op. cit.*, p. 80.

Without all the difficulties Humphrey's candidacy experienced in 1968—the turmoil of the Chicago convention, his ties to Lyndon Johnson and the Vietnam War, his organizational and financial disarray—it is quite probable that the Vice President could have narrowed the theoretical 52.4 to 47.5 per cent gap (in a Wallaceless contest) and, picking up another 2.6 per cent of the vote, defeated Nixon outright. This would have been the case, even without the potential advantage offered by the eighteen-year-old vote not available to Humphrey in 1968.

McGovern's 37 per cent vote total in 1972 must be compared with what would have been a 47.5 per cent Humphrey total in 1968 without Wallace in the race, and Humphrey's projected ability to win at least one out of three Wallace voters should be compared with McGovern's showing, in polls immediately prior to the election, of fewer than one out of five Wallace voters.

Furthermore, it makes little sense to argue that this poor McGovern showing among Wallaceites was inevitable for any liberal-to-moderate Democrat running in 1972. In fact, as late as June 1972, polls indicated Wallace voters as favoring Nixon over McGovern by margins of less than two to one. But it was only after the California primary, when McGovern's personal image suffered such serious damage—especially, among Wallace voters, due to the increasing perception of McGovern as a captive of a New Politics purist constituency—that Wallace voters defected to Nixon by the four- or five-to-one margins seen in the November elections. Indeed, despite the CPS study's attempt to describe the McGovern showing in 1972 as the same as Humphrey's (except for Wallace's absence from the race), the authors point out that McGovern's personal image problems were unprecedented. They refer to him as the "least popular Democratic candidate of the past twenty years," [3] and among Wallace voters, they point out, he was "exceptionally unpopular." [4] And they concede that, despite all of Hubert Humphrey's political difficulties in 1968, he was "more popular in 1968 than McGovern was in 1972." [5]

3. CPS study, p. 54.
4. *Ibid.*, p. 64.
5. *Ibid.*, p. 54.

An analysis of the Nixon-McGovern returns in the state of Wisconsin, the scene of McGovern's most important primary triumph and his best political organization, graphically shows McGovern's serious loss of support among blue-collar and other traditional Democrats as compared to Humphrey in 1968. In fact, such an analysis more than vindicates those who warned that McGovern's weak showing in blue-collar areas in the primaries portended difficulties in the general election. It might be recalled, for example, that a Washington *Post* article had described McGovern's 26 and 27 per cent vote totals in Kenosha and Racine, respectively, as "stunning" evidence of his "inroads" into blue-collar constituencies. However, in the general election, Nixon thrashed McGovern soundly in both cities—by a 54 to 44 per cent margin in Kenosha, and by 56 to 41 per cent in Racine. In 1968 Humphrey had carried Kenosha by a comfortable margin and had run just about even with Nixon in Racine. McGovern's vote totals in Kenosha were 9 per cent below the Humphrey-Muskie ticket and Nixon's had gone up 41 per cent; in Racine, McGovern dropped a percentage point compared to Humphrey's total in 1968, while Nixon had gone up 35 per cent.

Nor can McGovern's showing in Wisconsin be explained by a simple transference *in toto* of Wallace's 1968 vote to Mr. Nixon's 1968 vote. Such a wholesale switch to Nixon, if it occurred to that degree, would still not explain the repeated instances throughout Wisconsin of McGovern's loss of vote totals as compared to Humphrey in 1968—made all the worse because of the presence of the student vote, which, as was mentioned above, helped McGovern in 1972 and was not available to Humphrey in 1968.[6] In addition, Nixon's increases in vote totals in Wisconsin were almost always larger than the 1968 Wallace voter totals, meaning that many more than just Wallace voters were defecting to Nixon in 1972. In Kenosha, for example, Wallace had received 3500 votes in 1968; but Nixon had advanced his totals over 1968 by 7000 votes. In Racine, Nixon received a swing of 3000 to 4000 votes beyond the Wallace totals. In

6. Since McGovern was so heavily benefited by the student vote in some areas, running even with Humphrey's 1968 totals indicated significant losses across the board in other groups in the electorate. For example, McGovern in 1972 ran about even with what Humphrey had received in Dane County (Madison) in 1968—meaning that the estimated 20,000-to-25,000 vote margin McGovern received in 1972 from the student vote in Dane County were given back to Nixon by other voter groups.

Waukesha—also primarily a blue-collar city—Nixon increased his vote totals over 1968 by 12,000 votes—compared to an apparent switch of about 3000 Wallace voters to Nixon.

An analysis of Wisconsin's statewide totals in the 1972 presidential race also shows the extent to which McGovern's candidacy had alienated an unprecedented number of non-Wallace, traditional Democrats. Even subtracting Wallace-switchers, Nixon still would have won in Wisconsin by about the same margin he won in 1968—this despite the fact that (a) McGovern benefited by as many as 75,000 youth votes which Humphrey never had in 1968 and (b) a number of 1968 Wallace voters stayed home in 1972.

McGovern's poor showing among Wallace voters in 1972 cannot be used to predict what other liberal-moderate Democrats could have expected in 1972, or could expect in the future. Obviously, portions of the Wallace vote, especially in the Deep South, are still racism-based, and no liberal Democrat who is committed to civil rights and equal opportunity can expect their support. On the other hand, those who project a natural coalition of Wallace voters and traditional conservative Republicans fail to see the substantial nonracist, economic basis of George Wallace's appeal.

When Kevin Phillips first published his *Emerging Republican Majority,* that appeal was less obvious, leading Phillips to predict that, since Wallace's "statewide success" in 1968 was confined to the "Deep South," his "movement cannot maintain an adequate political base, and is bound to serve, like past American third parties, as a waystation for groups abandoning one party for another." [7] The 1972 campaign clearly indicated that Wallace had made significant breakthroughs among low-income, blue-collar voters in the North and the South as a result of his economic populism, especially his attacks on corporate power and tax laws which favor the rich over working people. This economic populism could cut more against the upper-class/big-business types whom many voters perceive as dominating the Republican Party than against the traditional middle- and low-income constituency of the Democratic Party. A liberal Democrat who avoided the pitfalls experienced by Senator McGovern in 1972—especially the perception of being the captive of

7. *The Emerging Republican Majority,* pp. 462–63.

a leftist counterculture constituency—could, by stressing economic-populist issues, significantly cut into the Wallace constituency and even carry it outright.

Inroads into Republican Constituencies

Not only are the proponents of a "new Republican majority" overoptimistic about the Wallaceite affinity to conservative Republicanism, but they fail to understand fully that, since 1968, there has been a dramatic political trend in the contrary direction—the substantial inroads by the Democratic Party into formerly Republican constituencies of suburban, upper-middle-class professionals and into what William V. Shannon has called the "growth areas of American politics—the young, the huge academic-and-research complexes, the better-educated independent-minded voters."

The growth of Democratic Party strength among these voters may well be the most significant legacy of the New Politics movement. During the early days of the McCarthy campaign, it became apparent for the first time that, in normally Republican upper-middle-class suburbs, there was significant support for Gene McCarthy's brand of anti-Vietnam War and reform liberalism. During the 1968 primaries, it will be recalled, McCarthy consistently ran well in suburban Republican areas.

While a number of these upper-middle-class professionals returned to the Republican column in the Nixon-Humphrey contest in 1968, they did so in insignificantly smaller numbers than in the 1960, 1956, and 1952 presidential elections. Even Kevin Phillips conceded that the 1968 elections seemed to indicate a countercyclical trend among "Yankee, Megalopolitan silk-stocking voters and Scandinavians from Maine across the Great Lakes" and through the Pacific Northwest—what he calls the "morality belt," which appeared to be in transition from moderate Republicanism to liberal Democratic. For example, says Phillips, Nixon won "only 38 per cent of the total 1968 presidential vote on Manhattan's rich East Side; he took only 44 per cent of the ballots in Scarsdale, the city's richest suburb; New England's Yankee counties and towns produced Nixon majorities down 10 to 15 per cent from 1960 levels; fashionable San

Francisco shifted toward the Democrats and Scandinavian Minnesota and Washington state backed Humphrey, as did the Scandinavian northwest of Wisconsin." [8]

This trend toward the Democrats in traditional Republican upper-class areas was continueb in the 1972 elections, although McGovern's competence-and-credibility-image problems cost him dearly among these voters. Nevertheless, despite the heavy landslide margins Nixon rolled up across the country, McGovern ran considerably ahead of his national percentage, and Nixon considerably behind, in Maryland's Montgomery County, which has a higher per capita income than any other county in the country, in Los Angeles County (which he won outright), and in the Republican upper-class suburbs of New York's Westchester County, the suburbs of Boston, Philadelphia, Chicago, San Francisco, and Milwaukee, and Republican counties and suburbs in the "morality belt" states mentioned above, especially Wisconsin, Minnesota, Iowa, and Oregon.

Michael Barone, co-author of the *Almanac of American Politics*, has pointed out that such countercyclical trends "have become the sites of the losing party's greatest gains in later elections." As examples, he cites the fact that Stevenson's strong showing in the Republican farm states and the West in 1952 was later reflected by Kennedy in 1960; and Goldwater's strong showing in the Democratic South and in blue-collar, Catholic areas in the urban North was later vindicated by Nixon's gains in these areas in 1968 and 1972. Thus, Barone argues, Democratic inroads into the Republican upper-class constituencies in 1968 and 1972 should indicate a significant political trend for the next decade.

Pollster Louis Harris documents what he perceives to be a growing "coalition for change," which he defines as "those under thirty years of age, those who call themselves independents rather than affiliated with either political party, persons who live in the suburbs, those who have had some college education, and persons in the $15,000-and-over bracket"—in other words, the groups which were the essential components of the New Politics constituency. Harris depicts this constituency as increasingly liberal on the issues. They "feel strongly about the quality of life, and want tougher

8. *The Emerging Republican Majority*, p. 465.

measures taken to curb air and water pollution." They helped pass referenda in 1972 on the environment, such as the anti-Olympics referendum which passed overwhelmingly in Colorado. They tended to favor "legalized abortions up to three months pregnancy, two in three are not upset by long hair, mod styles, and manners among young people." In short, says Harris, "a majority of these people are committed to change—concrete and pragmatic, not ideological, but real."

Not only were former Republican and independent voters from these upper-middle-class areas becoming more progressive, but their numbers seemed to be increasing relative to the constituency which Harris calls the "antichange coalition"—defined as older people, those with only eighth-grade educations, union members, small-town residents, and those who earn $5000 to $10,000 per year. This is the group, says Harris, which has been called "Middle America." Harris describes this group as opposed to busing, amnesty, and the legalization of marijuana, and tending to believe that law-enforcement authorities are too permissive. However, his description of this group as "antichange" on the basis of these kinds of "cultural" issues is misleading, for, as we have already seen, on a number of important economic and social issues, numerous surveys (including the Michigan CPS study) indicate this group favors change as much as Harris's prochange group.

But even accepting Harris's categories, the numbers appear to favor the "prochange" over the "antichange" group. In 1968, the so-called antichange group numbered approximately 55 per cent of the electorate, whereas the "prochange" group numbered 45 per cent. In 1972, the antichange group had dropped to 50 per cent, while the prochange group had increased to 50 per cent. By 1976, Harris predicts, the prochange group will grow to 55 per cent of the electorate.[9]

Numerous political analysts have commented on the significant rise in the number of "independents" over the decade of the sixties. Gallup reported immediately after the 1972 elections and *prior to* Watergate that voters who considered themselves "independent"

9. This and the above statistics and quotations are taken from the address by Louis Harris, previously cited in chapter 11, delivered on November 10, 1972, before the National Press Club in Washington, D.C.; see p. 10 of speech.

now constituted the largest alternative voter bloc next to the Democrats. The figures immediately after the 1972 elections showed the Democrats with 43 per cent, a figure which has remained constant since 1940 except for a brief upsurge due to the Johnson 1964 landslide; independents with 33 per cent; and the Republicans at 24 per cent.

This trend in favor of independents is not necessarily bad news for the Democrats. As mentioned earlier, the Democratic Party is perceived by most voters as the more liberal party. And the data indicate that independent voters have, on the whole, undergone the same kind of liberalizing trend on the issues as the rest of the population. The Michigan CPS study found that on a large number of issues, including the Vietnam war and urban unrest, independents exhibited a "relatively more rapid shift toward the left," compared to Democratic and Republican voters.[10]

The Youth Vote

The New Politics movement, through its early identification with young people and their importance in the political system, helped give the Democratic Party an early advantage in capturing the bulk of the youth vote. The youth vote as a whole—including non-college-student young people—was never as liberal and politically activist as some of us in the New Politics movement mistakenly presumed. In fact, President Nixon ended up winning a small majority of the overall youth vote (although McGovern won the college-student vote by a substantial margin).

But Nixon's small advantage over McGovern must be regarded as atypical. McGovern had led Nixon among young people by sizable margins prior to the Eagleton episode. After that incident —especially McGovern's promise of "1000 per cent" support and then his reversal—there was a dramatic shift away from McGovern among the young, even among some of his most stalwart supporters on the elite college campuses. Harris reports that "the net impact of the Eagleton episode was that [McGovern] lost his lead among young

10. CPS study, pp. 14 (table 1), 15.

people under thirty. For by two to one, the group on whom McGovern had staked so much felt he had taken an insensitive stand on a sensitive issue, besides behaving like a conventional politician." [11]

In any event, the registration statistics for the overall youth vote, on and off campus, cannot be comforting to the Republican Party. Gallup found that young people were opting for the Democratic over the Republican Party by almost a three-to-one margin, although the number of young people who choose to register as Independents is equal to the number who identify with the Democrats.[12] In places like Orange County, California, where total voter registration favors the Republicans by a comfortable margin, the sons and daughters of conservative Republican families were registering Democratic by a large margin. Moreover, on the issues, young people have been found to be more liberal than their parents. It might be recalled, for example, that young voters supported "improving the opportunities of minorities" more than older voters, and fewer young people were opposed to forced busing for racial integration than older voters.[13]

It is true that young voters historically turn out in low percentages relative to the rest of the population. In 1972, 59 per cent of the eighteen- to twenty-four-year-olds registered, and 83 per cent of these voted, as compared to a 72 per cent registration nationwide, with an 87 per cent turnout of registered voters.[14] However, another 16 million new voters will have become eligible to vote between 1972 and 1976 (added to the 25 million between eighteen and twenty-four in 1972), and another 18 million become eligible between 1976 and 1980—a youth population boom of unprecedented dimensions. Hence, even with a close split in favor of the Democratic candidate—say 53 to 47 per cent—the number of voters, even with a below-average turnout, is still large enough to give the Democratic candidate a vital—perhaps decisive—vote margin in a close election. (In fact, a number of studies indicate that had the eighteen-year-old

11. Harris, National Press Club speech, p. 6.

12. Gallup poll, May 1971: young people (eighteen to twenty-four) identified themselves as 16 per cent Republican, 42 per cent Democrat, 42 per cent independent. Subsequent youth-registration statistics reflect the same pattern.

13. See chapter 10.

14. Bureau of the Census, December 1972, Series P-20. No. 244.

vote existed in 1968, and had the youth vote, in a low turnout, split 55 to 45 per cent in favor of Humphrey over Nixon—what the polls in 1968 projected would have been the case—Humphrey would have been elected president.)

The Democratic Party's current advantage among young voters is largely attributable to at least two nonideological, non-issue-oriented factors. The first is the general perception that the Democrats are more concerned than the Republicans about youth participation in their party. And that perception is another important legacy of the New Politics movement. Just at the peak of the youth population boom, in the middle and late sixties, the New Politics movement politicized millions of young people around the issue they cared about most—the Vietnam War. Then, just at the time of the passage of the eighteen-year-old vote, the New Politics movement was giving the Democratic Party high visibility as being specially interested in the concerns of the young and their involvement in party affairs. The New Politics-inspired McGovern Commission guidelines, with its specific requirements of representation at the National Convention of young people in "reasonable proportion to their numbers in the population," was in stark contrast to the Republican Party, which refused to make a similar reform effort between 1968 and 1972. In fact, throughout 1971 and 1972, the Republican National Committee openly refused to cooperate with the Democrats in a common voter-registration drive among new voters—obviously understanding that any such efforts would result in the registration of one Republican new voter for every two Democratic voters.

The second nonideological factor actually offers the Republicans some hope for the future as well—and that is the importance of candidate charisma and personality in winning the youth vote. Once again, just at the time the youth population was growing increasingly aware of its own cultural and political role in American society, the Kennedys—especially President John Kennedy—gave the Democratic Party an image of youth and vigor, the "passing of the torch" to a new generation of political leadership. Senator Edward Kennedy continues to carry that political identity. He beats every political figure of either party, among college students and young workers alike, by huge margins; against most, by more than two to one. However, sensitivity of the young voter to personality and image factors can obviously cut both ways. If the Democrats nominated a nondescript liberal or a conservative whose style and approach to issues did not generate excitement among the young, the Republicans might have an opportunity to capture a majority of the youth vote with a candidate who had a more progressive and youth-oriented image.

Another legacy of the New Politics, harder to measure in the numerical terms of the youth vote but perhaps more significant in the long run, is the unprecedented use of young people at all levels of political campaigns. In the past, the power of the traditional urban machines had come from its ability to bring politics to the personal level of door-to-door canvassing and vote pulling on election day. As we have seen, the liberal student activists who worked for McCarthy and McGovern, while unrepresentative of the youth population as a whole, were able by virtue of their energy and organizing skills to exert an influence on the outcome of elections far disproportionate to their numbers.

This is not to say that effective youth activists are confined to liberal Democratic candidates. Some conservative politicians have attracted youth activists to their campaigns—notably, New York's Senator James Buckley. However, in terms of numbers, conservative student activists are *far* outnumbered by the liberals. Gallup reported in February 1972, for example, that self-identified liberal students outnumbered conservatives by a ratio greater than two to one; among registered voters, the ratio was almost three to one in favor of liberals.

Out of this evolution of the New Politics movement has arisen a new generation of political managers and strategists. Greg Craig, Tony Podesta, Eli Segal, Art Kaminsky, Rick Stearns, Gene Pokorny, and Joe Grandmaison are unknown to most of the general public. But these young veterans of the New Politics–reform movement of the past four or five years are likely to be running congressional, senatorial, gubernatorial, and presidential campaigns in the future. Some may be running for these offices themselves. Their expertise in grass-roots political organization—especially the ability to organize large numbers of young people previously uninvolved in political campaigns—will benefit Democratic Party candidates at all levels of government for years to come.

Building a New Coalition

The third premise underlying the theory that the old New Deal majority coalition is dead stresses the ideological and cultural inconsistencies within that old coalition. These intraparty divisions, the argument goes, are such that only one of two strategies is now available for the Democratic Party: write off the New Politics forces and return to the pre-1968 days when the party professional-Southern-organized labor axis ruled the party; or build a New Politics Democratic Party, a coalition of the top and the bottom, inviting the conservative South and the Archie Bunker vote in the North to join the Republican Party.

Anti-New Politics groups which arose in the Democratic Party in response to the 1972 McGovern drive for the nomination—groups such as the new postelection organization named the Coalition for a Democratic Majority, backed by some leaders of the AFL-CIO—will make a serious mistake if they try to write the forces of the New Politics out of the Democratic Party. One result of such an effort, if it succeeded, would surely be to halt—and perhaps reverse—significant Democratic inroads into the formerly Republican and ticket-splitting independent constituencies. Another would be to risk the alienation of the thousands of youth activists and voters who offer so much grass-roots organization and political power to the Democratic Party.

On the other hand, New Politics activists will make an even greater mistake if they accept the premises of the "conservative Republican majority" thesis and write off the South and the working class. Not only would such a strategy be pragmatically futile, since it would guarantee the Democratic Party a permanent minority status; it would also be contrary to the social goals for which New Politics liberals claim to be striving. In effect, it is a strategy for dividing working-class people along racial lines, and thus cannot possibly bring about fundamental and necessary changes, most of which have an economic basis. Battles against tax laws which favor the rich, against the corporate complex, and the power of money in politics and government cannot be won so long as low- and middle-income people are pitted against each other over symbolic cultural or racial issues. Such divisions would nullify efforts to combine forces in a coalition based on economic self-interest.

To win an enduring majority committed to real social and economic change, the Democratic Party must build a new political coalition, one which combines the components of the old New Deal labor-minorities-Southern alliance with the New Politics constituency of youth activists and upper-middle-class professionals.

Such a coalition obviously has some potential racial and cultural tensions. In the early sixties, the national Democratic Party's commitment to civil rights legislation for blacks caused tensions with the party's conservative Southern wing. In the mid- and late sixties, Lyndon Johnson tied the race problem to the problem of poverty and social oppression of blacks and other minorities, especially in the inner cities, and caused some alienation among formerly Democratic blue-collar workers, a deterioration hastened by the threat of suburb-to-inner-city forced busing.

The New Politics movement did little to bring these alienated Democrats back into the party. Many with close ties to organized labor and the party professionals grew to perceive the New Politics liberal activists as part of an exclusive culture, a set of values and social attitudes alien to their own. For many of these blue-collar Democrats, George McGovern's candidacy epitomized the worst of it: peace and protest, "radical chic" permissiveness and pot, lawlessness, drugs, and welfare.

Every coalition is composed of political groupings with divergent interests and perspectives. The question is, and always has been, a relative one: Are there common interests which override the differences? In fact, the projected "new Republican majority" coalition of Kevin Phillips and others contains far more fundamental internal inconsistencies than the new coalition of traditional Democrats and New Politics voters suggested here. The Phillips coalition is, after all, the joining of the working class with the corporate-managerial class. The only way to make that kind of merger stick is to so encourage blue-collar fear of minorities and cultural hostility to New Politics liberals as to outweigh the frequently divergent economic interests between workers and their employers.

The fact is, working-class whites and low-income blacks have much in common. Monsignor Gino Baroni, a specialist on blue-collar white ethnics, has pointed out that blacks and ethnics, living side by side in many cities, have "geography, income, the need for public services . . . [and] family and community priorities" in common. "Common problems," Monsignor Baroni said, are the "greatest equalizer."

During Al Lowenstein's 1972 campaign for the Democratic congressional nomination in Brooklyn's 14th Congressional District, I canvassed in the black neighborhoods in the Fort Greene section of Brooklyn, as well as the heavily Italian neighborhoods of Carroll Gardens. Working-class whites and blacks articulated nearly the same set of problems: crime; the failure of government to deliver public services adequately; inflation and jobs—in short, the very real day-to-day economic and social problems which people of low and middle incomes share.

As it happens, just at the time when the Democratic Party has made its greatest inroads into the formerly Republican and Independent upper-middle-class constituencies, the issues which most tended to alienate the blue-collar worker from the old Democratic coalition have become either obsolete or considerably less important. The Vietnam War, the chief cultural and generational polarizer within the Democratic Party in the late sixties, is over. The heavily publicized activities of the violent radicals and long-haired hippies, which the Republicans successfully identified at various times with the Democratic Party, have largely run their course. Even the issue of busing appears to have lost much of its steam, as the courts—and many liberals—have pulled back from always supporting busing as a means of correcting *de facto* racial imbalance in the schools.

With an emphasis on common class problems of low- and middle-income people, and with the additional political and financial support of the upper-middle-class professionals of the New Politics constituency, a majority coalition seems clearly to be available to the Democratic Party. The political center—defined not as a place where tough issues are avoided but where a majority of people can be convinced, on the basis of some common interests, to build a political coalition—is still viable. If anything, such a political center is ideologically to the left of where it was when John Kennedy ran in 1960. Furthermore, a study of the election results at the state and congressional level since 1968 indicates that the Democrats have already begun to create this new coalition.

In 1970 the Republicans pursued a strategy designed to exploit racial-cultural tensions within the Democratic coalition and thereby distract low- and middle-income voters from their growing disillusionment with the Nixon administration's probusiness economic policies, especially high interest rates and high unemployment. The strategy failed miserably. The Democrats won 54 per cent of the congressional vote and the components of the new Democratic coalition, with few exceptions, elected many liberal-populist governors, senators, and congressmen over conservative opponents in all parts of the country.

Political analysts, writing after the 1972 elections that the Democratic Party stood in unprecedented disarray,[15] paid too much attention to the results of the McGovern-Nixon contest. In fact, the 1972 elections below the presidential line showed a continuing coalescing of a new majority Democratic coalition. A significant number of liberal Democrats defeated conservative Republicans—for the Senate, the House, in the governors' mansions and in the state legislatures—despite one of the greatest presidential election landslides in American history. In fact, for the first time in American history, a political party that won 60 per cent of the presidential vote did not carry both houses of Congress.

In 1972, despite the Nixon landslide, the Democrats actually gained two Senate seats—increasing their majority from 55 to 45 to 57 to 43. Of the thirteen incumbents defeated for reelection in 1972, nine senators could be considered conservative, three, moderates, and one, liberal. Of their replacements, seven could be considered conservative, one moderate, and five liberal, a turnover which *Congressional Quarterly* described as an ideological shift making the Senate more liberal.[16]

While the Republicans in 1972 picked up twelve House seats, in

15. The University of Michigan study was titled, in part, *A Majority Party in Disarray.*
16. *Congressional Quarterly*, November 11, 1972, p. 2951.

large part due to reapportioned seats weighted in favor of the Republicans, the gain was considerably below expectations of most political observers and many Republican leaders. In fact, the new 1972 House, like the new Senate, was decidedly more reformist and liberal than in 1970 or 1968. The *New Republic*, for example, estimated that the reform forces had gained by 25 to 40 seats in the 1972 House. Black labor leader Bayard Rustin pointed out that of the 64 House members who consistently supported the positions endorsed by the Leadership Conference on Civil Rights, all but one were reelected. As in 1970, the Democrats in 1972 won a majority of the votes at the congressional level.

Likewise, the Republicans were not able to take advantage of the Nixon landslide at the state level. A majority of the nation's voters supported Democratic gubernatorial candidates over Republicans. The Democrats ended up with a net gain of one governor, bringing their total to 31, as opposed to 19 Republican governors. The Democrats even gained in a number of state legislatures, which, given the lack of name recognition of most candidates for the state legislature, one would have presumed to be more affected by a landslide victory at the top of the ticket. The 1972 election resulted in Republican control of both houses of the legislature in eighteen states—the same as before the voting. However, despite the Nixon landslide, the Democrats were in control of both houses in twenty-five states—a net gain of two. The Democrats controlled the governorship and both state houses in 17 states—the same as before the 1972 election. The Republicans, however, controlled all three in nine states—a net loss of one.[17] In an unprecedented display of ticket-splitting, voters were able to make a distinction between their votes for president and their votes for political candidates below the presidential level, even including local candidates for the state legislature.

Proponents of the "emerging Republican majority" theory try to explain away this vote-splitting pattern by arguing that the true ideology of the country was expressed in the results of the 1972 presidential race, and that the races at the congressional and state level were largely influenced by local issues and personalities. This

17. *Congressional Quarterly*, November 18, 1972, p. 3048.

argument is fallacious in a number of respects. For one thing, most of the contests for the U.S. Senate and the House were subject far more to national than to local issues. Furthermore, even in those gubernatorial contests where state and local issues were important, Democratic victories still indicated that a political base existed which might be successfully reached by the right kind of national candidate.

The election of liberal congressional and gubernatorial candidates across the country, some of them in previously Republican strongholds, was the accurate political expression of the majority of voters as reflected in the public opinion surveys outlined in Chapter Ten. Again it is clear that the massive rejection of George McGovern occurred, for the most part, *in spite of,* not because of, his liberal positions. A region-by-region analysis of the political situation in the various states will bear out the fact that, in the aftermath of the 1970 and 1972 elections, the Democratic Party appears to be on the threshold of an enduring new majority coalition, a merger of the traditional Democratic coalition with the forces of the New Politics.

New England (Maine, Vermont, New Hampshire, Massachusetts, Rhode Island, Connecticut)

The overall pattern *favors liberal Democrats.* Even traditionally Republican states—New Hampshire, Maine, and Vermont—contribute to the trend.

Massachusetts is a prototype of the new coalition of blue-collars, blacks, and New Politics activists of which the Democratic Party is capable across the rest of the nation. In Massachusetts, that coalition managed to muster one of the two nationwide majorities for George McGovern (the other being the District of Columbia). More than that, since 1968, Massachusetts has elected the most liberal congressional delegation and the most liberal state legislature in the nation.

In Rhode Island in 1972, former Navy Secretary John Chaffee, running on a "new Republican majority" platform, tried to identify his opponent, Senator Claiborne Pell, with all McGovern's liberal positions on social and economic issues. Pell accepted fully the identification, hammered away on those issues, and won. Likewise, a young liberal Democrat named Tom Salmon, running for governor against a popular and well-known Republican in heavily Republican and conservative Vermont, ran on an avowedly liberal-populist program, especially on pro-environmentalist positions, and won a startling upset victory, running almost twenty percentage points ahead of George McGovern.

Maine and New Hampshire were once considered relatively safe states for the Republicans. With Ed Muskie and former Representative William Hathaway in the U.S. Senate (Hathaway, a pronounced and outspoken liberal, easily defeated conservative Margaret Chase Smith in 1972 for the Senate), liberal Democrat Peter Kyros as one of the two congressmen, and a liberal, Democratic governor, Kenneth Curtis, Maine must now be considered, under most circumstances, a liberal Democratic state. New Hampshire, while still essentially Republican, nevertheless voted for moderate (and dovish) Democratic Senator Thomas McIntyre by a 58 per cent margin in 1972. Population growth in the southeastern part of the state, largely the New Politics-type middle- and upper-middle-class professionals, indicates that a liberal Democrat who can combine these voters with support from the large population of blue-collar voters in Manchester, Nashua and other cities could carry the state in future elections.

Connecticut used to be a solidly Democratic state, but the split within the Democratic Party in 1970—largely caused by Senator Thomas Dodd's independent candidacy—helped elect a conservative Republican governor, Thomas Meskill. But Meskill's conservatism has put him in political difficulty, and a number of liberal Democrats already are leading Meskill in the polls for reelection in 1974. Connecticut's Senator Abraham Ribicoff, also up for reelection in 1974, has shown the ability to win support from both traditional Democrats and New Politics liberals, and he should be in a good position to win reelection.

Middle Atlantic (New York, New Jersey, Pennsylvania, Maryland, West Virginia, Delaware)

The overall trend here is in favor of liberal Democrats, although continued division between New Politics liberals and working-class Democrats, especially in Pennsylvania and New York, threatens that trend.

Feuding within the Democratic Party resulted in the Republicans winning both Senate seats in Pennsylvania and New York, and the governorship in New York. In New York, however, if Democrats could unite around a liberal such as Off-Track Betting president Howard Samuels or Representative Ogden Reid, both of whom have appeal among blue-collar voters as well as upstate conservatives, Malcolm Wilson, a conservative Republican who succeeded Nelson Rockefeller at the end of 1973, could be beaten.

Democrats in both Pennsylvania and New York can learn from the experience of the New Jersey Democratic Party. Once again, the magic combination appears to be working-class ethnicity and committed liberalism. In Hudson County, that combination coalesced in 1971 to elect Paul Jordan, a vigorous reform mayor in Jersey City, overthrowing the corrupt John V. Kenney machine. Jordan, embarking on a widely acclaimed redevelopment project for the Jersey City Waterfront, combined his liberal-reform forces with the ethnic and black voting blocs to win reelection in 1972 by a landslide.

Statewide in New Jersey, an Irish-liberal Democrat named Brendan Byrne ran for the governorship in 1972 against a conservative Republican, Representative Charles Sandman. Sandman experienced the same kind of difficulties seen in the Duffey 1970 Connecticut senatorial campaign and the McGovern presidential campaign. He won his Republican nomination from a narrow, politically purist base—in his case, conservative Republicans who opposed the moderate Republicanism of the incumbent governor, William Cahill. Having gained the nomination in such a manner, however, Sandman could not unite his divided party. He could never escape the perception of most voters that he represented too narrow a political faction and too extreme a political viewpoint to hold statewide office. Meanwhile, Brendan Byrne, a former prosecutor, attacked Sandman for his conservative voting record and stressed his own liberal positions on the issues. With former RFK and Muskie aide Richard Leone running a professional campaign operation, Byrne put together a broad coalition which included blue-collar ethnics as well as the New Politics liberals, and defeated Sandman handily.

Although Maryland appears to be growing more conservative, Governor Marvin Mandel was elected in 1970 on a coalition of ethnics, blacks, and liberal suburbanites and a presidential candidate could potentially do the same thing. West Virginia remains an essentially Democratic state, despite Jay Rockefeller's loss to Governor Arch Moore in 1972 by a small margin.

Most dramatic in this region was Joseph Biden's 1972 victory in Delaware, a heavily Republican state, over the incumbent, J. Caleb Boggs, for the U.S. Senate. Biden ran a grass-roots campaign, drawing upon youth activists, suburban liberals, and working-class ethnic supporters from Wilmington and some rural Wallace-type voters in southern Delaware to eke out a 50.5 per cent victory—running more than eleven percentage points ahead of George McGovern. Once again the argument that national issues are separable in this kind of contest just doesn't hold water. Boggs attacked Biden's liberal positions on every national issue, Biden maintained his liberal positions unswervingly—and won.

Upper Midwest (Indiana, Ohio, Illinois, Michigan, Wisconsin, Minnesota)

The outlook here: with the exception of Indiana, more liberal Democratic than ever before.

Even Kevin Phillips admits that this region is the "mirror image" of what he perceives to be happening in the South: here, according to Phillips, in contrast with the South, Democrats appear to hold decisive political momentum. McGovern actually ran ahead of Hubert Humphrey in many areas of this Upper Midwest region—for example, in substantial parts of downstate Illinois, northern Ohio, central and southern Minnesota, and large portions of Wisconsin. Michael Barone, editor of the Almanac of American Politics, explains this "countercyclical McGovern trend" as follows: (1) The presence of the nation's second largest public higher-education system (next to California) in this area, with McGovern gaining substantial vote margins among college students and academic related voters; (2) the presence of relatively few military installations or large defense contractors; and (3) backlash among the relatively large numbers of moralistic Protestants of New England, German, and Scandinavian stock on the corruption issue (and, perhaps, exacerbated by Nixon's blatant efforts to win the Catholic vote).

Minnesota and Wisconsin already appear to have moved strongly in the direction of a liberal Democratic Party majority. In Minnesota, McGovern lost to Nixon by less than five percentage points; the Democrats won control of both houses of the (nominally non-partisan) state legislature; and Senator Walter Mondale, a widely respected liberal with presidential aspirations, was reelected by a landslide in 1972. In 1973, a thirty-three-year-old liberal Democrat, Al Hofstede, won an upset victory for mayor of Minneapolis over the incumbent, Charles Stenvig, a former cop who ran a tough law-and-order campaign.

In Wisconsin, David Obey won his congressional contest against a thirty-year GOP veteran, Alvin O'Konski, by a landslide margin—63 to 36 per cent (twenty points ahead of McGovern) in the largely rural, Republican Seventh Congressional District (northwestern Wisconsin). Senators William Proxmire and Gaylord Nelson and Governor Pat Lucey comprise one of the most liberal Democratic leadership in the Senate and the state house of any state in the country.

Adlai Stevenson 3d's 1970 election to the U.S. Senate in Illinois over a demagogic law-and-order campaign by Ralph Smith confirmed Illinois' basic liberalism (reflected also in the relatively liberal record of the Republican incumbent senator, Charles Percy). In 1972, Democrat Dan Walker won his campaign for governor on a populist platform and managed to build a coalition of anti-Daley New Politics liberal-reformers and downstate conservatives.

Governor John Gilligan of Ohio—like Ted Kennedy in Massachusetts and Brendan Byrne in New Jersey—possesses the rare ability to win support from both Archie Bunker ethnics and New Politics kids. His election in 1970 was one of the earliest indications that such a new Democratic coalition was possible. In 1972 Gilligan's progressive income tax was challenged by a conservative coalition of corporations, businessmen, and traditional antitax, anti-social service conservatives from southern and western Ohio. His 1970 campaign manager, Mark Shields (who had been a key political aide in the Muskie presidential campaign), advised Gilligan to portray the income tax in terms of a classic populist confrontation between the monied interests and lower- and middle-income people who would be most injured by a return to the regressive sales tax structure. The convincing victory of the pro-income tax forces in 1972—and, indeed, Gilligan's election in 1970—once again offers the lesson that a Democratic majority can be created out of an appeal to voters along class rather than racial or cultural lines.

Michigan offers an example of the dangers of a cultural/racial definition of issues for the Democratic Party. Senator Philip Hart's committed liberalism used to be fully representative of the sentiment of Michigan voters. But the busing issue—especially the Detroit District Court decision ordering white suburbanites to bus their kids into the inner city—has so alienated the heavy blue-collar population in Michigan that Hart, who refuses to oppose busing as a tool of integration, would have had a difficult time had he run in 1972. Senator Robert Griffin, who appeared to be in political trouble in early 1972, managed to defeat the Democratic state attorney general, Frank Kelley. Kelley's antibusing posture lost him support among liberals and blacks and was unable to stop the defection of blue-collar Democrats to Griffin, who had been a leader in the move to pass a constitutional amendment to bar busing.

Farm Belt/Midwest (North Dakota, South Dakota, Iowa, Nebraska, Kansas, Missouri)

This should be Republican country. Kevin Phillips wrote glowingly of the "new Republican majority in the Heartland." But traditional liberal Democrats have made significant breakthroughs even here in recent years.

Missouri, although still considered a border state, has two leading liberal Democratic senators—Stuart Symington and Thomas Eagleton—and nine Democratic congressmen, compared to only one Republican. South Dakota elected a liberal-moderate Democratic governor—Richard Kneip—in 1972, and an outspoken liberal Democratic Senator, James Abourezk—even while voting for Richard Nixon over its native son, George McGovern. In Iowa a young, liberal unknown, named Richard Clark, ran a vigorous populist Senate campaign, walking across the stage and pounding away at the tax-reform and corruption issues, never expecting to beat the incumbent, Jack Miller. To everyone's surprise Clark won by a solid margin.

Only in the Republican heartland of Nebraska and Kansas does the Nixonian conservative majority appear relatively solid, at least in the foreseeable future. However, in Nebraska, a moderate Democratic candidate for the Senate, Terry Carpenter, did manage to run eighteen percentage points ahead of McGovern and was barely defeated by the powerful incumbent, Senator Carl Curtis. In Kansas, Congressman William Roy, an energetic liberal Democrat, won by 61 per cent in the second congressional district, while Nixon carried the state with 68 per cent of the vote.

Rocky Mountains (Colorado, Nevada, Wyoming, Idaho, Montana, Utah)

Once again, this should be considered a stronghold of traditional Republicanism. In presidential voting, these states have given overwhelming support to the Republicans (with the exception of the 1964 election). However, there is evidence during recent years that this region too is undergoing a change in political character—from conservative Republican to moderate and, in some instances, liberal Democratic.

For example, Colorado's Gordon Allott was one of the most powerful conservative Republican leaders in the U.S. Senate. He was challenged in 1972 by an antiwar liberal and environmentalist named Floyd Haskell. Formerly a Republican, Haskell had switched parties after Nixon's 1970 invasion of Cambodia. It should have been no contest. But the issue of the funding of the Olympics, scheduled to be held in Colorado, came to highlight the special-interests-v.-

public-interest theme on which so many liberal Democrats had concentrated all over the country. A powerful coalition of New Politics upper-middle-class voters in and around Denver, heavy student voting in the universities, and good support from blue-collar voters managed to put Haskell over by a small margin—despite a 64 to 34 per cent Nixon-McGovern margin in the presidential contest.

Utah reelected moderate-liberal Democratic Governor Calvin Rampton, who had supported Muskie at an early point in his presidential campaign, by a 69 to 31 per cent margin, despite Nixon's 68 to 26 per cent win over McGovern in the state. Moreover, a young liberal and former aide to Senator Edward Kennedy, Wayne Owens, defeated a powerful and well-known Republican congressman, Sherman Lloyd, by a 55 to 45 per cent margin. Even in presumably conservative Republican Wyoming, while Nixon was beating McGovern by a 69 to 30 per cent margin, and Republican Senator Clifford Hansen was winning reelection with a 71 per cent vote total, liberal Democratic congressman Teno Roncalio, ran a grass-roots campaign for the lone statewide House seat and was reelected by a 52 to 48 per cent margin.

Idaho and Montana are also generally thought of as conservative Republican states in presidential voting. Nevertheless, Idaho's Senator Frank Church and Governor Cecil Andrus are both liberals who supported Senator Muskie in 1972. Both have clearly succeeded in putting together a majority coalition based on liberal principles. In Montana, outspoken liberal and antiwar Senator Lee Metcalf survived a 58 to 38 per cent Nixon landslide, as did the successful Democratic gubernatorial candidate, Thomas Judge. With a state leadership of Senators Metcalf and Majority Leader Mike Mansfield, Governor Judge and one out of two congressmen, Montana must now be considered as a state with a formidable progressive Democratic voter base.

West (California, Oregon, Washington, Alaska, Hawaii)

Kevin Phillips described the Pacific states in general, and California in particular, as a key component of his "new American majority" thesis. "No other region is so good a mirror of American political trends as the Pacific [area]," he wrote, especially "behemoth California, [which] is virtually a national sociopolitical microcosm." Phillips confidently predicted (in 1969) that "the forces which elected Ronald Reagan, [Senator] George Murphy and Richard Nixon appear to represent the political future of the most populous state in the Union." [18]

Notwithstanding Phillips' prediction, California has been undergoing a leftward trend since 1968, beginning with the election of liberal Alan Cranston to the Senate. In 1970 Jess Unruh's underfinanced populist-oriented campaign jolted Ronald Reagan, bringing Unruh within a few percentage points of victory. In 1970 incumbent Senator George Murphy and the Nixon "new Republican majority" strategists waged a harsh conservative v. liberal campaign against John Tunney, pounding away on law and order and antipoor, antisocial programs rhetoric.

A committed liberal with an excellent voting record while a member of the House, John Tunney had run in a hard-fought primary for the Democratic nomination against Representative George Brown, who, portraying himself as more to the left than Tunney, sought and won the solid backing of the California New Politics constituency.

When Tunney won the primary, he was perceived by the public as a liberal whose political sensitivity extended beyond the New Politics. In the general election, Tunney, remaining firmly committed to liberal social programs and opposition to the Vietnam War, put together the new Democratic coalition of New Politics liberals, minorities, blue-collar workers and middle-income families, and soundly defeated George Murphy. California Democrats in 1970 also increased their margin in the lower house of the California legislature by almost two to one.

Most recently, Los Angeles elected former city councilman Thomas Bradley as its first black mayor, leading former Sam Yorty to remark, "We're in the middle of a major shift to the left here in California."

Oregon's voting in 1972 was another example of a countercyclical trend in the McGovern-Nixon contest; for, as Michael

18. Phillips, op. cit., p. 412.

Barone points out, McGovern actually ran ahead of Humphrey's 1968 vote in many parts of the state. Oregon Democrats also captured control of both chambers of the state legislature. Washington state remains solidly Democratic. Despite Nixon's 56 to 39 per cent margin, all seven Democratic congressional candidates won. Alaska remains divided. It will be interesting to see whether Senator Mike Gravel experiences any difficulties in getting reelected since, after his election in 1968 as a moderate Democrat, he has become increasingly liberal during his first term in the Senate.

Southwest (Oklahoma, New Mexico, Arizona)

This region is still solidly Republican, voting heavily for Nixon in 1972—61 per cent in New Mexico, 65 per cent in Arizona, and 74 per cent in Oklahoma. Republicans appear to be in a strong position at the congressional and state level, with Dewey Bartlett's and Pete Domenici's Senate victories in Oklahoma and New Mexico, respectively, in 1972.

Despite this Republican strength, however, there is evidence of the kind of coalition Democrats could put together for a presidential campaign. In Oklahoma a young moderate Democrat and former protégé of Lyndon Johnson, James Jones, surprised the experts and bucked the Nixon landslide with a 56 to 44 per cent upset victory in the First Congressional District. In fact, five out of six congressmen in Oklahoma are Democratic.

In Arizona, liberal Congressman Morris Udall won reelection by a 64 to 36 per cent vote, despite Nixon's 65 to 32 per cent statewide winning margin. While Arizona remains predominantly Republican (two senators, the governor, and both houses of the state legislature), there is a potential liberal-moderate coalition which could unite in support of someone like Udall in a statewide contest. New Mexico, while still essentially a Republican state, reelected liberal Senator Joseph Montoya in 1970, despite the Nixon-Agnew law-and-order campaign to defeat him.

South (Virginia, North Carolina, South Carolina,
Georgia, Florida, Mississippi, Alabama, Louisiana,
Texas, Arkansas, Kentucky, Tennessee)

In the aftermath of the 1968 and 1972 presidential campaigns, there seems to be near-unanimity among political commentators, liberals, and conservatives that a Democratic presidential candidate who is committed to traditional liberal programs can just about write off the South. "A liberal's mere nomination," wrote Joseph Alsop shortly after the 1972 elections, "will automatically concede the whole South—or more than half of the electoral votes needed to win—to the man the Republicans nominate." The fact is, without an alleged Republican trend in the South, the entire Kevin Phillips thesis of an "emerging Republican majority" falls apart.

The central catalyst in this alleged turnabout in the South from the Democrats to the Republicans is the race issue. The old Democratic coalition, wrote Phillips, was unable to hold the conservative South while trying to placate the "Negro socioeconomic revolution." The 1968 election was an "historic first"—"the Negrophobe Deep South and the modern Outer South simultaneously abandoned the Democratic Party." This view is also generally accepted by liberal writer and former Kennedy-McGovern adviser Frederick Dutton. ". . . [M]ore than a century after the Civil War and over fifteen years after the start of an unparalleled if uneven exertion on behalf of equal rights, the racial prospect is still grim," Dutton wrote in Changing Sources of Power. Hence, he argues, the Democrats must concentrate on building a "more liberal Democratic Party" in the South and, in the interim, accept minority status there.[19]

I agree with Phillips and Dutton that the South is in a state of transition. But I disagree that the transition is from an antiblack, conservative Democratic South to an antiblack, conservative Republican South. Rather, substantial evidence indicates that the transition is actually away from the race issue and toward economic

19. Dutton, Changing Sources of Power, pp. 77, 93.

issues, a transition that favors the creation of a progressive Democratic Party majority through much of the South.

The primacy of the economic issue in the new South is not surprising in light of the continuing economic backwardness of the region relative to the rest of the country. For example, a 1972 Census Bureau survey indicated that the South is far behind other regions in median family income—with an $8079 median family income, compared to the West's $10,228, North Central's $10,115, and the Northeast's $10,454. None of the top six median family income states are from the South; five out of the bottom six are. Of the nine communities in the country with a median family income below poverty level for more than 20 per cent of their families, eight out of nine were located in the Southern states.[20]

The evidence is considerable that Southern voters are far more interested in candidates who are willing to attack the roots of the South's economic problems than in those who exploit the race question. Numerous opinion surveys show considerable support in the South for traditional liberal government programs to help solve basic economic and racial problems.[21]

Stephen Skardon, a young Southern political activist and writer, in an unpublished manuscript on the "new South," [22] quoted Senator Ernest Hollings of South Carolina on the South's new concern for nonracial, bread-and-butter issues. "Our concerns in the South are now the enduring ones," Senator Hollings said a few years ago, "such as jobs, national security, a healthy environment, educating the young. . . . Any candidate for high office who fails to address himself to these real issues, and who goes off instead on a tangent of nonproblems and image-building, might just as well write off the South. . . ."

Notwithstanding the poor showing of the Democrats in the 1968 and 1972 presidential elections in the South, there are still a number of hopeful signs there for the Democratic Party. One is the potential

20. *Congressional Quarterly*, November 25, 1972, pp. 3068–69.

21. Polls indicate, it will be recalled, that there is a substantial majority constituency, in the South as well as the rest of the country, in favor of increased government spending on basic social problems, such as education, health, jobs, and mass transit. On race, more than three out of five Southern voters said they would be more likely to vote for a candidate who favors "improving the opportunities of minorities."

22. I am indebted to Mr. Skardon for his thoughtful and detailed analysis of the "new South" and its implications for the Democratic Party in the future. The untitled manuscript was drafted in June 1973.

of the Southern black vote. In 1968 and 1972, the black vote made up only 20 to 25 per cent of the Southern electorate, well below the levels which could be reached if larger percentages of Southern blacks registered and voted.

In addition, while it is true that there has been a significant decline in Democratic registration over two decades in the South—from 74 per cent Democratic in 1948, to 55 per cent in 1960, to 43 per cent in 1972—there has *not* been a commensurate rise in Republican registration over the same period of time. In 1944 21 per cent of the South was registered Republican; in 1968, the figure was 27 per cent; and in 1968—the year Kevin Phillips described as an historic watershed for a new Southern Republican majority—the Republican registration figure had dropped back to where it had been in 1944—about 22 per cent. During this same period there has been a trend in favor of independent voters—from 8 per cent in 1944 to 18 per cent in 1960 to 35 per cent in 1968. This independent vote contributed substantially to George Wallace's vote totals in 1968, when he won nearly 40 per cent of the vote in many areas of the South.

It should be obvious that those who would urge the Democratic Party to ignore this constituency in the South are endorsing a strategy of default to the Republican Party. Even assuming that Hubert Humphrey's 30 per cent vote in the South in 1968 could be increased by higher percentages of black registration and voter turnout, such a course would offer little hope to the Democratic Party. The key to building an enduring majority coalition in the South—for either the Democrats or the Republicans—is to win the allegiance of the crucial Southern independent voter in general and, in particular, to cut into the Wallace constituency of white, low-income, largely rural voters. The only way a liberal Democratic presidential candidate can combine the traditional Democratic vote in the South with the Wallace vote is to emphasize economic problems shared by minorities and white low- and middle-income voters in the cities and rural areas.

In fact, this economic-class-oriented Democratic coalition, supported by upper-middle-class liberals, has to a great extent already emerged in the South during the past two or three years. This type of coalition is not new in the South. In fact, the early Populist movement in the 1880s had an extensive base in the rural, low-income agrarian areas, although most of the Southern Populist leaders were outspoken racists. In the 1950s Estes Kefauver of Tennessee won support from both low-income whites and blacks during his years in the Senate, although Kefauver's record in the Senate on civil rights was ambiguous at best.

Perhaps the most important turning point in the transition of the South toward nonracial politics occurred in 1960 in the Terry Sanford gubernatorial campaign in North Carolina. Sanford, a soft-spoken lawyer and a shrewd politician, defeated a racist Republican opponent on the strength of significant support from the predominantly white, rural, lower-income eastern regions of North Carolina which would later constitute the prototype of the George Wallace Southern constituency.

Sanford had been closely identified with the liberal-pro-civil rights wing of the North Carolina Democratic Party. The Republicans assumed they could defeat him easily by exploiting the race issue. Sanford held to his pro–civil rights positions, while running hard on issues which he believed united the lower-income blacks and whites, especially the crisis in North Carolina's public school system. His victory was one of the earliest signals of a new, nonracial phase in the political history of the South. Sanford, currently president of Duke University, ran for the presidency in 1972 and came close to beating Wallace in the North Carolina primary. In fact, Sanford's brand of Southern progressivism could be an asset to a national Democratic ticket in 1976.

Another significant indication that the old racially preoccupied South was changing occurred in South Carolina in 1968 with the election of Ernest Hollings to the Senate. During his Senate campaign, and thereafter in the Senate, Hollings had expressed opposition to the Vietnam War and supported cutbacks in U.S. troop levels in Western Europe. He went on to become one of the leading spokesmen in the Senate on the problem of hunger and malnutrition among the rural poor.

In his successful 1968 race for the Senate, despite his moderate-to-liberal posture on most issues, Hollings ran strongly in the pro-Wallace areas of South Carolina, as well as the black and liberal-moderate voter areas. For example, in Anderson County, almost half of which is composed of blue-collar voters, Wallace won 53.2 per cent of the vote—and Hollings won 66 per cent. In the rural areas of South Carolina, Wallace won 41 per cent and Hollings won 63 per cent of the vote. Yet, among black voters, while Humphrey won 74 per cent, Hollings was able to win 84 per cent.

The results of the 1970 elections in the South made it clear that the Sanford-Hollings brand of Democratic leadership, which emphasized economic and social issues as well as a commitment to racial moderation, represented the true wave of the future in the South—one which could combine the Wallace and traditional Democratic vote of blacks and urban moderates into a formidable majority coalition.

In South Carolina John West, a moderate who promised to appoint blacks in his administration (and kept his promise) was elected governor with the same type of support from Wallace blue-collar voters and blacks which had elected Governor Sanford in 1960 and Senator Hollings in 1968. Similarly, in Florida, a young state legislator named Reubin Askew was elected governor on a platform attacking corporate interests and supporting full integration, including the possibility of busing. In the Florida Senate race, a young moderate named Lawton Chiles, underfinanced and un-known, spoke out against wealth and corporate power and, once again, united blacks, liberals, and Wallace voters into a winning combination. In heavily proWallace Holmes County, in the northwestern panhandle—a county on which Kevin Phillips focused to show a Republican trend in the South—Chiles won 77 per cent of the vote over his Republican opponent, Representative William Cramer.

The pattern was repeated in Georgia, with the election as governor of Jimmy Carter, a racial and political moderate. In Arkansas, another young progressive Democrat, Dale Bumpers, was elected governor in 1970, and reelected in 1972 by a 70 per cent majority of traditional Democrats and white, rural voters who had supported Wallace. Even in Texas, where conservative Lloyd Bent-sen had defeated the champion of the liberals, Senator Ralph Yar-borough, in a bitter primary, Bentsen was able to win back some liberal and black support and defeat Republican George Bush for the Texas Senate seat in a surprise upset. (Since his election, Senator

Bentsen has compiled a respectable liberal-moderate voting record and now even expresses presidential aspirations.)

In 1972, another populist-style moderate Democrat, Walter Huddleston, won the Senate seat in Kentucky, running seventeen percentage points ahead of George McGovern, adding Kentucky—already led by progressive Democratic Governor Wendell Ford, an early Muskie supporter in 1972—to the list of Southern states in which a coalition of moderate Democrats, Wallace voters, and blacks seemed to be in control. And in Atlanta, Georgia, an articulate black civil rights leader, Andrew Young, formerly a close associate of Dr. Martin Luther King, won his congressional race with the support of suburban whites as well as a large turnout of black voters. The same moderate white-black vote elected Maynard Jackson in 1973 as Atlanta's first black mayor.

After the dust had settled in 1972, the Democrats still held nine governorships in the South compared to three by the Republicans; Democratic congressmen outnumbered Republicans by three to one; and out of twenty-four upper and lower houses of the state legislatures in twelve Southern states, *not one* was controlled by the Republicans. In other words, at the local grass-roots level—where political power ultimately rests—the Democratic Party still appears to be firmly entrenched through most of the South (with Tennessee and Virginia as the two major exceptions).

Even in a seemingly conservative Republican bastion like Virginia, a self-styled populist, Henry Howell, running as an independent, managed to come within a single percentage point of defeating former Democrat Mills Godwin in the 1973 gubernatorial campaign. Howell drew strong support from rural low-income whites in Southwestern Virginia who voted heavily for George Wallace in 1968. Stressing economic issues and attacking corporate and other special interests, Howell showed that these Southern Wallace voters can be attracted into a coalition that also includes blacks and liberal whites.

Over and over, the key ingredient to Democratic success in statewide and congressional elections in the South has been a progressive, economic-populist program that appeals to low-income voters, black and white alike, and to middle-income voters who are more interested in candidates committed to solving basic Southern economic and social problems than in exploiting racial tension.

It should be added that in the South, as elsewhere, voter perception of a candidate's personal qualities can often be more important than the substance of his speeches and position papers. If a candidate is perceived as a "Northern liberal" who is telling the South how racist or how backward it is—precisely the perception many Southern voters had of George McGovern in 1972—the substance of his program will be utterly irrelevant.

Senator Lawton Chiles proved graphically that among low-income and rural whites—the heart of George Wallace's voter base—style is often substance. Chiles' walk across Florida in his 1970 campaign was not perceived by these voters as merely a publicity stunt. They saw Chiles as someone who, like them, was alienated by the upper-class-establishment-run politics of Florida and by government which seemed indifferent to the concerns of ordinary people.

As important as this alienation factor is among many voters, Democrats cannot assume it will be sufficient as a means of building a new majority coalition, either in the South or any other region of the country. Some coalitions built on essentially negative sentiments can hold together temporarily. But the social costs are great, as the Republicans should have learned in the 1970 congressional campaigns. And, inevitably, most people will turn away from purely negative appeals and seek leadership they sense is honestly trying to deal with their problems. The emphasis must remain on positive programs which deal with economic problems affecting middle-income as well as low-income people.

The Democratic Party appears on the threshold of creating an enduring new coalition, which can combine the New Politics constituency with the traditional groups of the old Roosevelt coalition. The liberalizing trend on the major economic and social issues among a cross section of the population, the increased receptivity of working-class people to economic populism, the substantial inroads into upper-middle-class independent and Republican neighborhoods resulting from the New Politics antiwar and reform efforts—all these factors combined to give the Democratic Party significant successes in the House, Senate and gubernatorial races from 1968 to 1973 in all regions of the country.

A final question remains: If a new Democratic majority coalition has already emerged at the state and congressional level, what changes must occur within the national Democratic Party to help translate that majority into winning the presidency in 1976 and thereafter?

thirteen

SYSTEMS AND ATTITUDES

"Obviously the Democrats could rebuild a formidable coalition
for a presidential contest if they didn't make the kinds of mistakes
they've made the past few years. But I think I can depend on
people like you in the Democratic Party to prevent any significant changes from occurring."

—Kevin Phillips, author of *The Emerging
Republican Majority*, speaking to the Democratic Forum, a group of former campaign
workers from the Muskie, Humphrey, Jackson,
and McGovern campaigns, May 1973

SOMETHING HAPPENED to the Democratic Party on the national level
in 1972 that didn't happen to it on the state or congressional level. Or
some things.

There are those who like to simplify it all by blaming George
McGovern personally. Where the Democrats ran good candidates,
the argument goes, they won; where they ran bad candidates, they
lost. The logic seems plain enough. But, in fact, the problems which
produced Richard Nixon's landslide go far beyond George
McGovern's personal and political shortcomings.

To build a national majority coalition and recapture the White
House 1976, Democrats are going to have to do more than find a
better candidate than George McGovern. The nominating system
used in 1972 and before needed changing. And, more importantly,
many Democrats need to reassess some personal attitudes and
customary modes of political conduct.

That sounds like a formidable assignment. But the signs

are—from all parts of the spectrum in the Democratic Party, from all parts of the country—that many of the necessary changes have already occurred.

Reforming the Reforms

To begin with, the Democrats have already corrected the most important defect in the 1972 nominating system—the winner-take-all primary. By resolution the 1972 Democratic National Convention required that all state delegations to the 1976 convention be proportionalized—that is, that their votes for particular candidates be so allocated as to reflect the proportional votes the candidates received in the primary, caucuses, or state convention. In October 1973, the party's Commission on Delegate Selection and Party Structure, the successor to the McGovern-Fraser Commission, chaired by Barbara Mikulski, a Baltimore city councilwoman, abolished winner-take-all and imposed proportional representation at all levels of the delegate-selection process. The only major loophole remains those states, such as Wisconsin and Florida, which elect delegates by congressional district in an open primary. The winner in the congressional district wins all the delegates allocated to that district, even with a minority vote. Thus, statewide, he could win most or all of the delegates with a minority vote in a multi-candidate contest—essentially what George McGovern did in Wisconsin in 1972.

In the aftermath of the November elections, most of the controversy on the McGovern Commission reforms had centered on the guidelines requiring all state delegates to have numbers of young people, minorities and women "in reasonable relationship" to their numbers in the population. In practice this often amounted to a numerical quota system.

The party professional–organized labor axis within the Democratic Party denounced the "reasonable relationship" requirement as responsible for the lack of party professionals and labor leaders at the 1972 convention, and claimed that the nationally televised portrait of a Democratic convention filled with too many "unrepresentative" young people, minorities, and female activists hurt the party among the general public.

However, these labor leaders and party professionals were not represented at the convention, because they either backed the wrong man or refused to back anyone not because of the quota system. As far as "quotas" allegedly giving the advantage to the left wing of the Democratic Party, it must be remembered that George Wallace had no trouble meeting his "numerical goals" of blacks on his delegation in Florida. Senator Henry Jackson met his for young people on his Washington delegation. Moreover, it is simply a myth that the democratized 1972 Democratic Convention projected a negative political image in the country. For example, Lou Harris reported that 70 to 80 per cent of the public liked the sight of more young people, minorities and women being represented at a national convention and, by a 72 to 19 per cent margin, the public agreed that the Democratic Convention was more open than any before.[1]

Another theory floated by critics of the McGovern Commission reforms is that they had given the Democratic Party an excessive dose of democracy, permitting political activists to pack precinct caucuses and turn out in sufficient numbers to win state primaries for George McGovern. This too is absurd. While it is true that in some instances local caucuses were "packed" with student activists who managed to carry the vote for George McGovern, it is also true, as McGovern's political organizer Rick Stearns points out, that any candidate—especially one supported by organized labor—could have taken advantage of the caucus system with the right kind of advance preparation. Stearns doesn't see much difference between what he did for McGovern and what Mayor Daley does with his well-run organization on primary day. "Somehow 'stacking' a voting booth is good citizenship," says Stearns, "but encouraging a candidate's supporters to attend a caucus, which for half of the country is the only opportunity the ordinary party member is given to express a preference among the nominees, is 'stacking.' We did nothing more than the regular party has traditionally done."

There is some irony in the fact that both the reformers and the regulars accuse each other of representing political elites. Both sides represent elites: that is the basic reality of American politics which, self-delusion and hucksterism aside, ought to be recognized by

1. Address by Louis Harris, National Press Club, November 10, 1972.

reformers and regulars alike. The reformers may have a point when they say that they have been less prone to operating out of smoke-filled rooms; but, as the McGovern campaign showed, there was plenty of closed slate making in smoke-filled rooms by the new politicians in 1972. And the regulars have a point when they say the McGovernites overlooked and didn't represent the views of the average man on the street. Nonetheless, as Rick Stearns points out, "Political parties are governed in America (and elsewhere) by elites." The reformers are proud of their success in increasing the number of open primaries for delegate selection but, as Stearns says, "Even the presidential primaries, as welcome a popular device as they are, seldom attract as a whole more than a third of the party electorate. In the convention states, where the inconveniences of participation are greater, the participation rates are even lower."

Both sides must seek to facilitate *access* to the political process. The McGovern Commission reforms achieved this goal to a dramatic degree. The Mikulski Commission reaffirmed, without major controversy, all the 1972 rules regarding openness and democracy in party affairs. But it is unrealistic to use the rhetoric of "representativeness" (by the regulars) or "participatory democracy" (by the reformers) when discussing the workings of the political process. Concludes Stearns: "Short of forcing the voter to participate in a party, the best that any set of reforms can hope to do is to remove the barriers which the motivated party member has often found facing him. . . . Elites cannot be dismantled and at the same time parties preserved, but the competition among elites can be made fluid, their displacement can be made easier, and the devices which entrench them can be stripped away."

The problem with the 1972 system was not that it encouraged activists to participate but rather, as a result of the winner-take-all provisions of state primary laws, that the political consequences of their participation were disproportionate to their actual numbers within the Democratic Party. Surely this is obvious from the results of the Wisconsin primary—the most important primary and the turning point in McGovern's drive for the nomination. The political activists whom the party regulars seem to fear so much did turn out in large numbers for George McGovern in Wisconsin, but they could not muster more than 30 per cent of the statewide vote—or, more accurately, about 20 per cent of the Democratic vote (not counting

Republican crossovers). But the winner-take-all system in Wisconsin permitted George McGovern to win 100 per cent of the delegates in five of seven congressional districts, even though he won no more than about a third of the total vote in any one of them. The Mikulski Commission unfortunately permitted a continuation of the Wisconsin-type system of winner-take-all within a congressional district. Likewise, the winner-take-all system gave McGovern 100 per cent of the California delegation with only 45 per cent of the statewide vote in the primary.

As the Democrats learned in 1972, in a multicandidate primary, the winner-take-all system offers the greatest advantage to a candidate with a narrow but well-organized political base—who will probably be a weak candidate in the general election; and the greatest disadvantage to a candidate who has the broadest appeal among all segments of the party—probably a strong general-election candidate.

Clearly a political party interested in winning general elections cannot afford a system which too often results in killing off its best general-election candidates. Fortunately for the Democrats, the proportional system adopted at the 1972 Convention and by the Mikulski Commission should under most circumstances operate to the advantage of the candidate who has the broadest appeal in the party.

Replaying the 1972 Democratic race for the nomination under a proportional system, it is very difficult to calculate exactly how many delegates George McGovern would have had, since many of the state nominating systems used in 1972 are not easily converted into proportionalized voting. But one thing seems certain: George McGovern would not have had a majority of the delegates on the first ballot. Let us assume that McGovern would have had 35 or 40 per cent of the first-ballot votes—a relatively optimistic estimate—at the 1972 convention under a proportional system. Humphrey probably would have been second with, say, 25 per cent; Muskie and Wallace tied for third with 10 to 15 per cent; Jackson with 5 to 10 per cent. Assuming that McGovern's hypothetical 35 or 40 per cent total represented a ceiling of his political support—there is strong evidence that that would have been the case—then on the second ballot, Humphrey would probably have picked up delegates from

Jackson and Wallace (and maybe a few Muskie) delegates. If Humphrey reached as much as 30 or 35 per cent on the second ballot, many McGovern delegates at the same time would probably have begun to switch to Muskie as a better alternative than Humphrey. A strong argument could have been made to many of Humphrey's delegates that Muskie was surely more acceptable than McGovern and that he was in a much better position to restore party unity and to keep the New Politics liberals from bolting the party or sitting on their hands—both of which seemed to be an inevitable consequence of a Humphrey or Jackson nomination. It is likely that by the third or fourth ballot, there would have been enough slippage to Muskie from both Humphrey and McGovern delegates to have put him over.

Obviously this scenario of a Muskie nomination resulting from a deadlocked convention in 1972 (which, in turn, resulted from a proportional-voting system) may be viewed with skepticism from a number of standpoints. For example, a persuasive case can be made that in the event of such a deadlock, it would have been far more likely that the convention would have turned to some dark horse—such as Senator Harold Hughes of Iowa, Senator Walter Mondale of Minnesota, or Governor Reubin Askew of Florida—rather than a Humphrey or a Muskie, both of whom had had their public images seriously damaged by their primary campaigns.

What is important to note here, however, is that a proportional system in 1972 would have resulted in a *brokered* national convention, that is, a divided convention which would have been forced to work out a political accommodation before disbanding. Such a result would have been in the interests not just of the Democratic Party, which under such circumstances would probably have nominated someone who had the widest support among all segments of the party, but of the nation as well. This brokerage process is the essence of making a political coalition. It forces the interest groups who comprise a national party convention to put their immediate goals in perspective, to distinguish between what is desirable and what is possible, to consider larger shared interests over narrow differences, and to reflect on what kind of person would make the best candidate for president.

Even were the Congress to pass a national primary bill—which I strongly favor, assuming that provisions can be made for guaranteed access to the mass media by all serious candidates and spending and campaign-time limitations can be effectively imposed—the role of the national convention can still be maintained. Under a plan proposed by former ambassador and newspaper publisher, James Loeb, if no candidate received 40 per cent of the vote in a national primary, instead of a runoff, all candidates would receive delegate votes proportional to their vote percentages in the various states, and the delegates would then meet in a national convention (with delegates released from their candidate commitments after the first ballot).

The importance of maintaining the national convention in the nominating system relates to the larger issue of the role of the political party in American politics, one which, at this stage of American political history, has great relevance to the Republican as well as the Democratic Party.

With the trend toward direct primaries and the importance of broadcast media in political campaigns, the professional party apparatus in both major parties has played a diminishing role in presidential campaigns. While many of us who were active in the reform movement within the Democratic Party have liked to disparage the "hacks" who keep the party organization going, it has become increasingly apparent to reformers and regulars alike that the political party is a crucial institution which must not be allowed to deteriorate. A political party is the chief locus of coalition building. As such, it is the place not only where candidates are nominated but where issues can be debated, power distributed among factions and geographic regions, and accommodations reached.

Both the Johnson and the Nixon presidencies should have taught the lesson of the importance of maintaining a party organization strong enough to be independent of an incumbent president of the same party or at least efficient enough to make it desirable for an incumbent president to want to utilize its resources rather than ignore it.[2]

If it is important to strengthen the institution of the political party in the political process, then it should be desirable to increase

2. In this as in many other areas in this chapter, I am indebted to David Broder's influential and prescient analysis of party politics in America, *The Party's Over.*

the role of the party organization in selecting delegates to the national convention. For this reason, the Mikulski Commission decided to increase the allowable percentage of at-large delegates who can be selected by a state party committee from the 10 per cent permitted by the McGovern Commission guidelines to 25 per cent. The Mikulski Commission required that the state committees must be democratically constituted, consistent with the reform guidelines. Moreover, the at-large delegates would be required to cast their votes along proportional lines. This proportionalized at-large system is far preferable to one which would guarantee places on state delegations *ex officio* to uncommitted elected officials who, as a group, could wield a disproportionate amount of power in a divided convention.

While Republicans, in the aftermath of the Nixon presidential campaign and the Watergate affair, have come to realize the importance of a strong national party organization, the Democrats are one step ahead on this issue, as on the party-reform issue.[3] The 1972 Democratic Convention provided for the appointment of a national commission to write a "charter" for the Democratic Party.[4] The Charter Commission, chaired by Terry Sanford of North Carolina and composed of more than 150 Democrats from across the country, has proposed a charter aimed at strengthening the national Democratic Party organization. The commission's proposed charter broadens and strengthens the authority of the Democratic National Committee, provides for a professional, ongoing national staff, improves grassroots participation in party affairs and provides for a national conference to be held between presidential elections. Such an interim conference would give the national Democratic Party a focus for discussion of issues and organization activity in a setting independent of presidential campaign pressures.

No party organization can remain strong unless it gives itself a future. In politics a future means new adherents, a broadened political base. Because the New Politics movement has given the

3. The Republicans have established their own "reform" commission to report prior to the 1976 convention, though its mandate is far more limited than its Democratic counterpart.

4. The Democratic Party has never had a formally written charter or constitution. Rather, it was governed by the quadrennial Democratic Convention, which set rules and granted authority for the conduct of party affairs between conventions.

Democratic Party inroads into the growth sector of the population, it is important that anti-McGovern Democrats resist the temptation to undo the gains achieved in 1972 in opening up the party to grass-roots participation by young people, minorities, and women.

However, one can protect those gains and still correct some of the defects of the reforms. For example, the McGovern Commission clearly neglected to correct past underrepresentation at national conventions of working-class people, many of whom were members of ethnic groups, especially Polish, Irish, and Italian voters, who made up large segments of the Democratic electorate. Many of these ethnic blue-collar Democrats cannot afford to attend a national convention. A rule was established by the 1972 Democratic Convention providing for a special fund which would be available to help pay the expenses of these and other lower-income delegates.

There was nearly unanimous agreement between reformers and regulars on the Mikulski Commission that, instead of numerical quotas, state parties should be required to pursue specific "affirmative-action programs" to "encourage full participation [5] by all Democrats, with particular concern for minority groups, native Americans, women and youth . . . as indicated by their presence in the Democratic electorate." [6]

Thus, the Democrats appear to have corrected the major defects in the 1972 nominating system without turning the clock back to the pre-1968 undemocratic procedures. With its new charter, the Democratic Party has shown the ability to change itself, while the Republicans continue to hold on to the status quo.

5. The McGovern Commission had used the word "representation" rather than "participation."

6. With specific "affirmative steps," set forth prior to the presidential campaign, credentials problems at the 1972 Democratic Convention should be avoided. In 1972, the Credentials Committee was forced to decide credentials challenges on the basis of subjective judgments as to whether the state parties made good-faith efforts to increase the representation of young people, minorities, and women. This usually meant that votes were cast purely on the basis of presidential politics, or on a numerical-quota criterion. The new Democratic charter provides for an independent "Judicial Council" to decide future credentials challenges.

Bridging the Communications Gap

Changing the party rules and procedures won't mean much if the Democrats can't communicate their views to the public effectively.

Much has been written in recent years about what kind of Democratic Party program can lead to a new coalition of workers, minorities, and middle-income families. Jack Newfield's 1970 *Playboy* article "The Death of Liberalism" was one of the most influential early analyses of the political potential of a modern-day populist program. Only "by restoring the old dignity to the Populist attack on monopolies and abusive corporations and banks," he argued, "can [we] take liberalism out of the soft suburban living rooms and place it on the side of the workingman—the unskilled factory worker, the waitress, the gas-station attendant, the dishwasher, the taxi driver, the small farmer." This article led to Newfield's *The Populist Manifesto* (coauthored with former Lindsay speechwriter Jeff Greenfield), a brief survey of specific programs, including breaking up General Motors, requiring bank investments in socially useful areas, public ownership of America's telephone and electric utility systems, abolition of tax loopholes like charitable contributions, tax-free municipal bonds and depreciation, and limiting the private use and development of land in the country.

Proponents of these programs correctly identify issues with wide appeal. Unfortunately they also too often ignore the great distance between the substantive "rightness" of a program and the ability to persuade a political constituency of that rightness.

The experiences of the 1972 campaign—the civil rights movement, the antiwar movement, the McCarthy-Kennedy campaigns, and the Joe Duffey campaign in 1970—should teach us that the best party platform, the most creative new program, the most intellectually sound speech, is not enough unless it can be translated into the political arena. It is easy to forget that in politics you can't order people to agree with you or to trust that you mean what you say.

To concentrate on what a candidate is saying, or what a party stands for, while ignoring the communications barriers between the candidate and his audience, is fruitless. Political purists on the right and the left may rebel at such concern about style as well as substance. However, in a political system in which change can be won only through persuasion and the winning of public trust, more often than not, style *is* substance.

Sam Brown, Senator McCarthy's student coordinator and a leader of the Vietnam Moratorium, made this point repeatedly in a *Washington Monthly* article, "The Politics of Peace," published in the summer of 1970. The antiwar appeal, Brown wrote, "must be made in such a way that Middle Americans will not ignore the substance of the argument because of an offensive style. Personal appearance, language and life-style have nothing to do with the substance or purity of one's political views. Behavior that is offensive to Middle America neither establishes nor identifies real political differences; it merely offends Middle America."

Two years later, in a Washington *Post* analysis of why George McGovern's populism hadn't won him support from blue-collar ethnics, writer Peter Krickus made the same point. Despite all of McGovern's speeches on bread-and-butter issues, Krickus wrote, "he has failed ... to project a campaign that is populist in style to millions of voters who have lost faith in government and do not trust their leaders."

From the earliest days of the civil rights movement, New Politics liberals, myself included, learned a self-righteousness and moralism that led quickly to a double standard of judgment: we were quick to denounce conduct by others which we just as quickly justified when we did it. We hated all those Southern racists, while some of us ignored the racism in our own neighborhoods and families. Many of us who supported McCarthy in 1968 felt morally superior to all those Kennedy pragmatists, though we enjoyed the stories of canvassers who won votes by convincing anti-Communist voters that McCarthy was the guy who favored getting the Commies out of the State Department.

In 1972, McGovern and his supporters denounced as dirty politics Henry Jackson's and Hubert Humphrey's attacks on McGovern's record—just a few months after McGovern and his staff had refused to renounce publicly Stewart Mott's distortions of Ed Muskie's record and his innuendoes about the military record of Muskie's father. On the busing issue, there were all those liberals defending forced busing, while sending their own kids to private schools.

We also developed a doctrinaire, reflex approach to the issues, a corollary of which was intolerance of anyone within our ranks who insisted on seeing shades of gray we didn't see. This kind of absolutist thinking came out of the two issues which first politicized us—civil rights and the Vietnam War. The answers to these problems were simple: End racism and discrimination; pull out of Vietnam.

As time went on, we let ourselves be intimidated into overlooking certain conduct or ignoring certain issues for fear of being accused of a lack of liberal commitment. Liberals, for example, ignored the crime issue, permitting the conservatives to appear more concerned about it. In fact, few issues are as well understood by both low- and middle-income people, black and white and brown, as the problem of street crime. Civil libertarianism—a basic liberal value—is perfectly consistent with an all-out effort to make the streets safe from muggers and schools safe from vandals and heroin dealers.

But, somehow, many liberals let the conservative use of code words, such as "law and order," preclude adequate public discussion of the need for more police, improved court procedures, and better prisons. Instead, many liberals developed their own rhetoric: "Crime isn't the problem; you have to deal with root causes"—as a way to establish their liberal credentials.

Thus, many Democrats have too often reacted to issues in reflex, doctrinaire fashion. The failure to reassess old philosophic premises has resulted in a dangerous vacuity of new ideas and approaches to social and economic problems.

One evening early in 1973, political columnist and author David Broder met with a group of young political activists and professionals from Washington, D.C. who had been involved in various presidential and congressional campaigns. The group, which now calls itself the Democratic Forum, was primarily liberal in ideology. At the end of almost two hours of political discussion about the 1972 campaign with this group of young liberals, Broder was struck by the almost total neglect of issues in the questions and comments he heard. "If all of you were to find yourselves in power—if you had won in 1972—what would your program be?" he asked. There was an uncomfortable silence in the room. Somebody mumbled something about the Great Society, or an "extension of the New Deal." Then there was silence again.

It is not important that all Democrats agree on particular solutions to particular social problems. But what is imperative at this juncture is that Democrats show a willingness to ask the appropriate questions—to reassess the basic philosophic premises which the Democratic Party has followed reflexively since Franklin Roosevelt's first term forty years ago.

Today, some liberal democrats do question the exclusive reliance on federal government to solve social problems, and they are exploring the use of private marketplace mechanisms. Henry Aaron of the Brookings Institute, for example, does not believe that housing problems are always best solved by federal housing programs. He urges, instead, that a direct subsidy be given the poor as a "housing allowance." Such an allowance would permit the poor to make their own decisions on the housing they want, and the private marketplace, according to Aaron, would then respond by increasing the supply of low-income housing.

Suggestions for turning to the private sector sound too similar to traditional conservative theology not to draw instinctive resistance from many progressive Democrats. There is a good answer to such resistance in a story concerning Robert Kennedy's efforts to rebuild the Bedford-Stuyvesant ghetto in Brooklyn. Kennedy's plan substantially relied on private incentives. His proposals for tax inducements, accelerated depreciation, and capital investment incentives, were immediately praised by conservative writer William F. Buckley, Jr. "Senator Robert Kennedy was distributing a statement on the poverty program so sensible that it made [the same] recommendations I made three years ago," Buckley wrote in a nationally syndicated column. Not surprisingly, Robert Sheer of *Ramparts* magazine wrote that the Kennedy approach "involves return to the market economy, and he has described the Bedford-Stuyvesant project in terms more reminiscent of Ronald Reagan than Herbert Lehman." Democratic Socialist Michael Harrington also criticized Kennedy for putting "too much trust in private business, which remains motivated by profit, rather than by social and aesthetic goals."

Kennedy was asked at one point whether he saw any differences between himself and the conservatives on his willingness to use incentives to the private sector to help the poor and make the distribution of wealth and political power in America more equitable. Kennedy is said to have responded that there was indeed a great difference between them and the difference could be summed up in these words, "I mean what I say."

Finally, and most important of all: in addition to a new willingness to challenge old premises, Democrats—especially from the activist ranks of the New Politics—must return to the concept of building political coalitions. Many New Politics activists had "grown up," for the most part in narrowly based, relatively homogeneous, and what was seen as ideologically pure movements—civil rights, antiwar, political reform. Our early experience taught that we were strongest when we maintained our purity and weakest when we permitted ourselves to compromise. That sort of attitude might be valid for a social movement aimed at influencing policies from outside the political process. But when we brought that kind of antipolitics purism into politics in the 1968 McCarthy campaign and helped make the McGovern nomination possible in 1972, we failed to see that it was, in Sam Brown's words, "the opposite of the political instinct, which is to include as many people as possible in the interest of achieving an objective."

In the aftermath of the 1972 elections, the evidence suggests that the coalitionist principle has gained wide acceptance by all factions within the Democratic Party. The Coalition for a Democratic Majority, organized after the November election as an anti-New Politics group, stated in a report critical of the McGovern Commission guidelines: "The only way the Democratic Party can hope to win elections is for it to reconstitute itself as a broad coalition which includes all Americans who have an essential interest in progressive social change." The liberal, New Politics-oriented Americans for Democratic Action, in a report supporting the McGovern Commission reforms, similarly stated, "If a political party, and particularly a party which prides itself on being open to new ideas and new people, becomes the private property of the elite, its base will gradually narrow, it will not be able to fulfill anew its coalition-making function, and it will surely die."

There is also much evidence that many New Politics activists have come to accept coalitionist political strategies. Throughout the country, New Politics leaders have spoken out on the need to break out of elitist liberal movements and build effective coalitions with working-class people:

In Wisconsin Julie Minich, a McGovern campaign leader in Madison, now admits that "we liberals can't foist ourselves—or a candidate—on the rest of the country. We've got to begin dealing with the needs and problems of the average citizen." Mike Bleicher, McGovern's statewide coordinator in Wisconsin, supported a mayoralty candidate in Madison in 1973 who had supported Muskie rather than one who had supported McGovern. "The mayor candidate most deserving of Democratic support," Bleicher explained, "must have two outstanding characteristics—he must show great promise of being an effective and innovative mayor after having been elected, and he must show the greatest promise of being elected in the first place." Paul Soglin, twenty-eight, the McGovernite mayoralty candidate in Madison whom Bleicher didn't support, a former student radical and political purist, ran a coalitionist campaign. He sought and received the endorsements of the AFL-CIO, the state Fireman's Association, and the Teamsters—and won.

Marge Tabankin, former president of the National Student Association, is now working to build local organizations of young people and working people. "Young people are more seriously committed than ever before to building larger coalitions, to learn a skill and a profession which they can use effectively to bring about the changes they believe in," she says.

Barbara Mikulski, born and raised in an ethnic working-class Baltimore neighborhood, was elected to the Baltimore City Council as an outspoken liberal and reformer. That mixture of sensitivity to ethnic working-class concerns and liberal commitment appears to be the most effective combination for building a new coalition within the Democratic Party. Ms. Mikulski's leadership, and the continual coalitionist prodding of the Democratic Party chairman, Robert Strauss, enabled the Party Reform Commission in 1973 to resolve serious internal divisions and produce a unanimous report.

And there is Joe Duffey, who moved from active leadership in the antiwar and McCarthy campaign efforts, to a Connecticut Senate campaign in which he tried to create a coalition including working people as well as student activists, and finally, to support of Ed Muskie over George McGovern for the presidency on the ground that Muskie was better suited to build such a coalition.

In an epilogue to a book written about his campaign,[7] Joe Duffey called on New Politics liberals to increase their efforts "to understand and to speak for the great majority of voters who are sometimes called 'Middle Americans.' Many of our policies have been formulated as if the nation were composed of only two major groups—the affluent and the welfare poor. But somewhere between affluence and grinding poverty stands the majority of American families living on the margins of social and economic insecurity."

The New Politics activist, he wrote, has too often directed the call for sacrifice "toward those Americans who could least afford the burden" while showing no willingness to accept some of the burdens himself. "There must be proposals, and terms by which to formulate them, pointing toward a more equal America which recognizes the plight of overtaxed working families as well as the welfare poor and minorities," Duffey concluded. "And those terms will call upon secure and comfortable Americans to share more of the cost and sacrifice."

Thus, as we have traced Joe Duffey's story through the pages of this book, we have seen the distance which so many of us have come as we have journeyed through the ups and downs of the New Politics movement: the growing awareness of how much we have changed or, more accurately, the degree to which our political sensitivity and understanding have broadened, and, most importantly, our increasing perception as to the roots of our past failures and our sense now of where we must go, and what we must do, to build a majority coalition for significant change in the years ahead.

7. Eric Rennie and Howard Goldbaum, *A Campaign Album: A Case Study of the New Politics* (Philadelphia: United Church Press, 1973).

WATERGATE VALUES
—WHERE BAD HABITS BEGIN

> "Put loyalty to the highest moral principles and to country above loyalty to persons, party or government department."
> —First Commandment, "Code of Ethics for Government Service," prepared by U.S. Congress

> "I had caught myself falling in with it. As long as I hoped for something from McCarthy, I was no more immune than the others."
> —Jeremy Larner, speechwriter for Senator Eugene McCarthy's presidential campaign

HAPPINESS IS BEING ABLE to say "I told you so" after the guy you lost to in the election turns out to be the bum you said he was during the campaign.

Many Democrats gloated as they witnessed the Watergate hearings, the Agnew investigation and resignation, and the crisis over Mr. Nixon's impending impeachment. We watched with some satisfaction as Mr. Nixon's popularity drastically declined. In October 1973, immediately after the firing of special prosecutor Archibald Cox, the Quayle poll showed George McGovern soundly defeating Nixon in a mock rerun of the 1972 election.

"Don't blame me—I voted for McGovern," we smugly put on our bumper stickers, or "Don't blame me—I'm from Massachusetts," or "We were right from the start—and now you've got to admit it."

Notwithstanding this initial euphoria and self-righteousness, post-Watergate events offer some important warning signals for the

259

Democratic Party. On the one hand, interpretations of their political impact have obscured the gains the Democrats achieved at the state and congressional levels prior to these events, beginning with the emergence of the new Democratic coalition in the 1970 congressional elections. On the other hand, the Watergate and other Nixon scandals may encourage Democrats to assume they have it made. Hence, they may pay too little attention to what must be done, notwithstanding Watergate, to keep that new coalition together.

Some advantages obviously will accrue to some Democratic candidates as a result of post-Watergate developments. These events focus public attention on a traditional Republican vulnerability—the influence of big money and corporate power within the Republican Party. A number of voters will hold the Republican Party as a whole accountable for the transgressions of the Nixon-Agnew administration. However, it would be a serious mistake to assume that Watergate alone will be a sufficient foundation on which to build an effective, durable new Democratic majority coalition.

Basic changes in the party's presidential nominating system and in some attitudes and approaches to issues are still necessary within the Democratic Party or, Watergate or not, the Democratic presidential nominee in 1976 may have to bear those political burdens, and barriers to trust and communication, experienced by George McGovern in 1972.

There should be no minimizing of the serious threat to the political process and to a democratic system of government represented by the Watergate-related activites—not just the break-in and cover-up, which received most of the public's attention, but, in many ways more insidious, the Donald Segretti political sabotage and Anthony Ulasewicz investigatory operations. Nothing in past political history can compare in degree or in kind to the complex of illegal and police-state activities of Nixon's White House and the Committee to Re-elect the President.

But Democrats must be careful about pointing the finger too self-righteously at the Republicans concerning the Watergate scandal. While liberal Democrats may be less likely to engage in these kinds of activities, given their civil libertarian traditions, many Democrats tend to suppress the more uncomfortable thought that some of the values that made some aspects of the Watergate affairs possible are not exclusively those of a Republican presidential campaign.

When Herbert Porter of the Nixon Re-election Committee explained that he did not resist cooperating in the cover-up because of "the fear of not being a team player," it was easy to feel contemptuous of that kind of amoral obedience. But anyone who has ever worked in a hard-fought political campaign, especially when the stakes are the presidency, should feel some identification with Porter's sentiments. At the heart of Porter's value system is loyalty —to the candidate, to his "team."

Once the primacy of loyalty to the campaign and the cause is established, other values and modes of conduct become acceptable: the discouragement of internal criticism of the candidate; the willingness to lie to the press and to political audiences to protect the candidates; and, most important, a double standard of morality whereby actions that would otherwise be unacceptable on ethical or legal grounds are justified because they are in the best interests of the candidate and hence the nation.

I don't make this point lightly, for it troubles me to think that those of us who pride ourselves on our commitment to certain values and political principles are incapable of resisting the pressures within a political campaign and find ourselves doing and saying things which, outside the context of the campaign, we would be quick to denounce. For example, during the crisis in the Muskie campaign over whether Senator Muskie should go to Mississippi to campaign for Charles Evers, there was very little thought given to the moral problems of not being completely honest with Evers about why Muskie might have to back out of the appearance. When the staff agreed to recommend to Muskie that Evers be told that there was a scheduling conflict, no one stood up and said, "That's a lie. We have to tell Evers the truth—the appearance gives Muskie severe political problems among the Southern moderate governors." Nobody said that, because if he had, under the value system which prevails within most political campaigns, he would have been ridiculed, and his future influence within the campaign would have been seriously damaged. From that point on, he would have been called "soft," "unrealistic," "politically naive"—terms which, in the internal politics of a political campaign, are the most opprobrious of all.

The failure of McGovern and his top staff to denounce Stewart Mott's slanders of Senator Muskie—and their rationalizations for that failure—is yet another example of the primacy of expediency over principle even in the campaign of a liberal Democrat. While there may be a difference in the degree of compromise—or the importance of the issue at stake—somehow, in the face of the overriding goal of electing a man you believe in, and the atmosphere of dedication and loyalty within the campaign staff to the candidate and his cause, compromising truth becomes defensible. Once such compromises begin, who can say where they will end?

This analysis will undoubtedly be disappointing to those who look to particular villains responsible for the Watergate tragedy, who assume that the system is basically sound and that once we rid ourselves of a few bad apples, all will be well. In fact, there may be something inherent in the way we run people for the presidency which makes the primacy of loyalty, and the kinds of moral compromises which follow from that loyalty, inevitable.

This phenomenon is obviously not unique to a political organization. The "team player" ethic has long been a reality of the corporate world, for example. What makes the internal pressures of a presidential campaign so different is that the consequences of the bad habits of thinking and conduct affect more than a company's stockholders. People who have acquired these habits, who have learned, many for the first time, the ability to compromise formerly uncompromisable values, will—if they are successful—move all those habits from the campaign headquarters to the White House, where they will have little reason to unlearn them. Pressures to be loyal, to defend the president at all costs, to lie for the president if necessary, become worse.

Perhaps the heart of it is the attitude we have developed toward the presidency itself, our almost mystical reverence of the institution. The only answer may well be that, somehow, being president must be less important than it has become in recent years. The stakes must be lowered, the pressures diminished. Then, perhaps, there will be room for more straightforward considerations of "right" and "wrong" in presidential campaign decision making.

Until that time—and I would think it still very far off—our best hope may be to reflect on the full implications of the Watergate affair, to understand that there's a little bit of Herbert Porter in all of us. That insight may not prevent future campaign abuses, but it is a first step. It may teach us to be more honest, and more critical, about our own roles in future political campaigns. At a time of unprecedented deception and self-deception by countless people involved in government and politics, that would be no small accomplishment.

ACKNOWLEDGMENTS

I AM DEEPLY OBLIGATED TO a large number of people whose encouragement, suggestions, criticisms, research assistance, and friendship during the course of writing this book were indispensable to me.

First, my special thanks to G. Keith Haller and Ms. Signe Nielsen, whose assistance on researching various sections of this book was invaluable, and to Joseph Lieberman, Waldemar Nielsen, Tim Seldes, and Jethro Lieberman, without whose initial encouragement and help this book could never have been written.

I am also grateful to Charles Peters, publisher of the *Washington Monthly*, and John H. Rothchild, formerly a *Monthly* editor, both of whose skeptical eyes on everyone's conventional wisdom, as reflected in their work in the *Monthly*, helped shape many of the themes of this book; to Jack Newfield of the *Village Voice* and Tony Jones of *Harper's* magazine, both of whom gave me early encouragement to write this book; and to a number of people who were kind enough to read various parts of this manuscript and offer helpful criticisms, questions and suggestions, including Eli Segal, Anne Wexler, Maria Carrier, Berl Bernhard, Art Kaminsky, Stephen Skardon, and Alan Krauss; to the more than sixty people from the McGovern and Muskie campaigns and various liberal movements of the past decade who talked with me about various aspects of this book, especially Joe Duffey, whose perception of what the political process is all about was a central influence on me as I wrote this book; Rick Stearns, who also permitted me to quote from private McGovern campaign personal memoranda and an excellent manuscript (unpublished) on his organizing activities in the nonprimary states; Mark Siegel, who has shown, by his work at the Democratic National Committee, a rare ability to serve as a bridge to both reform and regular factions of the party; Steve Robbins, Tony Podesta, Mark Shields, Gregory Craig, Clinton Deveaux, Simon Lazarus, Marge Tabankin, Cleta Deatherage and Duane Draper, Mary Zon, Gordon Weil, Phyllis Segal, Bob Shrum, Penn Kemble, Ben Wattenberg, former ambassador James Loeb, Ken Bode, Leon Shull, and Kevin Sullivan; and to my editor, Mary Solberg, for her counsel, her professionalism, and her friendship.

I am also deeply obligated to the men in politics for whom I have worked and whose example has taught me again and again that there is a place for decency and integrity in the political process—Richard C. Lee, Mim Daddario, Senator Abe Ribicoff, Senator Edmund Muskie, and Allard Lowenstein.

Finally, I am grateful to those who had to live through the writing of this book, and whose capacity for patience and tolerance has sometimes been pushed far beyond the call of duty—to Maryann McNamee, my secretary, who typed and retyped most of the manuscript; to my close friend and adviser, Sheldon Hochberg, who knows better than anyone I know how to mix skepticism with idealism; and especially to my sister, Tama, and both sets of parents—Mort and Fran Davis and Sid and Jeanette Charney—whose faith in me has been an important source of strength these past few years.

And most of all, my thanks to my family—to my children, Marlo and Seth, whose love and laughter reminded me always about what is important in life and what is unimportant; and to my wife, Elaine—my best friend, my most thorough editor, my toughest critic, and the nicest human being I have ever known—and loved.

Silver Spring, Maryland
September 1973

INDEX